A Comprehensive History
of the
Austin Seven 'Grasshopper'

'It is debatable as to whether the T.T. Ulsters or the Grasshoppers are the more celebrated of the works two seaters. The specification of each was tailored to the more sporting conditions prevailing in their day and each gained considerable competition success, which resulted in much welcome publicity for the Austin Motor Company.'

Martin Eyre, <u>Austin Seven Competition Cars 1922-1982</u>

Peter Hornby and Michael Hanna

Published by:

The Pre-War Austin Seven Club Ltd.

www.pwa7c.co.uk

© 2014 P. Hornby and M. Hanna

ISBN: 978 0 9572426 3 0

Printed by Adlard Print & Reprographics Ltd. Ruddington, Nottingham NG11 6HH.
www.adlardprint.com

Contents

Acknowledgements

Our thanks to the following for their very willing assistance in the preparation of what follows:

Colin Ayre - who visited Portugal and produced information and photographs of AOX 3
Martin Baker - whose request for information for the Speedy Register sparked the beginning of this book
Graham Beckett and Chris Garner of the Pre-War Austin Seven Club for arranging publication
Jim Blacklock - for his assistance in tracing the current Portuguese owner of AOX 3
Patrick Collins - Motor Research Service Beaulieu – for his help in accessing archived material
Manuel Costa - for his help in tracing AOX 3
Michael Dorsett - for information on AOV 343 and the loan of many photographs
Ian Ferguson – A friend and the Librarian of the VSCC who is to be thanked for his patience and enthusiasm
Antonio Cardoso Lima - owner of AOX 3, for sharing the history of his car
Ted Walker - Ferret Fotographics for permission to include many of his contemporary photographs
Bob Wyatt - for permitting his rare archive of Austin Magazine to be examined and copied where necessary

Special thanks are due to Ian Moore, who over the years has provided much background information, letters, magazine articles, photographs and encouragement, all of which have had a very significant effect on the final product.

We acknowledge the input we have drawn from the pages of contemporary magazines, including 'The Light Car', 'Motor Sport', 'The Autocar', 'Motor' and from 'The 750 Bulletin' and are grateful for the assistance from Bibliothèque nationale de France with whose help we finally confirmed the identity of the Grasshopper which competed in the 1938 Paris-Nice Rally.

Our thanks, also, to the many other people who have assisted, past and current Grasshopper owners, and particularly The Austin Seven Clubs Association, without whose help in mobilising members and friends, the whereabouts of the Portuguese Grasshopper would not have been tracked down.

Front Cover Illustrations
1935 Le Mans 24 Hour Race – BOA 58 (No. 60), Dodson and Richardson, merged with 1937 MCC July Rally showing BOA 58, Buckley and his wife, leading BOA 60 with Hadley and Simpson. A modern-day BOA 59 in the foreground, observes the action.

Rear Cover Illustrations
1937 MCC Lands End Trial – Orford and AOV 343 climb Bluehills Mine; a modern-day UI 3345 awaits its turn at the foot of the hill.

The illustrations used for the various section headings are borrowed and adapted from Seeing Britain and the Continent from an Austin, by Alison D. Murray, compiled and published for the Austin Motor Company by Ed. J. Burrow and Co. Ltd. c1930s.

Introduction

The Grasshopper Austin Seven, despite being very special, had a relatively brief life as a Works car from the Lands End Trial in April 1935 to its zenith in April 1938 when 8 cars were entered for that year's Trial. By June 1938 some of the cars had been sold to private individuals, and the last Works appearance was a single entry for Bert Hadley in the Plymouth Motor Club Reliability Trial in May 1939. By that time the Austin Seven had had its day and the Works had for some time been putting much of their effort into later models. At the start of the war in 1939, three of the original cars had been scrapped by Austins and one had been written off. In 1947 a further car was 'butchered', to provide the basis for a 'modern' trials car, with the body scrapped. The car subsequently disappeared. Three of the remaining cars flew the flag for a few years in MCC and similar type trials in the early fifties before disappearing from the competition scene.

From the early sixties onwards therefore, it was unusual to encounter a Grasshopper. Little had been officially recorded and there were few photographs, except for what was available from the motoring magazines of the thirties and early forties. Memories had faded, and whatever information appeared in print often included a degree of speculation. There were exceptions, and notably Martin Eyre's publication 'Austin Seven Competition Cars 1922-1982' has an excellent section on 'The Grasshoppers' which gave a very accurate picture of the construction and development of the cars. There was still however no real history of the individual cars and summaries of the competition careers.

In 1995 however, the MG Car Club Triple M Register organised an event at The Bear of Rodborough, a famous Lands End Trial venue, to celebrate the 60th Anniversary of the 'Cream Cracker' MGs' appearance in the Land's End Trial, and invited Grasshopper owners to attend. Five of the remaining seven cars were present, which was probably the largest collection of Grasshoppers in one place since 1938. This event certainly stimulated the interest of enthusiasts and owners, and thereafter, Grasshoppers have appeared in trials and other events, particularly those held by the MCC and MG Car Club. By the nineties many photos of Grasshoppers in pre-War trials and races had emerged, and from these and contemporary programmes and literature it has been possible to build up the histories of individual cars, at least when they were in Works ownership. Only recently for example, have the identities of the cars which took part in the 1935 Le Mans race been confirmed from a newly discovered photograph.

This book has its origins in a register of Austin Grasshoppers which was drafted about ten years ago, but as time went on the project expanded. We have attempted to bring the story of each car up to date. As you will see there are gaps which we have not yet been able to fill and some myths and speculation are highlighted. Many photos from many sources have been used throughout the book. Some of these are by now almost 80 years old, and some have been copied from magazine articles where the originals are not available. Poor quality was however felt more acceptable than omitting them from the story.

It is sad that none of those involved in building or racing the cars is still alive and so a big opportunity has been missed to unravel the questions and myths which still challenge us. In writing this book however we have hoped that some readers may be able to supply missing information and possibly help resolve some of the speculation. We very much welcome such feedback.

Background

THE GRASSHOPPER WAS ANNOUNCED TO THE PUBLIC IN THE 19ᵀᴴ APRIL 1935 EDITION OF THE *LIGHT CAR* Magazine in a brief article entitled *'For the Lands End'*, saying that *'three Austin Specials'* were to take part in this annual event over the Easter weekend. The leading paragraph explained that these cars were 'Speedy' Sports models with entirely new bodies, to be driven by Orford, Milton and Richardson. The chassis, it was understood, followed the usual 'Speedy' specification including a *'full-pressure lubrication system'*.

1. Austin Publicity Photos – April 1935 *Authors' Collection*

The bodies were clearly influenced by the then current Singer Le Mans or J type MG, having a completely new style of slightly sloping radiator cowl, with a centre rib, based on the cowl of the Austin 10 Ripley or 12/6 Sports. The bonnets were held down by four short straps. As the cars were intended for trials use, twin 19" spare wheels were fitted, and in front of these was a 6 gallon 'slab' petrol tank with a small 'Bonora' quick action fuel cap as fitted to the Singer Le Mans. The 2 seater body had a leather covered bench seat-back, with a separate pair of seat cushions. There was a full range of instruments, including 5" rev counter and speedometer, plus a large cubby hole complete with grab rail, in front of the passenger. Early publicity photos show a standard gearlever, but by the time of the 'launch' this had been replaced by the very effective remote control change, which was unique to this model. Also visible on the early publicity photos are the long pressure-fed nosepiece, and the large winged radiator cap which was standard on the Ripley.

Whilst the announcement described the engine as *'the usual specification'* (for the Speedy), it seems likely that at this stage it had the unique Grasshopper 2 bearing crankcase, block and alloy cylinder head, whilst using normal Speedy manifolding, with a 30VEI carburettor. Doubtless, different cam profiles were tried and used over the period of Works ownership. The chassis was based on the standard Ruby with its extensions to support the tank and spare wheel arrangements, but with sports front axle and springs. The 'D type' rear axle was used, and it is generally accepted that the final drive ratio was 5.5 to 1.

The three cars entered in the Lands End Trial (19ᵗʰ-20ᵗʰ April) had a reasonably successful debut, with Orford (**AOV 343**) gaining gold and Milton (**AOX 3**) silver awards, but Richardson (**AOX 4**) retiring with carburation problems. It is interesting to note that the *Light Car* report on the event included *'The new Le Mans type Austin Sevens were pleasant to watch'* as preparations were in hand for three entries in the 24 hour race 2 months later!

The 1935 Le Mans race took place on 15ᵗʰ-16ᵗʰ June, and the Works built 4 further cars (**BOA 57, BOA 58, BOA 59** and **BOA 60**) in preparation, these being registered on 24ᵗʰ May. The cars were very similar to the first series with the same deep doors, the main changes being the use of cycle type mudguards to replace the steel trials version, a bigger 10 gallon fuel tank with larger 4" quick action filler cap, a single spare wheel, scuttle mounting sockets for aero screens and quick action filler on the radiator. The front number plate was removed for the race.

Only 3 of the Grasshoppers were entered: Driscoll/Parish (**BOA 57**), Dodson/Richardson (**BOA 58**) and Goodacre/Turner (**BOA 59**) plus the much modified Speedy (**CZ 6324**) of Carr/Barbour. The result was a disappointing performance with **BOA 57** & **BOA 59** retiring, and Dodson/Richardson finishing last, 3 laps behind the Speedy. The cars then returned to the Works where they were altered to trials specification being fitted with the trials mudguards, but retaining the Q/A filler caps and also the larger 10 gallon fuel tank, which necessitated modification of the spare wheel arrangements to mount the second spare wheel behind the rear cross tube.

The first trials appearance of these cars was the 1935 Exeter Trial, which was held on 27th /28th December, where drivers Sewell, Goodacre, Scriven and Hadley won a bronze and 3 silver awards respectively. Early the following year, in the search for more power, Buckley's car (**BOA 58**) was fitted with a Centric 125 supercharger for the Sunbac Colmore Trial on 22nd February 1936. All 7 Grasshoppers were entered and won 2 first, 3 second and a third class award. Subsequently all the **BOA** cars were fitted with blowers to be followed by the **AOX/AOV** cars for the Torquay July Rally of 1936. The first reference to the name 'Grasshopper' appears at the Coventry Cup Trial in March 1936, when the drivers adopted the team name of 'Grasshoppers'. Bill Sewell, apparently, first coined the 'Grasshopper' tag, inspired by the cars' behaviour on take-off, a tag retrospectively attached to all the cars.

By early 1936, the Works had begun construction of 4 new cars for the forthcoming Le Mans race. These were different in a number of respects to the **BOA** cars, having door-less bodies to save weight and a new 3 bearing pressure fed unblown engine with the oil feed to the centre main bearing via a copper pipe from the main oil gallery. They featured cycle-type wings and the radiator cowl was painted body colour. The wheel size remained at 19". These cars were registered on 12th May (**COA 118, COA 119, COA 120** and **COA 121**), but due to industrial action in France the race was cancelled.

2. Dodson leads a streamlined Adler - Le Mans 1937 *Authors' Collection*

Three of the cars, now fitted with 17" wheels, were entered for the 1937 race. Bert Hadley recalled that for the event, Jamieson *'produced a better head, improved camshaft and Laystall crankshafts'* and that he *'specified flexible braided internal oil pipes but was overruled and solid copper pipes were fitted'*. According to Hadley, the camshaft was part number 8B1083 and the engines developed 27 bhp at this stage. Sadly, 1937 produced an equally disappointing result as 1935, with all three entries retiring with fracture of the copper pipes supplying oil to the centre main bearing.

Following Le Mans, the engines were rebuilt with flexible oil pipes, and the cars were entered in the Donington 12 hour sports car race on 24th July, where they ran without mudguards and finished 2nd, 3rd and 5th in class and runners-up for the team prize. The final race appearance was Charles Dodson in the TT at Donington on 4th September (**COA 121**), but he retired after 61 laps with engine problems.

By this stage, **COA 120** had been written off (allegedly by an apprentice), and following the TT, **COA 121** was converted to blown trials specification with shallow doors. All the trials cars had now been fitted with straight front axles and raised suspension. **COA 119** was painted mid blue and was entered in the Paris Nice Rally in July/August 1938 to be driven by Kay Petre and Mme Itier where it won its class and finished 26th in overall classification before being converted to full trials spec on its return. **COA 118** does not appear to have been converted to trials specification, and was not used by the Works after the Donington 12 hour race.

There were now 9 Grasshoppers converted to high chassis, blown trials specification with the 'cottage loaf' bulge on the bonnets, (the exceptions being **COA 118** and **COA 120**). At this point the twelfth and final Grasshopper was constructed on low chassis and with 'trials' wings, but there is no record of any Works competition before it was sold to its first owner in Northern Ireland, being registered **UI 3345** in December 1937.

In the 1938 Lands End Trial there was a total of 8 Grasshoppers competing; they were always individual rather than team entries, and cars varied significantly in detail as the drivers modified them to their own specific tastes. Generally speaking drivers stuck to the same car throughout the season or longer, and all the Works single seater drivers at one time competed with them in races or trials. Three of the cars (**AOV 343, AOX 4** & **BOA 59**) were sold to Scottish trialists later in 1938 to form the 'Tartan Grasshopper' team north of the border, and a further 3 (**BOA 57, BOA 58** and **COA 121**) appear to have competed on occasion as a team with 'Grasshopper 1, Grasshopper 2 and Grasshopper 3' painted on their bonnet sides.

3. Grasshoppers at Lands End finish – 1936 *Authors' Collection*

Chassis

As recorded in the previous section, the Grasshoppers used standard Ruby chassis of the time, initially with lowered suspension from the current sports models. For the **AOV/AOX** and **BOA** cars the standard sports radius arms would have been used, although it is possible that extra reinforcing from the arm to the top of the kingpin may have been employed. The standard braking system was used, and damage to the brake fulcrum and underside generally led to the cars being converted to high chassis specification from late 1937. This was achieved by use of military scout car springs and the later Girling type of front axle and stronger radius arms.

4. 'Girling' Sports Radius Arm - **UI 3345**

The 1937 Le Mans cars were fitted with a 'dropped' version of this late type axle and special stronger 'swan neck' radius arms (part nos. F236 o/s and F237 n/s), to suit the later axle; this set up was unique to the Grasshopper, and of course disappeared when the cars were converted to high chassis spec.

5. Radius arms

The steering box, part number 9E96, is inclined 33.5 degrees and the column is 28.5" long to the point of contact with the box.

The rear extensions support a sub frame, which provides mountings for the spare wheel carriers and for the body panel on which the petrol tank sits. The straps supporting the tank are bolted through the body panel to the vertical face of the sub frame. At the rear of the sub frame is located the cross tube. On the early cars, with a 6 gallon tank, a pair of 19"spare wheels fitted snugly between this tube and the tank; later cars with the bigger tank had one wheel fitted each side of the cross tube. Clearly the design of the sub frames differed depending on tank size

6. Rear sub frame **UI 3345**

Bodywork

The first 2 batches of cars had steel floorpan, scuttle and rear panel under the fuel tank, elsewhere aluminium bodywork, bonnet and sides, but steel 'flowing' mudguards in trials mode. Possibly the Le Mans cycle type guards were aluminium although it is not known.

The third batch of (Le Mans) cars had single skinned door-less bodies as refitted to **COA 118** in the 1960s when owned by Mike Eyre.

The seat back rests against a bar running across the body at the front of the luggage compartment, and the exact specification of this varied from each batch of cars. Hood frame arrangements varied; some cars had a simple tubular hoop frame for the hood, and this could be fitted into 2 slots behind the seat to support the hood. It folded in half for stowage in the relatively small space behind the seats. The first batch **'AO'** cars and **UI 3345** have a very sophisticated (in comparison) arrangement which slides upwards and forwards and is constructed from flat bar rather than tube.

The seat bases are leather cushions with 'float on air' internals, held fore and aft by wooden supports located by steel pegs passing through one of three holes drilled in the floor.

7. Dashboard of **AOV 343** at Rodborough, 1995
Michael J. Dorsett

The dashboard was fitted with a comprehensive range of instruments including 5" rev counter and speedometer. Some cars had 120mph speedos matched with 8000 rpm rev counters, others 80mph and 5500rpm instruments. It is possible that the former were initially fitted to the Le Mans cars, and the latter were standard for trials use, but there is no real evidence. In addition, each car had a Smiths clock, ammeter, plus oil pressure or combined oil pressure and water temperature gauge and the usual switchgear. The steel dashboard was beautifully fabricated and, certainly on the **BOA** series, was originally finished in a painted woodgrain effect. The steering wheel was flat spoke or spring steel 'Bluemels Brooklands' type as seen in contemporary sports models, with the standard ignition/hand throttle controls. The trials cars were fitted with a passenger grab handle beneath the 'cubby hole'.

All cars manufactured in 1935 had deep doors, with small internal pockets and a pair of brackets attached on the inside at the top of the door to take the removable two-piece side screens. The later Le Mans cars were subsequently fitted with deep (**COA 119**) and shallow (**COA 118** and **COA 121**) doors. **COA 119** also had external door handles. **UI 3345** had deep doors and a non standard dashboard with speedometer and rev counter fitted in the centre of the dash. Body colour was mid green, with apple green upholstery.

The cars are fitted with probably the best remote gear lever extension produced for an Austin Seven. The short gearlever sits in an alloy casting bolted via a bracket to the propshaft tunnel. A special casting replaces the standard gearbox top and the connecting link to the lever passes inside a tube which is joined to the castings at each end by flexible hose and worm-drive clips. This takes care of the chassis flexing on trials. The reverse gear 'detent' is also arranged in the gear lever casting.

8. Gear lever extension on **UI 3345** (non original handbrake)

Engine

The engines, whilst similar to the contemporary Speedy and pressure fed Nippy engines, were unique to the Grasshoppers.

9. Pressure relief valve (rhs) and secondary oil filler (2 bearing engine)

In the original 2-bearing engine an obvious difference was apparent in the crankcase which had fixings for a 10 stud block, and visible on top of the flange on the nearside an adjustable pressure relief valve to the rear of the petrol pump mounting, and a secondary sump oil filler union, presumably for use in long distance races, forward of the petrol pump. Most of the 2-bearing crankcases had Part Number 9B3414 cast above the petrol pump mounting.

Three bearing bottom ends were introduced for the **COA** series of cars which first saw the light of day in May 1936. For this engine the secondary oil filler was omitted and the oil pressure relief valve returned to its standard position. Other than the extra holding down studs on the deck, the crankcase was indistinguishable from the 3 bearing sports item fitted at extra cost to Nippies at the time. It has been reported that special, stronger cranks were developed for both 2 and 3 bearing engines.

The cylinder block was a very special item being stronger than standard, with a wide base, 10 stud fixing and reinforcement up the sides of the cylinders. The inlet ports were set about ½" lower than standard, which allowed cooling water to circulate around and above the updraught ports. Valves were ¾" longer than standard, tappets were significantly shorter and non adjustable with clearance effected by grinding/shimming the 'mushroom' buttons. The setup was therefore significantly lighter than the standard items.

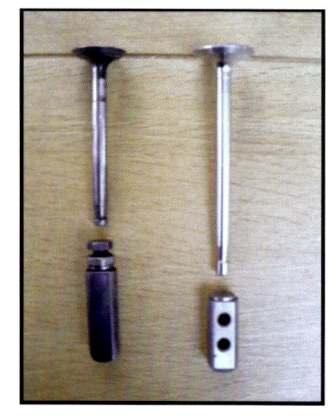

10. Grasshopper valve and cam follower (rhs), compared with standard items.

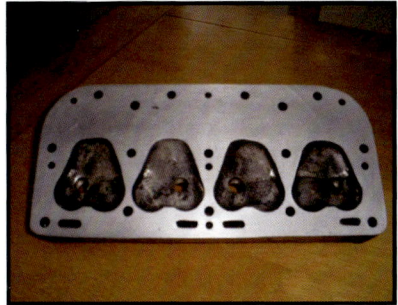

The aluminium cylinder head had extra slots on its face, positioned above the exhaust ports, to match the changes made to water flow in the block. There were 2 types of head produced. The early version had the combustion chambers similar to the Ulster. The later version (illustrated), probably introduced for the 1936 Le Mans cars, benefited from a long water off-take and the early use of 14mm plugs. The part number was 8B1084.

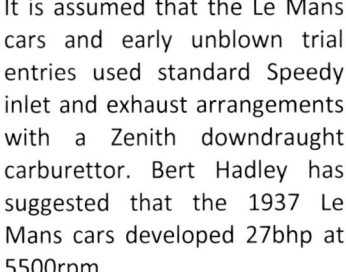

It is assumed that the Le Mans cars and early unblown trial entries used standard Speedy inlet and exhaust arrangements with a Zenith downdraught carburettor. Bert Hadley has suggested that the 1937 Le Mans cars developed 27bhp at 5500rpm.

11. 1⅜" Downdraught SU carburettor.

The blown engine fitted to the trials cars used a Centric 125 supercharger surmounted by a 1⅜" downdraught SU carburettor, part no. BA18404, making a very tall package and resulting in the familiar 'cottage loaf' bonnet bulge. The blower drive again was a 'first'. A special dynamo housing was cast, and in the near side of the housing the blower drive is via a pulley shaft supported on 2 ball races and driven by a gear between the races, which is meshed with the camshaft gear wheel. The blower is driven by a 'V' belt, tensioned by a swinging fan blade mounting, with a strut anchoring the blower casing to the timing cover. The fan, which now rotates in the opposite direction to the standard 'Seven' is identical to the Big Seven item. The blower sits on the forward end of an aluminium manifold, with a blow off valve located at the rear.

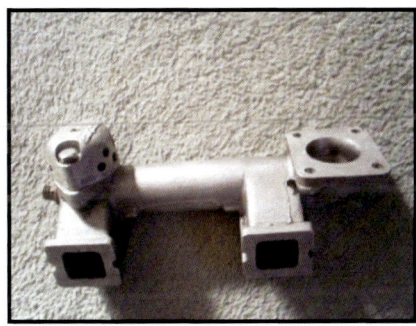

A new cast iron exhaust manifold completed the transformation. The cars were originally blown at 5 - 6 psi which was subsequently increased to 9psi.

The standard 4 speed and sports gearboxes were probably used in these cars, but they would have needed significantly different speedometer drive gears for the special instruments. With a standard drive, the Grasshopper speedo reads more than 50% slow! The rev counter drive was taken from the base of the distributor drive shaft, with the outer cable attached to the dynamo end plate, directly below the distributor shaft.

One mystery remains however. The **BOA** series of cars were entered in trials from March to October 1936 as 'supercharged'. All currently available photos from that period show that the cars competed without the bonnet bulge. One suggestion is that a horizontal Solex carburettor similar to that used on the 'Duck' racers was mounted on a short right-angled manifold and sat above the cylinder head under the standard bonnet. The change to the downdraught SU was in search of better performance. Alternatively, perhaps they used some sort of 'crossover' manifold between the blower and a horizontal carburettor, of the sort fitted to **UI 3345**, and decided that they could get better 'response' from the engine by bolting the carburettor directly onto the blower? Whatever the case, it is believed that this is the first factory fitting of an SU carburettor on an Austin Car.

12. 3 bearing engine with 'crossover' inlet manifold to Centric blower (as **UI 3345**)

The table below illustrates the disparity between the first reported use of a supercharger in trials events, and the first visual evidence of the car sporting the 'cottage-loaf' bonnet bulge.

Grasshopper	First reported use of 'blower'	Source	First picture of 'cottage loaf'	Photo No.
BOA 57	14 March 1936 Coventry Cup Trial	Wheelspin, M, LC, A	7 November 1936 MCC (Buxton) Sporting Trial	159
BOA 58	22 February 1936 Colmore Trophy Trial	Autocar	14 November 1936 Bristol Fedden Trophy Trial	163
BOA 59	14 March 1936 Coventry Cup Trial	Wheelspin, M, LC, A	1-2 January 1937 MCC Exeter Trial	168
BOA 60	14 March 1936 Coventry Cup Trial	Wheelspin, M, LC, A	1-2 January 1937 MCC Exeter Trial	170
AOV 343	17 July 1936 MCC (Torquay) July Rally	Cowbourne, MS	26-27 March 1937 MCC Lands End Trial	184
AOX 3	17 July 1936 MCC (Torquay) July Rally	Cowbourne	26-27 March 1937 MCC Lands End Trial	187
AOX 4	17 July 1936 MCC (Torquay) July Rally	Cowbourne	26-27 March 1937 MCC Lands End Trial	178

Key to Source: M – The Motor, LC – Light Car, A – Autocar, MS - Motorsport

Survivors

Of 12 cars constructed a total of 7 still remain. These are:

AOV 343	(West Midlands)
AOX 3	(Portugal)
BOA 59	(Surrey)
COA 118	(London)
COA 119	(Argyllshire)
COA 121	(Hampshire)
UI 3345	(Surrey)

Considering that 4 were written off or scrapped by the Works before the war and one is known to have been converted into a semi-production special in the 1940s, it is an excellent return!

13. A 'Plague' of Grasshoppers – Rodborough, April 1995 (MMM Register Cream Cracker 60th Anniversary)

First batch, 'AO series' - General

The first series of cars, **AOV 343, AOX 3** and **AOX 4** were registered in March & April 1935 in readiness for the Lands End Trial to be held on 19th/20th April. The publicity photos, taken shortly before the event, showed the cars with 'Ripley' radiator filler caps and standard Austin Seven gearlevers. By the time the cars appeared at the trial, these had been changed for the more usual Grasshopper items. This initial series was unique in that it was built purely for trials use.

14. April 1935 - The team publicity photo on announcement *Ian Moore Collection*

AOV 343

Date of Registration:	25th March 1935.
Original Chassis No:	XE 1018
Engine No:	M217306 (2brg)
Works drivers:	
J. G. Orford	(1935 - 1937)
T. H. Cole	(1938)
Private Ownership:	
G. Valentine	(1938 - 1950)
Charles Martyn Smith	(1950 - 1956)
Peter Forgaard	(1956 - 1959)
Peter Cutler	(1959 - 1963)
Michael Dorsett	(1963 - current)

15. Orford 1937 Lands End *Ferret Fotographics*

AOV 343 was one of the team of 3 Grasshoppers prepared for the Exeter Trial in 1935. It was the first to be registered, beating its team mates by 11 days. Consequently it was probably the car which appeared in the early publicity photographs. It was equipped with standard flared trials wings, deep doors and twin spare wheels which fitted between the early, narrow trials fuel tank and the rear cross tube. For the first two and a half years of its life, it was driven with notable success by J. G. Orford, who managed a total of 3 Premier Awards in successive Lands End Trials. T. H. Cole drove the car in the MCC Members' Day Brooklands event, winning a Premier Award before taking it over for the first 5 months of 1938 winning gold in both Lands End and Exeter.

In Orford's hands, it sported a 'Boyce' temperature gauge atop the radiator cowl, and at some point the 6 gallon fuel tank was replaced with the larger 10 gallon version - with the necessary modification to the spare wheel mountings. A blower appears to have been fitted by the time of the MCC Torquay Rally of July 1936 and it was probably converted to high chassis spec early in 1938 prior to its disposal. By June 1938 the car had been sold to George Valentine (at a rumoured £50), to become a member of the Scottish Tartan Grasshopper Team.

16. George Valentine (AOV 343) takes to the water at Drumtain Ford, 1939 Caledonian MC Summer Trial Michael J. Dorsett Collection

AOV 343 distinguished itself in Valentine's hands, and he kept it until 1950, when it was sold in original blown specification to Martin Smith who kept the car until 1956, when it was sold by Rugby Autocars to Peter Forgaard of Hagley. Whilst in Forgaard's hands the original blown engine was replaced with a Ford 10 unit and gearbox and the original engine, gearbox and remote gearlever extension were disposed of. By the early 60s they had come into the hands of the Sheffield racing and trials driver Cuth Harrison.

Forgaard, who appears to have had good service from the car, sold it in 1959 to Peter Cutler of Clent, from whom it was purchased by the current owner, Michael Dorsett, in 1963 for the sum of £30.

Over the next few years, the car was twice restored, Michael Dorsett initially fitting a standard engine and gearbox (with standard gearlever) in 1965/66, and later rebuilding the car on low chassis to its original spec but with a modified standard engine. It sports green paintwork and cream upholstery including hood, tonneau and original style sidescreens, has short bonnet straps and runs on 19" wheels. The dashboard retains original instrumentation and Bluemels steering wheel. The rebuild has been to a high standard.

Finally, in 2002, the original engine, gearbox and gearlever extension (ex Harrison, Rob Davies, John Sutton, Martin Eyre & Barry Clarke) were purchased, rebuilt and were reunited with the car in 2004/2005.

The car has appeared in public on a number of occasions in the last 20 years, including the 1995 MG Trials Cars reunion at Rodborough, the 1997 Austin Seven Rally at Gaydon, plus the Austin Seven 90th Anniversary meeting at Warwick in 2012. It currently shares a garage with the Dorsett Lotus Cortina and Dellow.

18. AOV 343 with side-screens in place

17. AOV 343 left out in the rain
Michael J. Dorsett

AOX 3 (Portuguese Registration TM-10-49)

Date of Registration:	4th April 1935.
Original Chassis No:	XE 1019
Engine No:	M217442 (2brg)
Works drivers:	
W. J. Milton	(1935 - 1937)
T. H. Cole	(1938)
W. C. Butler	(1938)
Private Ownership:	
Mario Gonçalves	(1938-1952)
Not known	(1952-early 1970s)
Fernando/Maria Raquel Cardoso Lima	(early 1970s – late 1990s)
Antonio Cardoso Lima	(late 1990s – current)

19. 1938 MGCC Midland Centre Trial – T.H. Cole *Authors' Collection*

AOX 3 was first registered on 4th April 1935 in time to contest the Lands End Trial 2 weeks later, driven by W. J. Milton who was the sole Works driver of the car from 1935 to 1937. T. H. Cole took over for 2 events in 1938, and W.C. Butler drove it on its final appearance as a Works car in the 1938 Lands End Trial, where he retired. In the 3 main MCC trials over the 3 years, it won gold, 2 silver and 3 bronze awards. Like its team mates, it started life on low chassis with flared mudguards and deep doors. It was supercharged for the MCC Torquay Rally in July 1936 and was on high chassis early in 1938 for its final events, prior to being sold to Mario Gonçalves, the son of a Portuguese Austin agent, and exported to Portugal in September 1938.

20. AOX 3, now TM-10-49, probably a post-war picture, and other than the wings, not significantly different from when it was first exported to Portugal in 1938. The owner, Mario Gonçalves, stands to the left in the picture, dressed in white overalls. *Picture shown courtesy of the Lima family*

It is fair to assume that the specification of the car was as it appeared above in the 1938 MGCC trial; high chassis, trial mudguards and deep doors and other contemporary photos show a 10-gallon fuel tank – generally the 'standard' trials specification of the time. The current owner relates that Gonçalves "raced it in several events from the beginning" and confirms that he exchanged it for a shotgun in 1952, by which time the 'blower' had disappeared.

The car was purchased by Maria Raquel Cardoso Lima in the early 1970s and passed on to her nephew, the current owner, in the late 1990s.

16

The car was photographed at a classic car meeting in France in 1996, and was seen by a VSCC member, Colin Ayre, who visited the owner in September 2008, and whilst clearly a Grasshopper, it is a significantly different vehicle from that which left the Works in 1938. The car has been restored and is in good condition, but is fitted with a 6 gallon fuel tank with small 'Bonora' Q/A cap, and twin spare wheels sitting *between* the tank and rear cross bar - the specification of the early cars which were quickly converted to take the larger tank. It was painted white from previous dark silver in 1969/70, with white radiator surround replacing the chromed version, and has been fitted with an unusual louvred set of cycle type mudguards. The original bonnet with its 'cottage loaf' blower bulge has been replaced with a well louvred single piece version, and the original short bonnet straps have been replaced with longer versions, fixed below the bonnet sides. The front section of the body appears to have been re-skinned and the 'rear' of the scuttle repositioned at some stage. At some point the car has acquired a 'three-plane' hood.

21. Photographed in France – 1996 *Authors' Collection*

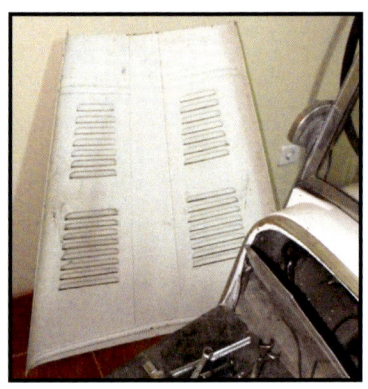

The engine appears to be a mixture of standard Austin Seven, with 'sports' and Grasshopper elements. The original crankcase seems to have survived. It has been skimmed removing most of the engine number. It is understood that a 'shadow' of the original number remains and is just sufficiently readable to confirm that this could be the original crankcase from **AOX 3**, but the block may have been replaced with a 10 stud Ulster version fitted with a Nippy cylinder head.

It looks to have Nippy manifolding and the 1⅜" downdraught SU carburettor used with the blown Grasshopper engine.

The original Grasshopper fan and mounting arrangements are in place, which would allow a Centric blower to be fitted.

The detailed colour pictures in this section are
reproduced courtesy of Colin Ayre

Inside the car the seats appear to be original or
close copies, although the front of the squabs
appear non-standard, and a Grasshopper
gearlever extension is fitted. The original
instruments are fitted into a (replacement)
wood dashboard, and the propshaft tunnel has
sprouted what appears to be a pair of 'fiddle
brake' levers. It now has shallow doors with
non-standard external hinges in place of the
original deep versions.

It has always been assumed that this Portuguese car is **AOX 3**. It is however difficult to understand how or why it
should have been modified (back) to this mixture of original early specification and non-original features such as
the mudguards. Most surprising is the change to the doors; not a simple task, nor one which would make the car
more 'user friendly'. It must be assumed on the balance of probability that **AOX 3** is alive and well in Portugal.

AOX 4

22. 1936 Lands End Trial and R.J. Richardson *Authors' Collection*

Date of Registration:	4th April 1935.
Original Chassis No:	XE 1020
Engine No:	M217443 (2brg)
Works drivers:	
R. J. Richardson	(1935 - 1938)
Private Ownership:	
J. H. Blyth	(1938 - 1941)
R. K. N. Clarkson	(1941 - 1947)
R. H. Dyson (Ausfod)	(1947)
David Findlay (Ausfod)	(1947 - no trace)

AOX 4, registered on 4th April 1935, was the final car of the first batch and its first competition was the 1935 Lands End Trial. R. J. Richardson drove the car for the whole of its Works career, winning silver, bronze and gold in the Lands End Trial in 3 successive years. As the other 'AO' cars, it was initially constructed with flared mudguards, deep doors, on low chassis and unblown. It was supercharged for the 1936 MCC July Torquay Rally and would have been converted to high chassis by the time of the February 1938 Colmore Trial. Richardson's last event in the car was the Lands End Trial on 15th/16th April 1938, when he went out in a blaze of glory winning a Premier Award.

The car was purchased by J. H. Blyth, and became a member of the Scottish Tartan Grasshopper team, his first competitive outing with it being on 11th June 1938.

23. 1938/1939 in Tartan mode - Blyth *Authors' Collection*

24. Clarkson in 1946 *Light Car February 1946*

In an article in ***Autocar*** – 9th May 1941 based on an interview Blyth revealed that the car had covered only 6000 miles when he bought it. It must have been hardly run in. Blyth was very successful with the car, but during the war he was persuaded to sell it to his friend R. K. N. Clarkson who fitted LMB independent front suspension and campaigned it in 1946/1947. A dental surgeon by trade, Bert Hadley described him as 'a curious chap'. Hadley was persuaded to drive the car in the 1946 Colmore, despite the engine sounding 'a bit clapped'. The crankshaft broke and the car was towed to Hadley's lockup in Stirchley, where it remained for weeks awaiting collection. Although Hadley was invited to purchase the car, he declined the offer.

Frustratingly for Clarkson, the replacement engine suffered big end failure within sight of the finish line at the close of the April 1947 Scottish Sporting Car Club's Highland 3 Day Trial. It made one last appearance in Grasshopper form for the Liverpool MC Jeans Gold Cup in May, before it passed into the hands of R. H. Dyson, who used it as the basis of the original Ausfod, a limited production special with a more modern abbreviated trials body and supercharged Ford 10 engine in the original chassis. He sold the car to David Findlay that year and J. M. Findlay competed successfully in the final Scottish event before petrol restrictions effectively killed off the sport for the next two years. **AOX 4** subsequently disappeared.

25. Ausfod Special outside the Russell Street, Chorlton-on-Medlock premises, 1947 *Ian Moore Collection*

April 1948 Light Car

There is no trace of the original engine or body, and the car is no longer registered with the authorities. The Ausfod Motor Engineering Co. Ltd was officially dissolved in June 1956, its former premises demolished in the 1960s.

Second batch, 'BOA series' - General

These cars were built shortly after the first batch and registered on 24th May 1935 in time for the imminent Le Mans 24 Hour Race in June. They were very similar to the first batch, the main differences being larger fuel tanks, cycle type mudguards, bound springs and larger headlights. The crews of each car included one of the Works racing drivers teamed with a private individual, but the cars did not distinguish themselves in the race, the remaining car at the end of the race finishing last and being beaten by a privately entered Speedy (albeit with a degree of Works preparation). This Speedy, now restored to its Le Mans state, has been a regular and successful participant in recent Classic Le Mans events.

26. 1935 Le Mans line-up *Authors' Collection*

Following this inauspicious arrival on the scene, all four cars were converted to trials specification in time to join the first batch for the MCC Exeter Trial held that year at the end of December.

As can be seen from the above photo, **BOA 60** was not included in the team for Le Mans in 1935.

BOA 57

Date of Registration:	24th May 1935.
Original Chassis No:	XE 1024
Original Car No:	XE 2025
Engine No:	XE 21 (2brg)

Works drivers:
L. P. Driscoll / C. D. Parish   (Le Mans 1935)
W. H. Scriven (Trials and Brooklands MCC Meeting)

27. 1936 Colmore *Authors' Collection*

BOA 57 made its competition debut at Le Mans on 15th June 1935, driven by Pat Driscoll and C. D. Parish, a garage owner from Hull who had entered a number of races at Brooklands the previous year with one of the 'Duck' racers. The car was retired after completing 1430 kms. Its competition number was 59 being officially classified 39th.

It began its trials career, with minor modification to its specification, in the Exeter Trial on 27th December, driven by Bill Scriven who used it for the whole of its subsequent career which finished, still as a Works car, with the Colmore Trial on 25th February 1939.

It was supercharged with the other **BOA** cars in February / March 1936, and in this form, and still on low chassis, was driven by Scriven in the MCC Members' Meeting at Brooklands on 26th September 1936. It was converted to high chassis specification at the end of 1937. Scriven won golds in all 3 Lands End Trials and 2 silvers and gold in the 3 Exeter Trials he entered in this car.

BOA 57 remained in Works hands for the whole of its career.

After its third class award in the 1939 Colmore, it was deleted by the Birmingham Tax Authorities, and therefore presumed scrapped as recorded by Mike Eyre in his article *'Austin Seven Grasshopper Model'* published in the 750MC Bulletin in 1968.

28. Land's End 1938 *Ferret Fotographics*

29. 1937 MGCC Abingdon (Scriven) Note how the front number plate is tilted forward *Ferret Fotographics*

BOA 58

Date of Registration:	24th May 1935.
Original Chassis No.	XE 1025
Original Car No:	XE 2026
Engine No.	XE 22 (2brg)

Works drivers:
C .J. P. Dodson /R. J. Richardson
(Le Mans/Donington1935)
C. L. Goodacre   (1935 Exeter)
C. D. Buckley
(Trials and Brooklands MCC Meeting)

30. Le Mans 1935 - Charlie Dodson at speed in BOA 58 *Authors' Collection*

Built specifically for the 1935 Le Mans, **BOA 58** was registered on 24th May 1935 and driven in the race by Charlie Dodson and R. J. Richardson, the **AOX 4** trials driver. Fundamentally the same as the first batch of trials cars; it did however have lightweight cycle type mudguards, a larger 10 gallon fuel tank and ran with a single spare wheel. It was the only one of the team of 3 Grasshoppers to finish, and unfortunately 3 laps adrift of the Carr/Barbour Speedy! The final position was 28th having covered 138 laps. The car was put away for a few months to be modified for trials use, retaining the large fuel tank however and initially the cycle type mudguards which were still in evidence at the 1936 MCC Sporting Trial held in the Buxton area on 17th November.

As a trials car, it was used almost exclusively by Dennis Buckley, the son of the Austin Sales Manager. The only exception was its first event, the MCC Exeter Trial on 27th December 1935, when Charles Goodacre piloted it to a silver award. For the next three and a half years Buckley produced some excellent results with many premier awards particularly in MCC trials.

BOA 58 was the first car to be fitted with a blower for the Colmore Trophy Trial on 22nd February 1936, and this lead was immediately followed by the remaining **BOA** cars. It competed at Brooklands in the Members' Meeting on 26th September that year, and with Buckley driving, finished behind Scriven in **BOA 57**. It was converted to high chassis at the end of 1937 with beneficial results.

Its final event was the Lawrence Cup on 20th May 1939 when Buckley won the 'Special Test Tankard'. In 1939 this car with such a historic record of Works competition was scrapped and deleted by the Birmingham Tax Authorities.

31. 1936 MCC Sporting Trial – Buckley is a 'High flier in the hairpin' (Jenkins Chapel) - note cycle-type mudguards
Ferret Fotographics

32. 1937 Exeter Trial *Michael J. Dorsett Collection*

33. 1938 Fedden Trophy Trial - Nailsworth Ladder
Authors' Collection

34. 1939 Colmore, Buckley *Authors' Collection*

BOA 59

35. Le Mans 1935 *Authors' Collection*

Date of Registration:	24th May 1935.
Original Chassis No:	XE 1026
Original Car No:	XE 2027
Engine No:	XE 23 (2brg)
Works drivers:	
C. L. Goodacre/R. F. Turner (Le Mans 1935)	
Trials	
C. L. Goodacre	(1936, 1937)
W. S. Sewell	(1937)
A. H. Langley	(1937-1938)
Private Ownership:	
B. L. Carlaw	(1938 - 1942)
Ivor Paige	(194?)
Ray Morley	(1952 - 1957)
William Delafield	(1958 - 1998)
Peter Hornby	(1998 - current)

Registered on 25th May 1935, **BOA 59** was entered in the Le Mans 24 hour race 3 weeks later. Driven by Charles Goodacre and R. F. Turner, who had achieved notable success racing his privately owned blown 'Ulster', it carried race number 61, and covered 1200 kms before retiring with gearbox failure, being officially classified 45th. This proved to be its sole outing as a 'racing car', thereafter being converted for use in trials, initially in Goodacre's hands, when the Le Mans cycle type guards were retained.

Its first trial, like the other '**BOA**' cars, was the MCC Exeter on 27th December 1935, and it completed 3 more trials in 1936; the Colmore, the Coventry Cup and Lands End Trial in Gooodacre's hands. In the latter two trials, the car was blown. At some point it is rumoured that Goodacre fitted a 'Duck' engine to the car, but according to Bert Hadley whilst the car had bags of power at the top end, it was quite unsuitable for trials use with very little power low down. Perhaps this was on the 1937 Sunbac Inter Team Trial where there were no awards gained!

At the start of 1937, Bill Sewell, who was Herbert Austin's Competitions Manager, took over the car for the Colmore and the 3 major MCC trials ending with the Edinburgh on 14th May, but sadly appears to have non started in the Lands End and Edinburgh. From October 1937 to April 1938, Alf Langley had the car for its most successful phase with the Works, achieving 8 awards in the 8 trials entered.

36. Langley - Queuing for Hustyn, 1938 Lands End
Authors' Collection

37. Morley - Exeter Simms 1955 *Authors' Collection*

In May 1938, **BOA 59** was sold to Carlaw, to become one of the 3 members of the 'Tartan Grasshopper' team trialling north of the border. Thereafter, the car passed through a number of owners including an army major in Glasgow in 1942, and Ivor Paige, before September 1951, when it was purchased for £215 from Mercury Motors in South Harrow, by Ray Morley, a successful trials driver of the 1930s in AC cars, *'in poor condition, from a salesman who was unaware of its origin'*. After some fettling, *'a tidy up, repaint and new tonneau cover'*, **BOA 59** recommenced its trialling career at the end of May 1952 in the MCC Edinburgh Trial.

Ray Morley, who named his Buckingham home 'Hustyn', flew the Grasshopper flag over the next 5 years in a number of events; he achieved 2 silvers and a gold in the Lands End Trials and silver in the 1955 Exeter. Following its gold in the 1957 Lands End, the decision was made to sell and it was taken to Moores of Ellesborough to be sold in October that year. Ray Morley remembered that *'it gave me a wonderful time in spite of all sorts of snags... A lovely little car'.*

In September 1958, William Delafield, of Leighton Buzzard, purchased *'one used Austin as seen tried and approved, Regn No: BOA 59'* for the sum of £300. He was a student at Oxford, and the green 'student light' still fitted to the radiator grille dates from that time. He subsequently became a gentleman farmer at Deddington near Oxford. In his possession the car was very carefully maintained and appeared notably at the 1995 MG Trials Cars reunion at Rodborough and the 1997 Austin Seven Rally at Gaydon. Having preserved the car in its very original form for 40 years, he sold it in March 1998 to Peter Hornby.

38. Ray Morley and William Delafield (passenger) 1990

39. Land's End Centenary 2008

In Ray Morley's hands a number of changes were made, the most significant being the altering of the spare wheel mounting to take 16" wheels and larger tyres (1952) and the fitting of supplementary telescopic shock absorbers to the rear axle in 1955.

Since passing to the current owner, the engine has been rebuilt and the blower refitted in 2003. In addition the telescopic shock absorbers have been removed, and the dished Bluemels Brooklands steering wheel has been replaced with a Bluemels flat spoke wheel.

Whilst nowhere near concours condition, it is probably the most original of all the remaining cars, retaining all major original fittings, including engine/chassis and body/wings, upholstery and seats, and the main instruments - and never having been 'restored'.

The car took part in the MCC Centenary Lands End Trial in May 2008 and the Centenary Exeter Trial in 2010, plus other events including the 2013 Welsh Trial and a number of MG Kimber Trials.

It currently shares a garage with **UI 3345**, two Corgi folding scooters and an Austin 'Pathfinder' pedal car.

40. MG Kimber Trial 2008

41. Supercharger **BOA 59**

42. Cockpit **BOA 59**

43. **BOA 59** in repose

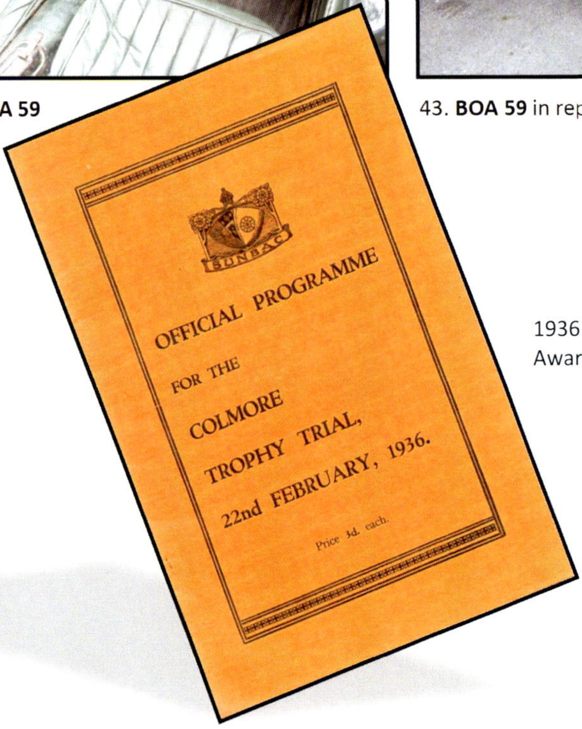

OFFICIAL PROGRAMME FOR THE COLMORE TROPHY TRIAL, 22nd FEBRUARY, 1936.

Price 3d. each.

1936 Colmore – Goodacre won a First Class Award in **BOA 59** at this event.

BOA 60

Date of Registration:	24th May 1935
Original Chassis No:	XE 1027
Original Car No:	XE 2028
Engine No:	XE 24 (2brg)
Works drivers:	
H. L. Hadley	(1935 - 1938)
W. S. Sewell	(1938)

44. 1935 Exeter *Ferret Fotographics*

BOA 60 was constructed to compete in the 1935 Le Mans race, but it did not make the team and may possibly have been used as the spare car. It was subsequently converted to trials Grasshopper specification exactly as the '**AO**' series of cars, except that the 10 gallon tank was retained and the second spare wheel was therefore mounted outside the rear cross tube.

In its first event, the Exeter Trial on 27th December 1935, the car was driven by Bert Hadley, who gained a Simms Hill Medal and a silver award. Hadley then drove the car for the next 2 years in various trials, and with much success, finishing with a Premier Award in the 1938 Exeter Trial on 7th – 8th January.

Bill Sewell took over the car for what was to be its last event, winning a Third Class Award in the Colmore Trophy Trial on 26th February 1938. Whilst Hadley had entered the Lands End Trial in April, he was a non-starter, taking over **COA 119** in October that year. Canning Brown reports that following the Colmore event *'BOA 60 was subsequently destroyed by fire',* although in later years she was unable to recall the source of this claim. The car was scrapped by the Works and deleted by the Birmingham Tax Authorities. The engine did however survive.

45. 1937 MGCC Abingdon *Ferret Fotographics*

46. Hadley (BOA 60) at the foot of Fingle Bridge, 1938 Exeter Trial
The Motor 11 January 1938

Third Batch, 'COA series' - General

Registered in June 1936, the **COA** series of cars was different in a number of significant ways to their predecessors. As they were produced for racing rather than trials, they wore lightweight door-less bodies. They were fitted with a new 3 bearing engine and also ran with painted radiators. The cycle-type wings were unusual in that they now covered the same section of tyre as the front wings. Their first appearance was at the 1937 Le Mans race, but by the end of the season their circuit racing days were over and 2 were eventually converted to full trials specification.

47. Kay Petre with Charles Goodacre (?), **COA119**; Goodacre's **COA 118** parked behind, and Dodson's **COA 121** to the rear
Authors' Collection

The **COA** batch has survived well compared to the 1935 cars. The 3 cars in the above photo taken in June 1937 currently exist, whilst the fourth car of the batch, **COA 120**, was written off or scrapped very early in its career, allegedly following an accident when being driven by an apprentice. The slim possibility exists that this car might have formed the basis for **UI 3345** which was first registered in December 1937.

As no photographs or other specific details of **COA 120** have emerged, it has not been possible to include any further information in the following pages, but could the picture below be **COA 120**?

Snapped at the track last week: Charles Goodacre trying out one of the Austin Sevens which will be competing in the Le Mans 24-hour sports car race in June.

48. Goodacre and one of the **COA** cars prepared for the cancelled
1936 Le Mans, as it appeared in the **Motor** magazine, 2nd June 1936

COA 118

Date of Registration:	12th May 1936
Original Chassis No:	244518
Original Car No:	XE 2036
Original Engine No:	XE 29 (3brg)

Works drivers:
C. L. Goodacre /C. D. Buckley
Le Mans/Donington (1937)

Private Ownership:

W. H. Scriven	
G. Symonds	
J. Swinburn-Butterfield	(1958 - 1959)
Maxwell Bennett	(1959 - 1962)
Stuart Bennett	(1962 - 1963)
Mike Eyre	(1963 - 1983)
Adli Halabi	(1983 - current)

49. 1937 Donington 12 Hour Race - **COA 118** *Authors' Collection*

Originally built for the cancelled 1936 Le Mans race, **COA 118** was first registered on 12th May 1936. It competed in the following year's race on 19th and 20th June, driven by Goodacre and Buckley (but entered by John Carr), and was the first of the team to retire with the fractured oil pipe which afflicted all 3 cars. It managed only 432 kms to be classified 37th after completing 32 laps. Its second, and final, Works outing was the Donington 12 Hour Sports Car Race a month later on 24th July. Goodacre and Buckley once again drove, finishing 3rd in class and 7th overall (2nd Grasshopper), and this result helped Austin to runners up position for the Team Prize, won by the MG Midget team.

The trail on **COA 118** now goes cold for some time.

According to the Biggs article *'Entomological Dissection - The 'Grasshopper' Austin Sevens'* it appears that it was purchased from the Works by Bill Scriven at some point in the late 30s, and subsequently sold to George Symonds, in whose ownership probably it was significantly damaged by fire. Certainly at some stage during the war, it still retained the Le Mans door-less body as shown in photographs of the car with lights modified to comply with wartime blackout regulations, yet at some point, presumably in the 1940s the body was rebuilt with doors exactly as the trials cars were equipped. It is hard to imagine that such an expensive rebuild would have been justified unless the original body was damaged beyond repair. Views are at variance as to the cause of the fire; one possibility is that it was damaged in an air raid whilst at the Austin Works (for repair?); another view is that it was destroyed by a fire at Scriven's parents' home.

50. **COA 118** late 30s picture *Authors' Collection*

51. **COA 118** sporting wartime white flashes and headlamp cover *Authors' Collection*

Whatever the reason, when Max Bennett wrote his article in the 750 Bulletin in April 1962, it had what was effectively a trials body with a chrome radiator cowl, but fitted with cycle type mudguards.

Max paid £200 for the car and at this stage it had the Grasshopper engine with twin SU carburettors, non standard cycle mudguards, non original redwood dash, telescopic shockers and hydraulic brakes on the front axle, an air outlet on the bonnet top, shallow doors and twin spare wheels. It appears to have been fitted with a Centric 125 blower at some point as this came with the car, although not fitted, in the late 50s. It was apparently equipped with' *a negative/positive boost gauge'* which supports this view. The car briefly passed to Stuart Bennett before Mike Eyre bought the car in 1963.

52. **COA 118** prior to Mike Eyre's rebuild *Authors' Collection*

He carried out another significant rebuild, re-skinning the body to its original door-less Le Mans specification (retaining its original flitches, scuttle and floorpan), with a new steel dashboard of standard layout. It retained lowered suspension and the Centric blower was fitted to the rebuilt 3 bearing engine. He fitted a mesh dome above the high mounted downdraught SU rather than fabricate the cottage loaf bulge so characteristic of the trials cars. It also sported a single spare wheel and a return to the green painted radiator surround.

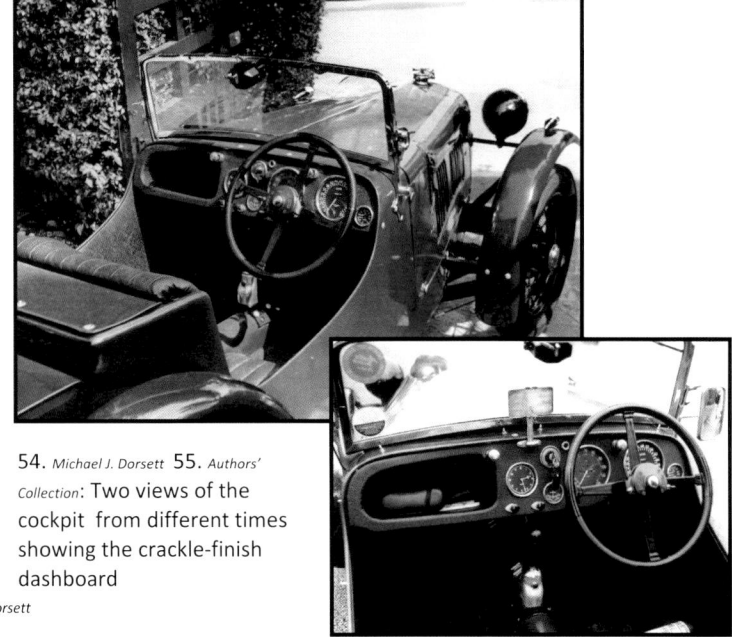

54. *Michael J. Dorsett* 55. *Authors' Collection*: Two views of the cockpit from different times showing the crackle-finish dashboard

53. Painted grille – mesh blower cover *Michael J. Dorsett*

COA 118 passed to its present owner in the early 80s, and apart from the radiator surround being re-chromed it remains substantially as it was rebuilt by Mike Eyre. It has a slightly shallower windscreen than the other examples, and short bonnet straps replace the longer versions which were on the car originally. It is finished in mid/dark green with black upholstery.

COA118 attended the MG Cream Cracker reunion at Rodborough in 1995, and has been seen over the years at Austin 7 Beaulieu meetings and some other 750 MC events.

56. Mike Eyre and Freddie Henry having fun at Silverstone
Ferret Fotographics

57. As it appeared in more recent times *Courtesy Motorsnippets.com*

The official programme for the Donington 12 Hours Sports Car Race in which **COA 118** finished 3rd in class, driven by Kay Petre and Percy Stevenson. It was to be its final pre-war competitive involvement.

COA 119

58. **COA 119** (No.3) competing in the 1937 Donington 12 Hours Race
Authors' Collection

Date of Registration:	12th May 1936
Original Chassis No:	244519
Original Car No:	XE 2037
Original Engine No:	XE 30 (3brg)
Works drivers:	
Kay Petre/G. Mangan	1937 Le Mans
Kay Petre/P. Stephenson	1937 Donington 12 Hrs
Kay Petre/Mme Itier	1938 Paris-Nice Rally
Trials:	
H. L. Hadley	(1938-1939)
Private Ownership:	
J. Wilson	(1940 - 2006)
Wilson Family	(2006 - current)

First registered 12th May 1936 and intended for the cancelled Le Mans race that year, **COA 119** emerged for the 1937 event, and was driven by Kay Petre and Guy Mangan. It was the second car of the team to retire with a fractured oil pipe having completed 970km, being classified 31st. The following month Kay Petre drove the car with Percy Stephenson, an Austin distributor from Southport, in the Donington 12 Hour Sports Car Race, finishing 16th overall and 5th in class. This was its final event in door-less form, as it was next seen a year later when it competed in the 1938 Paris-Nice Rally again driven by Kay Petre, this time partnered by Mme Rose-Itier. Cars competing in this event were required to carry full equipment including hood, and so **COA 119** was converted to low chassis trials specification, deep doors, still unblown, but with a single spare wheel. Its previous mid green paintwork was changed to the mid blue favoured by Kay Petre and the radiator cowl was now chromed. They were placed 26th out of 29 finishers.

Following the Paris-Nice Rally, the car was entered in the IMRC Phoenix Park International GP held on 11th September 1938, to be driven by Guy Mangan. It does not appear in the reports or results of this race so perhaps non started.

By the end of October it had been converted to full trials specification including blower and raised chassis and was campaigned by Hadley in trials for the remainder of its Works career. The door arrangements were also modified at this stage, the body being widened at the rear of the doors which allowed more cockpit space when shut. It was also the only Grasshopper to be fitted with external door handles. Hadley's first trial with **COA 119** was the Mid Surrey Experts' Trial on 29th October and his final outing was the Plymouth Motor Club 200 on 29th May 1939, where he set best performance, but was disqualified when he was delayed by an accident. This was also the car's final Works appearance, and it was sold to Mrs Wilson, wife of the Austin distributor at Dunoon for £55. It was to be used by her son John (Jock) Wilson after the war.

59. 1938 Experts' Trial *Authors' Collection*

60. A post-war trial with 'Jock' (Jack) Wilson *Authors' Collection*

'Jock' Wilson recalled that he took the car up to Scotland in March *1941 'It was in very good order, and my father kept it during the war when all sorts of people wanted to buy it, including the submarine commander at the Holy Loch'*. His first competition was in the 1946 Colmore Trial, and the supercharger seized as they went past the Austin Factory. A couple of trials in Yorkshire/Lancashire followed before competing in the Highland 3 day Trial, winning the Team Prize, but thereafter *'I carried on from there, and found that the Grasshopper.....didn't fit the bill, and I built myself a special with an A40 engine, Austin 7 chassis and rear axle and Ford 10 suspension'*. In this latter car he had great success *'winning the Highland and 18 of the 19 trials I did in Scotland'*. There was one further outing with the Grasshopper when he competed with **COA 119** in the RAC Championship in Cheltenham.

61. Photos taken at Dunoon in 1965

The car now disappeared from general view, sitting in the garage premises in Dunoon. At some point the car had been sent down to the Works for rebuilding and the engine subsequently went missing. When the car was photographed in 1965 in Dunoon, it was in a poor state, and Jock Wilson had no plans at that stage either to part with it or rebuild it. Most of the parts however, except the engine, were there. So it remained until 1994, when Jock heard about the planned MG Reunion at Rodborough and dispatched the car to a local fettler, who having dismantled it, went out of business. A few important parts were missing, including the radiator cowl, but these were fabricated with the help of original parts loaned from **AOV 343**! The car, fitted with a standard Austin 7 engine, duly made it to the event

It has since been seen at the MAC/MCC Centenary event at Brooklands in 2002 and some local Scottish events. Jock died in 2006 at the age of 86, and the car remains in the family.

62. Marine Drive, Scarborough '440' Trial (1946) *Authors' Collection*

63. Rodborough 1995 *Authors' Collection*

64. 'Jock' Wilson and COA 119 outside his home in Toward, Argyll *Michael J. Dorsett*

65. Scottish Western Thoroughbred Vehicle Club Summer Rally *David Clelland*

COA 121

66. 1937 Donington International Tourist Trophy Race
Authors' Collection

67. Dodson capturing the attention of the press
Authors' Collection

Date of Registration:	12th May 1936
Original Chassis No:	244521
Original Car No:	XE 2039
Original Engine No:	XE 32 (3brg)
Works drivers:	
H. L. Hadley/	(1937 Le Mans,
C. J. P. Dodson	1937 Donington 12 Hrs)
Trials:	
C. L. Goodacre	(1937-1938)
W. H. Depper	(1938)
A. H. Langley	(1938-1939)
W. H. Scriven	(1939)
Private Ownership	
Lloyd Evans	(1940 - 1949)
Ray Morley	(1949 - 1951)
Taylor	(1952)
Thomas Duffield	(1953 -1955)
David Carson	(1956)
Bill Johnson	(1956 - 1978)
Joe Lynn	(1978 - 1992)
R. Woodside	(1992 - 2004)
Ian Moore	(2004 - current)

COA 121 was first registered on 12th May 1936 to compete in the cancelled 1936 Le Mans race, but its competition debut occurred a year later in the 1937 event. Its competition number was 57, and entered by the Austin Motor Company its drivers were Dodson and Hadley. The latter tells an amusing story about a bet that they could lap the other team Grasshoppers by the 4 hour mark. This feat was just achieved, much to the surprise of Goodacre who was driving **COA 118**! It however befell the fate of the other 2 cars, retiring with a fractured oil pipe, having covered 998 kms and being classified 30th, just ahead of **COA 119**.

The same driver pairing competed in the Donington 12 Hour Sports Car Race on 24th July that year, the problem with the oil pipes having been resolved, finishing 7th & first Grasshopper.

Finally, on 4th September, Dodson took the car to Donington as a lone Austin entry in the Tourist Trophy which was run as a handicap race. Dodson, number 29, was the only entry in the 750cc class and retired after half distance with 'engine problems'. His fastest lap was a shade below 56 mph.

Thus ended its racing career, the car being converted to high chassis, blown trials specification, unusual shallow doors, with its unique large capacity racing fuel tank set into the rear body, significantly encroaching on the already small storage space behind the seat. In addition its radiator cowl was now chromed and it had abbreviated front wings more in the style of the production Nippy than the usual Grasshopper trials version. In this specification, driven by Goodacre, it tackled the SUNBAC Vesey Cup Trial on 6th November 1937.

For the next few months, it joined the usual 4 '**BOA**' and occasional '**AO**' cars, and after Goodacre won a premier award in the 1938 Exeter, Bill Depper took over driving duties for the 1938 MGCC Ludlow Trial, when Goodacre left the Company, and by this point the radiator cowl had reverted to green painted. Langley took over the car in May 1938, as by then his regular mount **BOA 59** had been sold to Carlaw. Its final event in Works hands was the Lawrence Cup trial in May 1939, when Scriven had a one-off drive.

The Official Programme for **COA 121**'s final track event.

68. 1937 Gloucester. Goodacre takes over - note chrome cowl *Authors' Collection*

69. Langley on Nailsworth Ladder, 1938 Fedden
Ferret Fotographics

Lloyd Evans, whose father had an Austin Dealership in Carmarthen, acquired the car in 1940, and on 12th July 1949 it was bought by Ray Morley from 'Evans Motors Ltd' in Carmarthen for £310. His first event was the MCC Buxton Trial in October that year. After a further handful of events, the crank broke in the Buxton Trial in 1950. Following failed attempts to replace the special crank, he purchased **BOA 59** in September 1951 and sold **COA 121** in April 1952 to Mr Taylor of Blackpool for £155.

The car then spent many years in Northern Ireland, being passed to Thomas Duffield of Ballynahinch around 1953, who recalled that *'it was fitted with standard engine and gearbox at the time, but had been fitted with a Ford 10 engine previously. I got the original engine which was special, having a pressure fed crank.....10 stud block, non adjustable tappets....and was supercharged by Centric blower and large SU carb.... also a 15 gallon petrol tank at rear'.* There is however no evidence that Mr Duffield rebuilt the engine and fitted it to the car.

In the mid fifties, the car, by now painted red, was bought by David Carson in Northern Ireland for £7 and sold on after a short time for £11, presumably to Bill Johnson who owned it for 22 years from 1956 to 1978. It seems likely that the car received a minor rebuild and repaint, possibly following accident damage early in its time with the new owner.

Joe Lynn in Ballymena owned the car from about 1978 to 1992. When bought, it had a standard Austin 7 engine; Joe Lynn had a 3 bearing pressure fed engine built by Andy Storer, with a '37 cylinder head, using a horizontal SU carburettor with standard Austin 7 manifolding. This was mated to the existing gearbox with its original Grasshopper extension. In 1992 the car passed to R. Woodside, and in 2004, after 51 years in Ireland it was purchased and 'repatriated' by Ian Moore. At that stage it had the following specification:

    3 bearing standard engine rebuilt/modified by Andy Storer
    Original mudguards and fuel tank
    Light wood dashboard, but including original speedometer and rev counter
    16" wheels / oversize tyres all round
    Bowed front axle with standard early radius arms and drop links
    Bluemels flat spoke steering wheel without throttle and advance retard mechanism.

The car, it is understood, is currently being returned to its Le Mans specification, but with doors and a Centric blower with modified carburettor mounting to avoid a bonnet bulge. It shares a garage with an ex- Works 'Duck' single seater.

70. 1938 Lands End – Depper *Ferret Fotographics*

71. A pre-2004 picture *Barry Clarke*

Fourth Batch, 'UI 3345'

Date of Registration:	December 1937
Original Chassis No:	XE 1037
Original Engine No:	XE 40 (3brg)
Works Drivers:	
None recorded	
Private Ownership:	
Mrs Gladys Watt	(1937 –
P. W. Widdowson	(1951 - 1952)
John Hodges	(1953 - 1955)
M. E. Grafton	(1960 -
John Kelly	(1963)
Peter Hornby	(1964 - current)

72. Wartime photograph of **UI 3345** Authors' Collection

UI 3345 is the only Grasshopper which was produced in 1937. It appears to have been unused by the Works prior to being registered to Mrs Gladys Watt of Culmore Road, Londonderry in December 1937. The photograph above shows the car during the war when it was owned by someone serving in the RAF.

From the photographs of the car taken at this time, its specification is that of an early low chassis, pre-blown car with body details as the first and second batches, with swept wings. It has the large tank and a single spare wheel, and 16" rear wheels. Whilst the Grasshopper instruments are there, including 80mph speedometer and 5,500 rpm rev counter, they are not in the usual positions, the speedo and rev counter being mounted in the centre of the dashboard with no 'cubby hole'. It is fitted with the large winged Austin radiator cap as seen in the early publicity photos and a flat Bluemels steering wheel. A Grasshopper gearlever extension is also fitted. The Grasshopper engine and chassis numbers indicate that it was manufactured shortly before it was sold to Mrs Watt. Whilst there is no record of a Works competition history, intriguingly there is an RAC stamp on the top face of the 3 bearing crankcase beside the engine number. There is evidence of blue, mid green (also evident on parts of **BOA 59**), red and finally cream paint in its later years.

73. This is likely to be an early photo of **UI 3345** taken in Ireland in the late 1930s. The driver is understood to be Tom Dickson with younger brother John. The car is reported to have been purchased through Harry Ferguson.

The photo is reproduced courtesy of Simon Thomas.

74. War years *Authors' Collection*

75. The car (then **8046 WW**), as acquired in 1964

By 1951 the car had been fitted with a Ford engine and swing axle LMB front suspension with the distinctive low chassis, late-Grasshopper swan-necked Girling radius arms being retained.

John Hodges owned the car from 1953 to 1955 at which time it was mid green and he recalls cooling problems with the Ford engine and some issues with the connection of the Ford gearbox and the propshaft! At this point a couple of air outlets had been fixed on each side of the bonnet top to aid engine cooling.

By 1963 a standard Austin Seven engine and gearbox had been fitted, and the car belonged to a student at Leeds University. When acquired by the current owner in 1964 (for £30), the independent front suspension remained, but the remote control gear lever had disappeared.

The car was rebuilt between 1964 and 1966 and a number of changes were made. The engine was changed for a 2 bearing pressure fed Nippy unit modified by Bill Boult, and a Nippy gearbox was fitted. With twin 1⅛" SU carbs and a 4 branch manifold it developed about 23bhp at the wheels. In addition, a Grasshopper style remote control based on a Singer Le Mans gearchange was fitted. The LMB front suspension was replaced by a Girling type dropped axle, retaining the original Grasshopper radius arms, a new mounting was fabricated to take twin spare wheels and the original mudguards were substituted for cycle type. Finally, hydraulic brakes were fitted and the very effective hood frame mechanism was modified to accept a '3 plane' hood.

76. VSCC Lakeland Trial 1983

77. MGCC Rodborough 1995

In this form the car covered 10,000 miles in the year 1966-67, much of it travelling between Leeds and Edinburgh, and was good for an indicated 75mph. In that time there were no engine failures despite harsh treatment, but having broken 2 halfshafts and a front axle, the decision was made to retire it from daily use. It subsequently raced in VSCC events between 1967 and 1970, and competed in the VSCC Lakeland Trial in 1983. It was exhibited at the Motor Museum at Bentley from 1984 to 1991, and came out of semi retirement for the MG Cream Cracker reunion at Rodborough in 1995.

78. Peter Hornby in action at Silverstone, 1968

79. **UI 3345** parked up at Silverstone – July 1982

80. Hustyn Hill on Lands End Centenary Trial 2008 – John Bennett, a close friend of the owner, in control

81. Kop Hill Climb c 2010 –John Bennett giving it throttle

It has taken part in the MCC Centenary Lands End Trial in May 2008 and the Centenary Exeter Trial in 2010, plus other events including the 2013 MCC Welsh Trial and a number of MG Kimber Trials in the hands of John Bennett who has also taken it on a number of occasions to the Kop Hill climb.

It was finally reunited with its original engine (fitted with the SUs from 1966) and a Grasshopper gearlever extension in 2001, and in 2010 the carburettors and manifolds were removed to be replaced by a Centric 125 blower and cross-over manifold, mounting the 1 3/8" horizontal SU on the offside of the engine, so avoiding the 'cottage loaf' bulge.

The car had been re-registered **8046 WW** in 1960, but its original registration was recovered in 1982. It currently shares a garage with **BOA 59**.

82. **UI 3345** cockpit

83. Blower with 'cross over' inlet manifold

Copies of Grasshoppers

Over the last 40 years a very large number of replica 'Ulster' Austin Sevens have been constructed, largely as a result of the relative simplicity of design, and cheapness of manufacture of the body shells. Some of these cars have been virtually indistinguishable from the original.

The challenge of producing a convincing copy of a Grasshopper is however significantly greater, with a much more complicated body, and an engine with many unique components. There are however a very small number which come close, and these have generally been based on bodywork constructed by Keith and Stuart Roach.

CH-6315 / BOA 60

In 1982, an Australian, Graeme Steinfort, who on a working holiday in London in 1967, had purchased the original engine from **BOA 60**, commissioned Artesi (Roach, Taylor, Clarke - RTC) to build a Grasshopper body for him. It arrived in Melbourne in April 1983. The doorless body, which is supported on a round tube frame, is mounted on a standard Ruby chassis with a dropped front axle and 1937 semi-Girling cable brakes. Modern instruments were installed as were bucket seats rather than the usual Grasshopper arrangement. Trials type mudguards were specified and originals copied. The body in shape and dimensions is a close copy of Grasshopper **UI 3345**, which was loaned to Artesi for the build; some parts such as the bonnet sides are probably interchangeable with equivalents on that car.

Once in Australia, the rebuilt Grasshopper engine was installed in the chassis with a locally produced close ratio gearbox and gearlever extension. In 1990, the engine was running on a 1½" SU carburettor, which was later changed to a 1¼" version. Graeme Steinfort competed with it from 1991 in Vintage trials and sprints, and road registered it in 2000. Its Australian registration was **CH-6315**. The build was featured in an article *'Grasshopper - An Australian Replica'* by Graeme Steinfort (Vintage Austin Magazine Summer 2000/1).

The car was subsequently bought by Ian Moore in 2003, and has been re-registered in the UK as **BOA 60**. In his ownership it is understood that a Grasshopper remote gearlever has replaced the Australian item.

The car changed hands in 2012.

84. Steinfort 'Grasshopper'. Pictures taken shortly after completion, and not yet road registered *Authors' Collection*

WD 5283

Another car constructed by Artesi in the mid 1980s for Geoff Winder in Yorkshire. Intended for trials, in doorless form, it has Grasshopper style instruments and layout, and a very good representation of a Grasshopper radiator cowl. It was trialled in VSCC events in the 1990s by Jo Winder, and was bought by Barry Clarke around the turn of the century. Although based to some extent on the RTC Mk2 it is a good likeness and often mistaken for an 'original'. Now owned by Martin Eyre, and continues an active life in trials events.

85. **WD 5283**, Martin Eyre driving, Cobham 2014   86. Jo Winder VSCC trialling *Authors' Collection*

SV 9061

87. Photos taken at the Roach premises prior to collection *Roach Manufacturing*

Another Roach 'Grasshopper' constructed in the early 2000s for Belgian Christian Lauffs. Little is known of the car, but from the available photographs it looks a very good copy. This car has deep doors and wing arrangements similar to **UI 3345**. It appears to be on a 'mid height' chassis setting, and with 17" front and 16" rear wheels is a very convincing copy. Currently abroad, it doubtless now runs on Belgian plates.

Other copies

A few more copies of Grasshoppers have been made; one of particular merit is **UF 6136**, built by Alan Riley in New Zealand in 1986. This was based entirely on details and photographs from contemporary books and magazine articles. It is constructed on an export Ruby chassis, with 16" wheels and Big 7 shock absorbers. The body is aluminium panelled over a wood frame, the front wings are modified Ruby and the rears formed from the outer halves of 4 Ruby rear wings! The radiator cowl and windscreen frame are also based on Ruby items. It is believed that Alan Riley still owns the car.

88. Alan Riley's New Zealand car *Authors' Collection*

John Bamber's example doing what a Grasshopper was intended to do. It appears to be an RTC Mk 2 bodied car with a Grasshopper style radiator cowl, one of a growing number of copies. No doubt more will emerge as Austin Seven parts are sourced for future 'specials', and some would say are a welcome change from the ubiquitous 'Ulster replica'.

89. *2003 Lands End trial* *Authors' Collection*

90. Ilkley, May 2006
(http://hoits.smugmug.com)

Living with a Grasshopper

It was noticeable at the event in 1995 in Rodborough that all but one of the owners, past and present, were of slim girth and no more than 'average' height for their generation. This was probably not a coincidence as the Grasshopper interior is intimate and rather tight. The exception was the late William Delafield, the then-owner of **BOA 59**, who whilst slim, exceeded 6 feet in height. Examination of that car reveals that the bodywork was probably at some time professionally modified to allow the seat back to be set a couple of inches rearwards. Whilst most of the Works drivers were both small and slim, when **COA 119** was converted to trials specification for Hadley, the door arrangements were modified to allow a little extra 'wriggle room' in the cockpit for *'portly little Bert'* who was somewhat rounder than his team mates. Like any Austin 7, when two-up it becomes quite an intimate experience and tackling a classic trials hill requires the passenger to grip the offside rear of the body, with arm behind the driver, and the top corner of the 'cubby hole' if there is a need for bouncing up muddy hillsides! - As they did in the thirties.

91. Early publicity photo *Authors' Collection*

92. **UI 3345** with modified hood 1967

The snug feeling becomes more intense when the hood and sidescreens are in place. The rear plane of the original two section hood is very close to the driver's head, particularly if of current average height, and indeed the air in the 'Float on Air' cushions needs to be minimised to permit the driver of today to see comfortably through the windscreen. Some cars (**UI 3345**, **AOX 3** and **COA 121**) now have a modified 3 plane hood arrangement which produces a more comfortable interior and a little more luggage space.

93. Boost gauge - Late addition

The instrument layout is comprehensive, only lacking a blower pressure gauge which of course was unnecessary when the cars were first built. At least two of the cars are now fitted with ex WW2 Air Ministry boost gauges to indicate blower pressure. Whilst the sense of 'cosiness' is enhanced after nightfall by the gentle glow of the 2 instrument lights (particularly with green filters), it is not possible to adjust them adequately to provide illumination for all the dials. The standard Austin 7 lighting systems provide the usual challenges in modern conditions and need modification if extended night work is anticipated - particularly if off road sections are included!

Many of the cars were originally fitted with 'Bluemels Brooklands' steering wheels which some feel are not ideal, being of overlarge diameter and often dished. Particularly where drivers are of modern day proportions, the smaller diameter flat spoke spring wheel, as fitted to the '65' model provides a suitable alternative. The remote gearchange is a pleasure to use, but the handbrake in the standard position can be a bit of a stretch in a hill 'restart'. **UI 3345**, which was converted to hydraulic brakes many years ago, is fitted with a 'fly off' handbrake, located beside the gearlever, which is much easier to use. The fold flat windscreen, unique to this model, is robust and simple in operation, and some of the trials cars had a movable spotlight attached to the nearside pillar for operation by the passenger.

94. Fly off handbrake **UI 3345**

Other than the view over the bonnet (with or without bulge) to the quick action radiator cap, as you would expect, the driving experience is very similar to any sports Austin Seven with a fair amount of power available. In full trials specification, with steel mudguards and twin spare wheels it is no lightweight and the blower makes a significant difference. Unblown, and even in racing form the performance was probably little better than a Speedy - as illustrated by the 1935 Le Mans result. According to Bert Hadley, even the 'lightweight' 1937 Le Mans cars were developing only 27 bhp. However, when driving a Grasshopper, it feels quicker; an unblown car with a few modern tweaks possibly nudging 75mph, and the blown cars good for 80mph (with a lot more torque).

95. Non-standard arm for front mounted trackrod

96. **UI 3345** - Revised track rod arrangements

As originally produced, the turning circle, like many Austin 7s, is rather large for modern day driving tests and trials. In 1937 **BOA 59** was modified, with new fabricated forward facing track rod arms (95), which allowed the track rod to be located in front of the axle. This significantly improved the turning circle, and the resulting lack of 'Ackerman' did not prove a problem. In recent years **UI 3345** has similarly successfully had its track rod moved in front of the axle, this time using the standard sports track rod arms. Again, there has been a noticeable reduction in the turning circle.

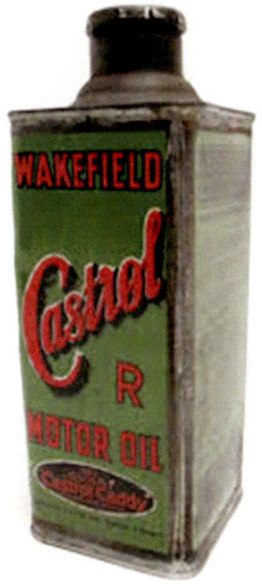

On first acquaintance with a Grasshopper, it is quite usual to find that you can override the detent when changing rapidly from 2nd to 3rd gear (probably a sign of the age of the equipment) and one tends to lean on the horn button when turning round to reverse, but these are minor irritations which are soon overcome. Some cars run Castrol 'R' in the blower oil tank, to give the driver the reassuring smell that the system is working. The blown cars have a discernible whine under acceleration which together with the Castrol 'R' vapours give the impression that you are *really* travelling! Stop and start tests on classic trials show that even compared with 50s and 60s equipment, the blown Grasshopper is very quick off the mark and still competitive.

Fifty years ago it was very rare for a Grasshopper on the public roads to be identified, with its unique radiator cowl often being mistaken for a BSA Scout or even a Singer Le Mans. The badge and styling were not as recognisable as the relatively ubiquitous MG with its slab tank and spare wheel. Nowadays they are better known, particularly in Austin Seven circles where they now appear almost regularly. Grasshoppers are quite comfortable cars to drive; drivers have been known to travel 4 hours at a stretch without a stop. In wet weather, with standard wiper it is either 'RainX' or screen down! In terms of creature comfort, the driving position has some adjustment, and there is limited luggage space behind the seat, and indeed beside the passenger's legs in the footwell.

97. Space for a weekend bag!

98. Owner Michael J. Dorsett in full flight

As the cars were built on Ruby chassis there is rarely a shortage of replacement parts for the running gear. The unique scuttle, floorpan, fuel tank base panel and trials wings are steel with the rest of the body constructed of aluminium. Body rot has not been a problem on the surviving cars although in a couple of cases accidents have led to some replacement panelling. The radiator cowl, usually of brass, is another unique feature although some replica cowls have been produced by Roach engineering in recent years. The Grasshopper engine does of course have few parts in common with the standard item, although replica parts are available, probably to the point where it would be possible to produce a complete engine, but at some cost.

99. Grasshopper with unique luggage-carrier *750MC*

Of all the sports Austin Sevens produced, the Grasshopper is the most user-friendly and practical. All were eventually fitted with doors, and the luggage space whilst certainly not large is easy to access and a practical shape for weekend luggage. **COA 118** was even fitted with a neat luggage rack above the spare wheel mounting, when owned by Max Bennett in the early 60s.

The cars are robust and like any car intended for trials, will take a fair amount of hard use without significant damage. The bodies do not suffer from rust damage, and most chassis parts liable to wear and needing replacement are available off the shelf. Many people would say that the Grasshopper was the best looking of the sports Sevens; it certainly had the 'thirties look', which until then had been somewhat lacking.

What a great pity that it never went into production!

A few reflections from some who have driven them:

J H Blyth on AOX 4: 'After taking over one of these wonderful little cars from the works in 1938, I found it so suitable for ordinary use, and so easy to start in any weather that I have since covered about 12,000 miles of competition and daily running to the office etc., without any repairs or replacements except one set of plugs; the car had done 6,000 miles when I bought it'   *'Talking of Sports Cars'* - **Autocar** May 9th 1941.

The Light Car on AOX 4: 'We have had quite a lot of motoring in the vehicle and it is surprising how the tiny green machine can cruise effortlessly at around the mile-a-minute mark, with a maximum of some 75 mph should you wish to scamper and snappy acceleration to match. The crackle from the exhaust is a trifle cop-attracting and you can see the nostrils of the boys twitch as the scent of Castrol 'R' hits them and brings all those nostalgic memories back' ' *A Grasshopper Without a Hop'* - **The Light Car** February 1946.

Ray Morley on BOA 59: 'BOA 59 gave me a wonderful time in spite of all sorts of snags.... A lovely little car.... I seem to remember how warm my feet always were in the snow hills, although the top half was the opposite!' - Ray owned the car from 1951 to 1957 and competed extensively in MCC and other trials.

Maxwell Bennett on COA 118: 'A comfortable pace in the trials 'Grasshopper' was around sixty mph; above this they were apt to jump around owing to their soft springs and high ground clearance. However, the Le Mans car was fitted with an Ulster type bowed front axle with forged drop ends to the radius arms... in the cockpit one is faced by a redwood dash containing a comprehensive set of instruments. The five-inch speedometer and rev counter dials are easily read between the steering wheel ... The driving position is comfortable and secure, and can be maintained for long periods.' *'The Grasshopper Austin'* - **750 Bulletin** April 1962.

Stuart Bennett on COA 118: 'I found the Grasshopper to be an absolutely delightful motor car to drive, and entirely different to other Austin Sevens. Its road holding was impeccable, and most exhilarating. It had unfortunately only two SUs to breathe by... and this rather limited its performance. It was a trifle temperamental in reverse as it would sometimes accelerate furiously, with me more often than not, not in full control. Very hairy! ... I would dearly like another Grasshopper...' - **750 Bulletin** early 60s.

Michael Dorsett on AOV 343: 'It would have to be the very last thing to go. I'd have to be really hungry before I sold it...' Owner since 1963.

Competition Reports from the Motoring Press and other sources

Austin

ALONGSIDE OTHER CAR MANUFACTURERS OF THE TIME RECOGNISED THE PUBLICITY TO BE GAINED THROUGH COMPETING IN TRACK AND SPEED EVENTS AND THE POPULAR RELIABILITY TRIALS. Both MG and Singer directly sponsored teams of cars piloted by leading drivers: MG's 'Cream Crackers' and 'Three Musketeers', Singer's 'Candidi Provocotores' and so to Austin's own 'Grasshopper' team. This strategy was not so popular with some private entrants, suspecting the factory teams to have a technical advantage over their own privately entered cars, and with the added advantage of factory support. In reality there was little difference between the factory sponsored cars and the standard production models. Whether this criticism extended to the 'Grasshoppers' is speculative, since these were not production models, albeit the construction was not so dissimilar, except in appearance, to the sports models available to the general public, and although the cars were not officially entered for events by the factory, they did receive extensive technical support from the Competitions Department, whether these were driven by the driver/mechanics directly employed at the Austin, or the 'loaned' cars with their invited drivers.

Prime 'trialling' country was shared in many club events and favourite hills were commonly used: Exmoor, the Cotswolds, the Shropshire Hills, the Welsh Marches, the Peak District and the South Downs were frequently exploited. C. A. N. May's experiences of these trials in 'Wheelspin' are particularly descriptive and Andrew Brown's similarly named website offers an extensive treasure trove of factual information covering the trials and the location of observed sections. Cowbourne's record of the main MCC trials is indispensable for its detail. The most entertaining accounts are to be found in the magazines of the day, a selection of which is reproduced in edited form, here, focusing unashamedly on the performance of the Grasshoppers. More sources of information can be found in the Reading List appearing at the end of this book.

The Grasshopper trials cars, initially, were entered for the MCC events throughout 1935, but with the introduction of the ex-Le Mans cars at the close of the year, drivers began competing in many other club events, primarily representing the North West London M.C. (NWLMC) and the Sutton Coldfield and North Birmingham A.C. (SUNBAC), often competing in the same events but registered independently, judging from the competition numbers assigned. Initially, the trials costs were paid out of Lord Austin's own pocket, and the Works drivers paid overtime for weekend work, eventually competing on a 'voluntary' basis and receiving only expenses. Successes saw invitations extended to a variety of other local club and national events, including those organised by their arch-rivals, the MGCC. A very busy trials calendar developed that was generally repeated year by year until the onset of war brought an end to competition.

It is easy to read about the exploits of these drivers and their cars in isolation, but it should not be forgotten that the years in which the Grasshoppers performed were austere for many: high unemployment, low wages, the shocking spectacle of hunger marches, the rise of Fascism in Europe, civil war in Spain; against this troubled background, the trials scene remained active and popular with those manufacturers and private car owners who could afford to indulge their time and money in pursuit of fun, personal glory, awards and potential sales, but also popular with the hundreds of enthusiastic spectators, from all walks of life, who braved whatever the elements had to offer to enjoy the spectacle first-hand.

The account of these potent, mud-plugging 'Special Austins' commences with the **1935 MCC Lands End Trial**, coinciding with the debut of the 'Three Musketeers' team of MGs, a tournament that was to flavour the competition from here on; so let the trials begin!

Sporting Events

Key

Photographic evidence	⊕
Video evidence	V
Detail(s) to be confirmed	Red text
Did not finish	DNF

English Trial
Scottish Trial
Track Event
International Event

1935 MCC Easter Lands End Trial 19-20th April — 23rd Event

W. J. Milton	268	AOX 3	Silver Award (MCC-V)
J. G. Orford	269	AOV 343⊕	Premier Award
R.J. Richardson	270	AOX 4⊕	No Award

First appearance of the 'AO' registered cars– **low chassis, unsupercharged.**

1935 MCC Edinburgh Trial 7-8th June — 28th Event

W. J. Milton	115	AOX 3	Retired

1935 24 Hour Le Mans 15-16th June

P. Driscoll/C. D. Parish	59	BOA 57⊕	DNF
C. J. P. Dodson/ R. J. Richardson	60	BOA 58⊕	28th out of 58 Entrants
C. L. Goodacre/ R. F. Turner	61	BOA 59⊕	DNF

Debut of the 'BOA' registered cars in race form, **unsupercharged.**

1935 MCC July Rally (Torquay) 26-28th July

W. J. Milton	20	AOX 3⊕	Silver Award (No. 17 Coachwork comp)
J. G. Orford	139	AOV 343⊕	Premier Award (No.16 Coachwork comp)
R. J. Richardson	140	AOX 4 ⊕	Premier Award (No. 15 Coachwork comp)

1935 MCC Members' Meeting (HST) – Brooklands 14th September

R. J. Richardson	47	AOX 4⊕	1 Hour Speed Trial Class L <850 Silver Medal

1935 MCC Sporting Trial (Buxton) 5th October — 15th Event

J. G. Orford	79	AOV 343	No award (MCC-V)
R. J. Richardson	80	AOX 4	Premier Award
W. J. Milton	81	AOX 3	No Award (MCC-V)

1935 MCC Exeter Trial 27-28th December — 21st Event

W. J. Milton	214	AOX 3	Bronze Award
R. J. Richardson	215	AOX 4	Non Starter
C. L. Goodacre	280	BOA 58⊕	Silver Award
W. S. Sewell	281	BOA 59	Bronze Award
W. H. Scriven	282	BOA 57	Silver Award
H. L. Hadley	283	BOA 60⊕	Silver Award & Simms Hill Trophy Winner

First trials appearance of the converted 'BOA' registered cars and BOA 60's first competitive event; **low chassis.**

1936 SUNBAC Colmore Trophy 22nd February

C. L. Goodacre (W. H. Depper)	23	BOA 59⊕	First Class Award
H. L. Hadley	24	BOA 60⊕	Second Class Award
W. H. Scriven	25	BOA 57⊕	Second Class Award
J. G. Orford	42	AOV 343⊕	Second Class Award
R. J. Richardson	43	AOX 4⊕	Third Class Award
C. D. Buckley	44	BOA 58⊕	First Class Award, Langley Cup Trophy

BOA 58 – first car to be fitted with a **supercharger.**

1936 NWLMC Coventry Cup 14th March

H. L. Hadley	33	BOA 60⊕	Second Class Award, Best Sunbac
W. H. Scriven	34	BOA 57⊕	
C. D. Buckley	56	BOA 58⊕	Third Class Award
C. L. Goodacre	58	BOA 59⊕	

Rest of 'BOA' cars fitted with **superchargers.** Goodacre reputedly installs Ulster/Duck engine in BOA 59.

1936 United Hospitals Trial (Cotswolds) 29th March

W. H. Scriven		BOA 57	First Class Award, **Team Award**
C. D. Buckley	30?	BOA 58⊕	First Class Award, **Team Award**
H. L. Hadley		BOA 60	First Class Award, **Team Award**

1936 MCC Lands End Trial 10-11th April   24th Event

R. J. Richardson	222	AOX 4⊛	Silver Award
J. G. Orford	223	AOV 343⊛	Premier Award
C. L. Goodacre	274	BOA 59⊛	Premier Award
W. H. Scriven	275	BOA 57⊛	Premier Award
H. L. Hadley	276	BOA 60⊛	Premier Award
C. D. Buckley	286	BOA 58⊛	Premier Award
W. J. Milton	318	AOX 3⊛	Bronze Award

1936 MGCC Abingdon Trial 9th May

| C. D. Buckley | 49 | BOA 58⊛ | Premier Award |
| J. G. Orford | 54 | AOV 343⊛ | Premier Award |

Runners-Up Team Award (Inter-team) Sunbac 'B' Team: W. C. Butler, J. G. Orford, G. L. Boughton

1936 MCC Edinburgh Trial 29-30th May   29th Event

| W. J. Milton | 95 | AOX 3 | Silver Award |
| H. L. Hadley | 206 | BOA 60 | Premier Award - Held Over |

1936 Lancashire AC Blackpool Rally 12-14th June

| C. D. Buckley | 96 | BOA 58 ⊛ | Starting Test Prize (Saturday) |

1936 MCC July Rally (Torquay) 17-18th July

W. J. Milton	34	AOX 3	Silver Award
J. G. Orford	106	AOV 343⊛	Premier Award
C. D. Buckley	108	BOA 58⊛	Premier Award
R. J. Richardson	109	AOX 4	Non-starter
P. H. J. Barugh	112	BOA 60⊛	Silver Award

'AO' series cars fitted with **superchargers**

1936 MCC Members' Meeting – Brooklands 26th September

R. J. Richardson	50	AOX 4's' 1 hour High Speed Trial <850 Premier Award, & relay car no.P2
C. D. Buckley	80	BOA 58's' 1 lap handicap <850 & team relay car no. P3
W. H. Scriven	82	BOA 57's' 1 lap handicap <850 & team relay car no. P1

1936 MCC Sporting Trial (Buxton) 7th November   16th Event

W. J. Milton	24	AOX 3⊛	Premier Award
R. J. Richardson	81	AOX 4	Non-starter
J. G. Orford	89	AOV 343⊛	Premier Award
W. H. Scriven	90	BOA 57⊛	Premier Award
C. D. Buckley	91	BOA 58⊛	Premier Award
H. L. Hadley	113	BOA 60⊛	Premier Award

BOA 57 fitted with 'cottage-loaf' bonnet bulge

1936 Bristol MC & LCC Roy Fedden Trophy Trial 14th November

C. D. Buckley	10	BOA 58⊛V	
W. H. Scriven	11	BOA 57⊛V	
R. J. Richardson	12	AOX 4⊛	
H. L. Hadley		BOA 60	Anthony Cup – Best Supercharged 1100

BOA 58 fitted with 'cottage-loaf' bonnet bulge

1936 SUNBAC Shell Cup/Vesey Cup 21st November

R. J. Richardson	7	AOX 4⊛	Second Class Award
J. G. Orford		AOV 343	Tankard
W. H. Scriven		BOA 57	Second Class Award, **Team Prize**
C. D. Buckley		BOA 58	Watson-Gwynne Bowl, **Team Prize**
H. L. Hadley		BOA 60	Vesey Cup winner, **Team Prize**

1936 NWLMC/SUNBAC London – Gloucester 5th December   26th Event

| C. D. Buckley | 75 | BOA 58 ⊛ | **Team Award** |

1936 MCC Exeter Trial 1- 2nd January 1937   22nd Event

H. L. Hadley	152	BOA 60⊛	Premier Award
C. D. Buckley	153	BOA 58⊛	Premier Award
W. H. Scriven	154	BOA 57⊛	Silver Award
W. S. Sewell	155	BOA 59⊛	Bronze Award

BOA 59 & BOA 60 fitted with 'cottage-loaf' bonnet bulge

1937 SUNBAC Colmore Trophy Trial 27th February

W. S. Sewell	4	BOA 59 ⊕	Second Class Award
R. J. Richardson	5	AOX 4	Third Class Award
C. D. Buckley	22	BOA 58 ⊕	Principal Award, Shell Cup
W. H. Scriven	23	BOA 57 ⊕	Second Class Award, Best 750 performance
H. L. Hadley	24	BOA 60 ⊕	First Class Award Trial to Trial Trophy
J. G. Orford	52	AOV 343 ⊕	Retired

1937 MCC Lands End Trial 26-27th March   25th Event

C. D. Buckley	275	BOA 58 ⊕	Premier Award (MCC-V)
H. L. Hadley	276	BOA 60	Retired (blown gasket)
W. H. Scriven	277	BOA 57 ⊕	Premier Award (MCC-V)
J. G. Orford	278	AOV 343 ⊕	Premier Award
W. S. Sewell	279	BOA 59	Non-Starter
W. J. Milton	280	AOX 3 ⊕	Bronze Award (MCC-V)
R. J. Richardson	281	AOX 4 ⊕	Bronze Award

1937 Liverpool MC Jean's Cup Trial 11th April

R. J. Richardson		AOX 4	Wade Trophy – best performance <1100cc

1937 SUNBAC Inter-Club Team Trial 24th April

C. L. Goodacre	38	BOA 59 ⊕	Worcestershire Austin O C 'B' Team
R. J. Richardson		AOX 4	Worcestershire Austin O C 'B' Team
C. D. Buckley		BOA 58	
H. L. Hadley		BOA 60	Worcestershire Austin O C 'A' Team?

1937 MGCC Abingdon 1st May

C. D. Buckley	59	BOA 58 ⊕	
H. L. Hadley	60	BOA 60 ⊕	Watkinson Cup (Best Visitor)
W. H.Scriven	61	BOA 57 ⊕	Novices' Award

1937 MCC Edinburgh Trial 14-15th May   30th Event

W. J. Milton	81	AOX 3 ⊕	Premier Award
W. S. Sewell	201	BOA 59	Non-Starter
C. D. Buckley	202	BOA 58 ⊕	Premier Award
W. H. Scriven	203	BOA 57 ⊕	Silver Award
H. L. Hadley	204	BOA 60 ⊕	Premier Award

1937 Bristol MC & LCC Whitchurch Airfield 22nd May

H. L. Hadley	1	BOA 60	5th in Class

1937 Lancashire AC Blackpool Rally 4-6th June

C. D. Buckley		BOA 58 ⊕	
W. H. Scriven		BOA 57 ⊕	

1937 24 Hour Le Mans 19-20th June

K. Petre/G. Mangan	55	COA 119 ⊕	DNF
C. L. Goodacre/ C. D. Buckley	56	COA 118 ⊕	DNF
C. J. P. Dodson/H. L. Hadley	57	COA 121 ⊕	DNF

1937 MCC July Rally (Torquay) 16-17th July

J. G. Orford	44	AOV 343 ⊕	Premier Award
C. D. Buckley	47	BOA 58 ⊕	Premier Award
H. L. Hadley	48	BOA 60 ⊕	Bronze Award
W. H. Scriven	49	BOA 57 ⊕	Silver Award
W. J. Milton	72	AOX 3 ⊕	No Award

1937 Donington 12 Hours Sports Race 24th July, 221 laps

C. J. P. Dodson/H. L. Hadley	1	COA 121 ⊕	finished 2nd (7th overall)
C. L. Goodacre/C. D. Buckley	2	COA 118 ⊕	finished 3rd (11th overall)
K. Petre/P. Stevenson	3	COA 119 ⊕	finished 5th (16th overall)

1937 Singer Motor Club, Midland Centre Annual Sporting Trial 7th August

W. H. Scriven		BOA 57	Patrick Challenge Trophy & Replica <1100

1937 XI RAC International Tourist Trophy, Donington 4th September

C. J. P. Dodson	29	COA 121 ⊕	DNF - 61 laps, 29th Engine problem

'AO' series cars fitted with 'cottage-loaf' bonnet bulge

First appearance of the 'COA' registered cars sporting doorless bodies and **unsupercharged**.

1937 MCC Members' Day Meeting – Brooklands 25th September

T. H. Cole	27	AOV 343	High Speed Trial (1 Hour) 69.45mph
			Premier Award; 2 lap handicap car no. 73;
			1 lap handicap car no. 68 (Events 6 & 11)
C. D. Buckley	28	BOA 58	2 lap handicap car no. 45; 1 lap handicap
			car no. 43 (Events 4 & 9)
W. H. Scriven	29	BOA 57	2 lap handicap car no. 44; 1 lap handicap
			car no. 42 (Events 4 & 9)

1937 Wye Valley Club (Hereford City Trophy) 10th October

W. H. Scriven		BOA 57	First Class Award
C. D. Buckley		BOA 58	First Class Award
A. H. Langley		BOA 59	First Class Award

Langley, former Singer driver, joins Austin as a trials driver.

1937 MCC Sporting Trial (Buxton) 23rd October   17th Event

W. J. Milton	40	AOX 3	Non-starter
J. G. Orford	41	AOV 343	Premier Award
R. J. Richardson	96	AOX 4	Premier Award

Milton and Orford vanish from the trials scene after this event.

1937 Mid-Surrey Automobile Club Experts Trial – Exmoor 30th October

W. H. Scriven		BOA 57	Retired (blown gasket)
C. D. Buckley	21	BOA 58 ⊗	Runner-up in Timed Tests (Tied)
A. H. Langley		BOA 59 ⊗	Class Winner (750cc)
H. L. Hadley	31	BOA 60 ⊗	

1937 SUNBAC Vesey Cup 6th November

W. H. Scriven		BOA 57	
C. D. Buckley	25	BOA 58 ⊗	Watson Gwynne Bowl
H. L. Hadley	26	BOA 60 ⊗	Second Class Award
C. L. Goodacre		COA 121	

First appearance of COA 121 in trial form – shallow doors, **high chassis and supercharged**.

1937 Bristol MC & LCC Roy Fedden Trophy Trial (Cotswolds) 13th November

W. H. Scriven		BOA 57	Third Class Award
C. D. Buckley		BOA 58	Winner Roy Fedden Trophy
A. H. Langley		BOA 59	Second Class Award
H. L. Hadley		BOA 60	No award
C. L. Goodacre	48	COA 121 ⊗	First Class Award

1937 Torbay and Totnes MC English Riviera Trial 20th November

W. H. Scriven		BOA 57	**Team Award**
C. D. Buckley		BOA 58	Winner, Premier Award, **Team Award**
A. H. Langley		BOA 59	Best Visitor, **Team Award**
H. L. Hadley		BOA 60	Runner-up, Eric Perry Cup
C. L. Goodacre		COA 121	

Hadley rolls BOA 60

1937 SUNBAC/NWLMC London-Gloucester Trial 4th December   27th Event

A. H. Langley	62	BOA 59 ⊗	Bronze Medal, Third Class Award
C. D. Buckley	63	BOA 58 ⊗	Silver Medal, Second Class Award
W. H. Scriven	64	BOA 57 ⊗	Bronze Medal, Third Class Award
C. L. Goodacre	75	COA 121 ⊗	Silver Medal, Second Class Award
H. L. Hadley	76	BOA 60 ⊗	Silver Medal, Second Class Award

'BOA' series cars now placed on **high chassis**.

1937 MGCC South West Boxing Day Kimber Trophy Trial 26th December

| C. D. Buckley | | BOA 58 | First Class Award |
| A.H. Langley | | BOA 59 | First Class Award, Spencer Trophy |

1937 MCC Exeter Trial 7-8th January 1938   23rd Event

W. H. Scriven	182	BOA 57 ⊗	Premier Award
A. H. Langley	183	BOA 59 ⊗	Premier Award
C. D. Buckley	184	BOA 58 ⊗	Premier Award
T. H. Cole	193	AOV 343	Premier Award
C. L. Goodacre	212	COA 121 ⊗	Premier Award
H. L. Hadley	213	BOA 60 ⊗	Premier Award

Hadley undergoes surgery and a period of convalescence, following this trial.

48

1938 MGCC Ludlow Midland Sporting Trial 13th February

W. H. Depper	20	COA 121⊗	Grasshopper Cup & 1st Class Award
C. D. Buckley	22	BOA 58⊗	Ludlow Cup
A. H. Langley	23	BOA 59⊗	Bryant Cup Winner
W. H. Scriven	24	BOA 57⊗	First Class Award
T. H. Cole	30	AOX 3⊗	
		Kimber Team Trophy: Buckley, Langley, Scriven	

1938 SUNBAC Colmore Trophy Trial 26th February

T. H. Cole	10	AOX 3⊗	Second Class Award
R. J. Richardson	11	AOX 4⊗	Retired
W. H. Depper	12	COA 121⊗	Third Class Award
W. H. Scriven	28	BOA 57⊗	Principal Award, Special Award
C. D. Buckley	29	BOA 58 ⊗	Principal Award, Shell Cup
W. S. Sewell	30	BOA 60	Third Class Award

1938 MGCC South West Skurray's Scramble Trial 13th March

W.H. Scriven	BOA 57	Second Class Award
C.D. Buckley	BOA 58⊗	First Class Award
A.H. Langley	BOA 59	First Class Award

1938 Hagley & District Light Car Club Spring Trial 12th March

| T. H. Cole | AOV 343/AOX 3 |

1938 West of England Motor Club Trial 19th March

W. H. Scriven	BOA 57	First Class Award
C. D. Buckley	BOA 58	MCC Cup winner – Best non-member
A. H. Langley	BOA 59	Class Cup winner (under 1000cc)
	Team Award - Knill Memorial Trophy: Buckley, Langley, Scriven	

1938 Liverpool MC Jeans Cup Trial 10th April

| R. J. Richardson | AOX 4 | First Class Award |

1938 MCC Lands End Trial 15-16th April   26th Event

R. J. Richardson	428	AOX 4 ⊗	Premier Award
C. D. Buckley	435	BOA 58⊗	Premier Award, **Team Award**
A. H. Langley	436	BOA 59⊗	Premier Award, **Team Award**
W. H. Scriven	437	BOA 57⊗	Premier Award, **Team Award**
W. C. Butler	438	AOX 3	DNF
H. L. Hadley	448	BOA 60	Non-Starter
W. H. Depper	449	COA 121⊗	Premier Award
T. H. Cole	450	AOV 343⊗	Premier Award

1938 SUNBAC Inter-Club Team Trial (Herefordshire) Worcestershire Austin Owners Club) 23rd April

W. H. Scriven	BOA 57	**Team Winner** WAOC
C. D. Buckley	BOA 58	**Team Winner** WAOC
A. H. Langley	COA 121	**Team Winner** WAOC
T. H. Cole	AOX 3	Sunbac 'B' Team

1938 MGCC Abingdon Trial Challenge Trophy 14th May

A. H. Langley	77	COA 121⊗	First Class Award
W. H. Scriven	78	BOA 57⊗	First Class Award
C. D. Buckley	79	BOA 58⊗	Watkinson Cup for Best Visitor

1938 Scottish Sporting Car Club, Royal Scottish AC Trophy and Scottish Team Trophy 11th June

G. Valentine	AOV 343	
J. H. Blyth	AOX 4	Winner of RSAC Trophy and **Team Award**
(Caledonian MC 'A' Team: J.E.Playfair, Frazer-Nash-BMW; J.P. Millar, Ford V8; J.H. Blyth, Austin Seven S)		

1938 Caledonian Motor Club Summer Half-Day Trial 18th June

G. Valentine	AOV 343
(J. H. Blyth)	AOX 4
B. L. Carlaw	BOA 59

Goodacre leaves Austin in February to work for Ethyl Export Company. T. H. Cole joins the trials team.

Depper steps in for Goodacre in COA 121.

BOA 60's last appearance AOX 3 competes for the final time before its September sale?

Richardson's final event. AOX 3 might have been used by W. C. Butler (Singer), number 438.

Langley takes on COA 121? Cole using either AOV 343 or AOX 3?

Scottish Tartan Grasshopper Team formed with the sold-off AOX 4, AOV 343 and BOA 59 cars.

1938 Paris-Nice Rally, Automobile Club de Nice 31st July to 5th August

K. Petre/A. C. Itier	72	COA 119 ⊛	26th out of 29 Finishers

> COA 119 reappears, **unsupercharged, low chassis** and doors.

1938 Kirkcaldy & District M. C. 27th August

G. Valentine		AOV 343	First Class Award, 2nd in Team Prize
W. K. Stewart	7	AOX 4 ⊛	First Class Award, 2nd in Team Prize
B. L. Carlaw		BOA 59	First Class Award, 2nd in Team Prize

1938 Lanarkshire MC and CC Shersbie-Harvie Trophy 29th October

G. Valentine	AOV 343	Second Class Award
J. H. Blyth	AOX 4	
B. L. Carlaw	BOA 59	First Class Award

Caledonian MC Team: J. P. Miller (Ford V8), Elliott Playfair (1 ½-litre Frazer-Nash-BMW), J. H. Blyth (Austin 'Grasshopper') won the 1938 Club Championship

1938 Mid-Surrey Automobile Club Experts Trial (Exmoor) 29th October

C. D. Buckley	15	BOA 58 ⊛	Class Award Runner-up 1100cc
A. H. Langley	17	COA 121 ⊛	Winner, Gliksten Trophy
W. H. Scriven	19	BOA 57 ⊛	Third in class
H. L. Hadley	29	COA 119 ⊛	
			Second in Team Award, Ballards Trophy

> Hadley returns to Trials with COA 119, now with **supercharger** but retaining low chassis. These are the final four Austin Works cars.

1938 SUNBAC Vesey Cup 5th November

W. H. Scriven	BOA 57	Watson Gwynne Bowl (under 1100cc)
C. D. Buckley	BOA 58	Ashtray
H. L. Hadley	COA 119	
A. H. Langley	COA 121	Vesey Cup Winner
		Team Prize: Langley, Scriven, Buckley

1938 Scottish Sporting Car Club Anniversary Trial 5th November

B. L. Carlaw	BOA 59

1938 Bristol M. C. & L. C. C. Roy Fedden Trophy Trial 12th November

H. L. Hadley	3	COA 119 ⊛	Second Class Award
C. D. Buckley	19	BOA 58 ⊛	
A. H. Langley	20	COA 121 ⊛	Alexander Duckham Cup (4th Best)
W. H. Scriven		BOA 57	

1938 Hagley & District Light Car Club 21st November

W. H. Scriven	BOA 57
C. D. Buckley	BOA 58

1938 SUNBAC/NWLMC London-Gloucester 3rd December — 28th Event

C. D. Buckley	BOA 58	Silver Medal, Second Class Award

> Hadley competed in the Touring Car class with a 900cc Austin Big 7 saloon.

1938 Ford Enthusiasts' Trial 27th December

H. L. Hadley	COA 119	Best Performance <1100

> COA 119 now placed on **high chassis**.

1939 Lanarkshire MC & CC Half-Day Trial 4th February

G. Valentine		AOV 343	
J. H. Blyth		AOX 4	Second Class Award
B. L. Carlaw	6	BOA 59 ⊛	Premier Award (best performance)

1939 NWLMC Coventry Cup Trial 11th February

H. L. Hadley	12	COA 119 ⊛	Runner-up, Whittingham Trophy and First Class Award

1939 MGCC Midland Centre Ludlow Trial 12th February

W. H. Scriven	37	BOA 57 ⊛	Best under 1100cc, Ludlow Cup
C. D. Buckley		BOA 58	Second Class Award
A. H. Langley		COA 121	First Class Award

1939 SUNBAC Colmore Trophy Trial 25th February (Saturday)

H. L. Hadley	67	COA 119⊛ Second Class Award
C. D. Buckley	70	BOA 58 ⊛ Second Class Award
W. H. Scriven	72	BOA 57⊛ Third Class Award
A. H. Langley		COA 121 Third Class Award

Langley's final appearance with COA 121.

1939 Southsea Club President's Trophy Trial 26th February (Sunday)

H. L. Hadley	COA 119⊛ 1,500 Cup and NWLMC Tankard

1939 Scottish Sporting Car Club Winter Half-Day Trial 4th March

L. Bissett	AOV 343	First Class Award, Team Prize (B Team)
J. H. Blyth	AOX 4	First Class Award, Team Prize (B Team)
B. L. Carlaw	BOA 59⊛	Premier Award in Opposite Class, First Class Award, Team Prize (B Team)

1939 West of England Motor Club Spring Trial 4th March

W. H. Scriven	BOA 57/COA 121	MCC Cup – Best Visitor

Potentially the last trial of BOA 57

1939 Caledonian MC Invitation Trial 11th March

J. H. Blyth	AOX 4	First Class Award
B. L. Carlaw	BOA 59	Premier Award in Opposite Class, First Class Award

1939 Edinburgh & District M. C. Trial 25th March

G. Valentine	AOV 343⊛	Second Class Award, **Team Prize**
J. H. Blyth	AOX 4	Premier Award, Challenge Trophy, **Team Prize**, First Class in Opposite Class
B. L. Carlaw	BOA 59	**Team Prize**

1939 Highland 2 Day Trial 8-10th April

G. Valentine	AOV 343	
J. H. Blyth	AOX 4	Premier Award for Best under 1500cc
B. L. Carlaw	BOA 59⊛	

1939 NWLMC Lawrence Cup – 'Red Road' 20th May

C. D. Buckley	51	BOA 58⊛ Special Test Tankard
W. H. Scriven	52	COA 121⊛

BOA 58's last trial. COA 121's final pre-war trials appearance.

1939 Plymouth Motor Club '200' Reliability Trial 29th May

H. L. Hadley	COA 119 Best Performance, but disqualified

COA 119's final pre-war trials appearance.

1939 Caledonian MC Summer Trial 10th June

G. Valentine	10	AOV 343⊛ Second Class Award, **Team Prize** 'B' Team:

G. Valentine (Austin Seven), J. Anderson (Anderson Special), W. K. Stewart (H.R.G.)

The event that launched the new team of Austins

100. The Austin Team, 13 April 1935 *Ian Moore Collection*

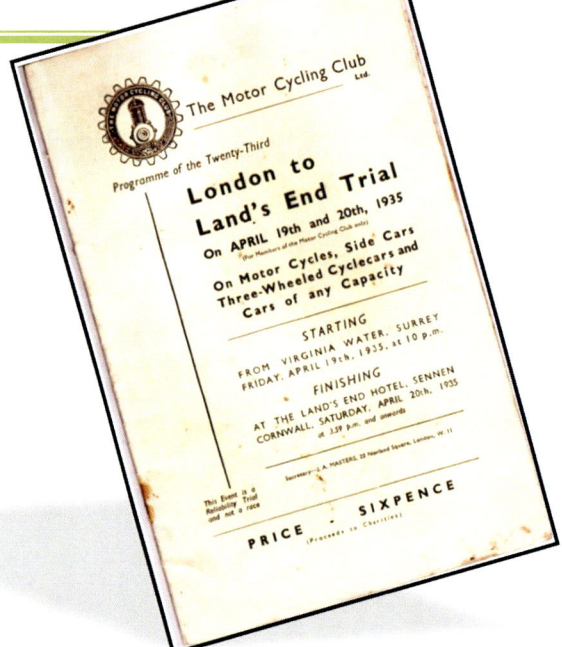

1935 MCC Easter Lands End Trial 19-20th April   23rd Event

Grasshopper Results			
W. J. Milton	268	AOX 3	Silver Award
J. G. Orford	269	AOV 343	Premier Award
R. J. Richardson	270	AOX 4	No Award

Of the 339 entries for Class IV (Cars) 313 were starters. The Austin Works entered the specially prepared Trials cars **AOX3, AOX 4** and **AOV343** driven by Milton, Richardson and Orford, respectively. The cars left the starting point at Virginia Water, Surrey, from 11.09pm on the Friday, driving through the dark to reach the Breakfast Control at Deller's Cafe, Taunton, from 2.38am. The finish was at 5.08pm and took in the following observed hills: Grabhurst (or Doverhay), near Dunster, Lynmouth, Station, Beggars' Roost, Barton Steep (Test), Darracott, Hustyn, Bluehills Mine and Rocky Lane (a newly introduced hill) that included a Test.

The Light Car (26 April 1935) makes meagre, but favourable mention of the Grasshopper team and their performance on Barton Steep with its restarting test under drizzly and greasy conditions: '*The new Le Mans type Austin Sevens were pleasant to watch, but R. J. Richardson, who was having [carburetion] problems, stopped.*' Contrast this with the 'Cream Cracker' drivers who *gave beautiful exhibitions... without unnecessary swank... and the three equally distinctive N-type Magnettes from the Evans stable who were no less impressive.*' The 'Grasshopper' drivers have yet to make their mark.

1935 MCC Edinburgh Trial 7-8th June   28th Event

Grasshopper Results			
W. J. Milton	115	AOX 3	Retired

The 'Edinburgh' was the third and final event of the three 'Classic' MCC Trials to qualify for a Triple Award. This event tended to attract marginally fewer entries than the more popular 'Lands End', and only one Grasshopper, Wallis Milton's AOX 3, competed, but retired, along with another 20 competitors who failed to finish. There were 177 Starters out of an original 191 Entries.

This Edinburgh event was made memorable for introducing the three starting points, Carlisle, Stratford-on-Avon and Wrotham Park (Barnet). The Carlisle Starters commenced from 8.15pm. All routes met at the Granby Hotel, Harrogate from 3.44am and finished in Edinburgh from 6.08pm on the Saturday, limiting the trial proper to the section between the breakfast and lunch stops and running the rest on 'go-as-you-please' rally lines. This year's event saw the introduction of three new hills: Summer Lodge, Wrynose Pass and Hard Knott Pass. Finally the weather: a strong south-westerly gale blowing throughout the night, heavy rainfall in the Lakes section followed by spells of bright sunshine for the final lap from Carlisle to Edinburgh. Summer Lodge was the most difficult of the new hills with its loose surface, sharp S bend and stiff gradient.

Park Rash claimed some victims with its bumpy surface, from the top of which a bumpy run over the moors led down to Carleton and on through West Witton, Newbiggin and the foot of Askrigg Hill to Summer Lodge, from which competitors descended Askrigg, tarred and innocuous, where the route made a complete loop before turning to Sedburgh, Kendal and Windermere. Soon after Ambleside main roads were forsaken for twisting, winding by-roads leading to the long and steep Wrynose Pass, tackled in bottom gear with its deep mud and jagged boulders on the loops of the old road. A run through the mountains led to Hard Knott, only three miles away through a howling rain storm, with its hairpins and a Non-Stop and Restart test that were not unduly severe. A tricky sinuous descent took the route through to Eskdale and on through Calder Bridge and Cockermouth and Carlisle for the lunch stop. From this point competitors motored to the finish in Edinburgh.

1935 24 Hour Le Mans 15-16th June

Results			
P. Driscoll/C. D. Parish	59	BOA 57	39th (750 Class) 106 Laps DNF
C. J. P. Dodson/R. J. Richardson	60	BOA 58	28th (750 Class) 138 Laps
C. L. Goodacre/R. F. Turner	61	BOA 59	45th (750 Class) 89 Laps DNF
J. Carr/J. Barbour	62	CZ6324 (A7 Speedy)	27th (750 Class) 141 Laps

The **'BOA'** series cars were built specifically to compete in the Le Mans. Only the first three cars raced, resulting in a *'somewhat inglorious performance'*. Although Murray-Jamieson was not involved in their preparation he remarked that the cars were, *'Too heavy, no thought given to streamlining and no punch.'*

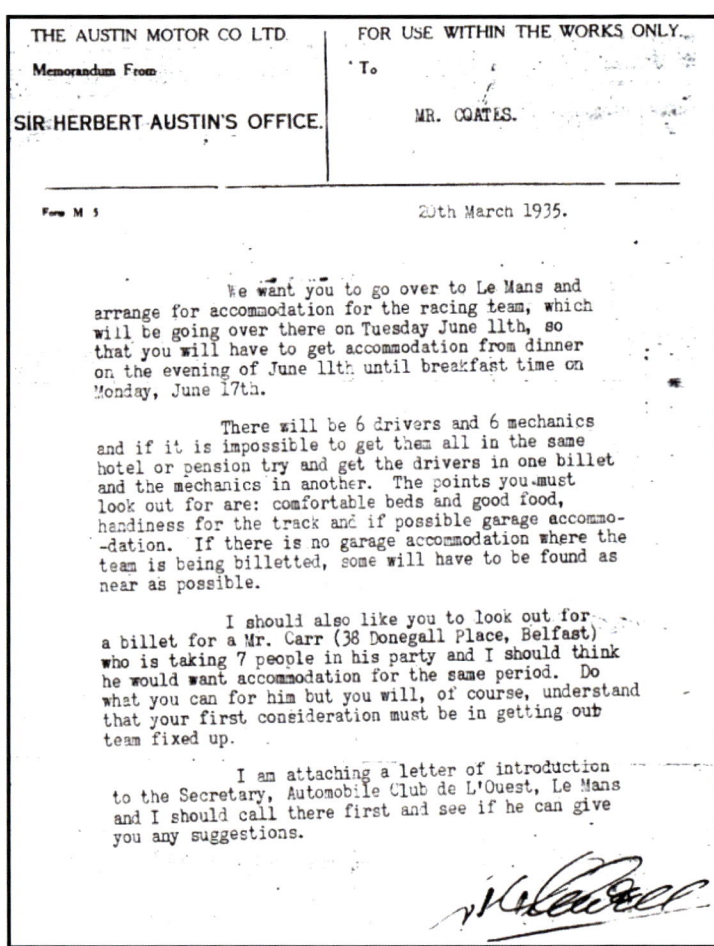

Memo from W. S. Sewell to George Coates with instructions to arrange accommodation for the Austin team's drivers and mechanics, and also for John Carr's Irish team.

George Coates was a fluent French speaker who served his apprenticeship with Austin and who, over the years, was often called upon to translate on numerous trips abroad.

(Reproduced courtesy of Ian Moore)

101. **CZ 6324** at the 2011 PWA7C Autokarna, Nottingham, and the car raced by Carr and Barbour.

On their return to the factory the Competition Department began converting the Le Mans cars for trials competition, following a consultation between Lord Austin, Goodacre and Hadley. Hadley was given permission to take **BOA 60** out on some of the Colmore sections in the Cotswolds and report back. He identified two key problems, both of which were eventually addressed: firstly, the unblown Le Mans engines lacked the sort of power required for the climbs, and secondly, the cars needed more ground clearance.

Both *The Light Car* and *Autocar* went all out to capture the atmosphere and excitement of this event with some quite descriptive literary flourishes. Although their coverage was fair, inevitably the main focus centred on the more exotic cars and drivers, and in a style that might raise disapproving eyebrows in this day and age.

With a customary eye to the prevailing weather conditions, *The Light Car* reported:

Contrary to the Le Mans tradition, the weather was, at best, only fair, and at worst chilly and wet...If the customary blistering sun was missing as the 58 operative cars were juggled into echelon formation before the bustling pits, there was no lack of the unique Le Mans 'atmosphere' – a thing defying analysis or description, yet so real and all-pervading as to be almost cutable with a knife: an unforgettable agglomeration of sights and smells and sounds...

The usual vast concourse of motor vehicles was invading the great car parks, as 4 p.m., the zero hour, drew near, and were being marshalled into that geometrical order which only the pure science of the French gendarme can achieve. The flags of many nations fluttered their friendly defiance at one another above the well-manned pits. Dark-skinned Latins barked excited commands, while their quieter Anglo-Saxon rivals went more stolidly about the tasks of last-minute preparation... And all the while the road surface, wet from a recent downpour, gleamed a warning to the men who soon would be battling for supremacy on that 8.38 mile circuit of sinuous curves and alluring straights... Then silence fell, an electric silence, pregnant with expectation. Seconds passed, the flag fluttered and the brave 58 were dashing helter-skelter to their waiting cars...As the last car disappeared from view, leaving the atmosphere heavy with the biting odour of burning oil, the multitude burst out afresh into excited exclamations and conjectures. Who would lead after the initial lap?... At this early stage no light cars figured in the foreground of the picture. Their turn would come later, when the time came to show stamina. This, after all, was a Grand Prix d'Endurance, not a mad sprint of a few miles...

The urgent methods of the leaders were, of course, not common to the whole field, for a considerable number were merely bent upon covering the distance necessary to qualify them for next year's Rudge-Whitworth cup: among these was George Eyston's women's team in the green P-type M.G. Midgets, who lapped consistently and with due restraint; likewise the little green Austins, manned by the duos Driscoll-Parish, Dodson-Richardson and Goodacre-Turner... **The Autocar** *commented:* Very sanely, which is extremely difficult, the M.G. team, Doreen Evans, Joan Richmond and Margaret Allan, held strictly to schedule in exact formation, keeping absolutely clear of the dog-fight around them, giving the faster cars ample room to pass, while the Austins, with a similar task, handled by Dodson, Goodacre and Driscoll were equally good. **The Light Car** *continued:* Night came down chill and dank, and a far greater proportion of the assembled multitude than usual hied to warm beds and firesides. Enthusiasm, however, still ran high, and many were the shouts of hilarity which arose from the two-storey pits as friends and attendants of drivers staved off the cold with various potions.*

The Autocar picks up from here: *Nine-thirty approached, the hour when the head lights must, by the regulations, be lighted, the hour when one realises for the first time how different and how magnificent Le Mans is. For the moment it was not raining, and as one by one the headlights appeared, the scene was eerie in the extreme. Imagine the dark mass of the grandstand brightly lighted within, silhouetted against the darkening sky, and opposite that the two-storeyed pits brightly illuminated, with lights shaded from the drivers' eyes, each pit a hive of industry on its ground floor, with men actively engaged with semaphore signals, parti-coloured, lined, or plain, illuminated by torches for the better guidance of the drivers.*

Back to **The Light Car**: *After half-distance had been covered at 4 a.m. the lead places were* constantly changing hands, pit stop after pit stop, a roaring succession of cars thrusting through the darkness, their headlamps cleaving the dimness with broad streaks of brilliant light.*

By the end of fifteen hours, **The Autocar** reports *unpleasant things were happening rapidly* – breakdowns and retirements abounded, but, *all this time the M.G.s and Austins had been lapping with that clockwork regularity which shows excellent control. Now there was trouble even among the small cars, for Turner, diagnosing something thoroughly wrong with the gearbox, came in with the official car, having retired. When the Austin eventually reached the pits, anxious friends of other teams enquired the trouble and were told in reply that the car had been 'overwound', but apparently it proved afterwards that the car could have continued, which was a sore blow to all concerned.*

So the only result for the Austin team was 12th position for Dodson and Richardson in the 1000cc class behind the privately entered Austin Speedy of the two Johns, Carr and Barbour.

1935 MCC July Rally (Torquay) 26-28th July

Grasshopper Results

W. J. Milton	20	AOX 3	Silver Award
J. G. Orford	139	AOV 343	Premier Award
R. J. Richardson	140	AOX 4	Premier Award

The cars were classified according to taxation groups, both for the Trial and Rally sections. As for the conditions, **The Light Car** summed it up in one – 'DUST!'

There were three Starting Controls at London, Birmingham and Bournemouth commencing at 10.00pm on Friday 26th July and ending with an Appearance Competition on the Sunday morning, 28th July. There were 153 Starters out of a list of 171 Entrants; 163 taking part in the Trial section, and only 8 in the Rally. All competitors converged at Exeter for a Breakfast Control and then followed a 54 mile Trial route to Torquay, taking in a number of observed hills: Windout, Pepperdon, Little John, Simms and Slippery Sam. Competitors not involved in the Trials section took a more direct route to Torquay, but all participated in a Timed Test on arrival, a short 'Woggle'.

1935 MCC Members' Meeting High Speed Trial, Brooklands 14th September

Grasshopper Results

R. J. Richardson	47	AOX 4	1 Hour Speed Trial Class L <850	Silver Medal

The Club's annual meeting attracted 200 competitors. The major part of the programme was formed by the one-hour trials, starting at 11.00am and running non-stop until 7.10pm Each trial consisted of an attempt to average for a period of one hour a certain set speed around the Outer Circuit. A series of two-lap handicap races followed and a series of one-lap scratch races to show the capabilities of the cars in high-speed work and their massed acceleration at the beginning of the race. The meeting was rounded off by a three-lap team relay event, run in three heats. Richardson, the only Grasshopper entrant for this year's event, completed 20 laps in the 850cc class One-Hour Trial and won himself a silver medal.

1935 MCC Sporting Trial (Buxton) 5th October   15th Event

Grasshopper Results

J. G. Orford	79	AOV 343	No award
R. J. Richardson	80	AOX 4	Premier Award
W. J. Milton	81	AOX 3	No Award

The Trial commenced at the Palace Hotel in Buxton and covered a distance of forty or fifty miles, lasting only a few hours. 116 Starters from a field of 129 left from 9.31am, 5th October, for a noon finish, taking in the observed hills of Jenkins Chapel (2 Sections) about 20 minutes from the start with its greasy first section and harmless hairpin. The difficult to find Blackwell Mill (Blackermill Hill) followed, with a standing start at the steepest pitch at the foot of the hill and a loose and greasy surface. Only 27 car entrants were successful at this point. Litton Slack had had its surface renovated, although it deteriorated as the day wore on and saw some failures. Bamford Clough was the steepest hill in the trial followed by the steep Winnatts Pass with craggy heights on each side but a relatively good surface giving little trouble on it.

1935 MCC Exeter Trial 27-28th December   21st Event

Grasshopper Results

W. J. Milton	214	AOX 3	Bronze Award
R. J. Richardson	215	AOX 4	Non Starter
W. S. Sewell	280	BOA 59	Bronze Award
C. L. Goodacre	281	BOA 58	Silver Award
W. H. Scriven	282	BOA 57	Silver Award
H. L. Hadley	283	BOA 60	Silver Award & Simms Hill Trophy Winner

Members of the Austin team maintained their dignity "under difficulties" when unanticipated spectators arrived.

This Trial was no longer the first Event of the three 'Classic' Trials in which a Triple Award could be earned. It was bypassed in the 1935 series, later to become the third and last event for the 1936 series (put forward to January 1937). Entry level was strong, with 289 starters (238 cars) and boasted a line-up of five Grasshoppers (R. J. Richardson was a non-starter). There was only one Starting Control at Virginia Water from 11.27pm, reaching the Breakfast Control in Exeter for 4.20pm and the Final Control at the Crown Hotel, Blandford, after midday. The observed hills were Fingle Bridge, Simms (where competitors who successfully climbed Simms Hill and kept time at all the Checks and completed the event under Bronze medal regulations were awarded a 'Simms Hill Trophy'), Harcombe (Test) and Harcombe (Non-stop) and Meerhay. H. L. Hadley was the only Simms Hill Trophy winner from the Grasshopper entrants. Disappointingly, *The Light Car* made no mention of the Austin entries' performance and the debut of the newly converted Le Mans cars; nor did *The Motor*, although it did contain a sketch of one of the Austins in difficulty, seen here, with caption. *The Motor* published the results in its 14 January issue, but all it offered was the Award tally. *The Autocar* also failed to report on any of the Austin Grasshoppers; so much for publicity! Any 'Grasshopper' follower might have been pretty miffed after stumping up the necessary 11 pence for these three issues.

1936 SUNBAC Colmore Trophy 22nd February

Grasshopper Results

C. L. Goodacre	23	BOA 59	First Class Award
H. L. Hadley	24	BOA 60	Second Class Award
W. H. Scriven	25	BOA 57	Second Class Award
J. G. Orford	42	AOV 343	Second Class Award
R. J. Richardson	43	AOX 4	Third Class Award
C. D. Buckley	44	BOA 58	First Class Award, Langley Cup Trophy

The 'Colmore' opened the **1936** Trials season for the Austin ensemble, entering all seven of the Grasshopper cars produced at the time. There were 126 listed entries of which 116 started. The course centred in the Cotswold area with the Starting Control at the Fish Inn in Broadway, leaving in pairs at intervals of three minutes from 10.00am Saturday. The course measured 59 miles in total and finished at the George Hotel in

Birdlip, taking in the following observed hills: Fish Hill, Stanton, Stanway (Stop and Restart Test), Guiting Wood (Driving Test), West Down, Mill Lane, Syde Hill (Driving Test), and Greenway Lane. C. D. Buckley in **BOA 58** teamed up with C. A. N. May (MG), and Norman V. Terry (Frazer Nash-BMW) to form the Sunbac 'A' Team and win the Langley Cup Trophy with a First Class Award.

As mentioned earler, reputedly, Goodacre had fitted a special Sprint Ulster, or 'Duck' engine to his **BOA 59** steed – perhaps he'd skimped on the spark plugs judging from the report below? At any rate, Hadley was later to write that he had advised against his team-mate using such an engine as it could not provide sufficient power delivery at the lower revs for the climbs. One has to question his memory here, because Hadley refers to Goodacre with **COA 121** and himself with **COA 119** at a later Colmore. The 1936 Colmore was the only one they attended together, and Goodacre had already left Austin months before Hadley began trialling with **COA 119**! Maybe he had remembered the location correctly, but confused the event and the cars, since many of the observed hills were common to a number of trials held over the years, and Goodacre didn't do too shabbily in this event?

The Autocar, February 28th 1936: *'Colmore Mud!'*

Driving rain! Sleet! Snow! Mud! These were the predominant characteristics of the Colmore Trophy Trial, held last Saturday by the Sutton Coldfield and North Birmingham A.C. Mud in particular was to the fore, in fact to the rear, the sides, and everywhere. Cars were covered in it. Windscreen wipers failing to keep the screen clear, drivers or passengers peered round the side, their faces, too, receiving a generous portion of the all-pervading substance.

Mud, too, caused the first hill, which followed only about a mile from the start at the top of Fish Hill, near Broadway, to be cut out after some seventy cars had tried it. This was not, as one might have thought, because the hill itself was severe, having but one sharp corner, but because cars could not even reach the starting line! Competitors had to descend a steep grass slope, turn round in a slippery field, and so approach the hill itself. The trouble was that the field soon got churned up, and the almost farcical spectacle was seen of horses being used to pull cars to the starting line! There they would be unhitched, the driver would spin his wheels once more in an attempt to restart in a sort of quagmire, and often the horses would have to be hitched on again... Sewell had an interesting blown Austin Ten Sports and managed to get going, but Charlie Goodacre's Seven had a plug cut out, so he stopped. Hadley's Seven needed a horse to get to the line, a gigantic beast dwarfing the little green car, but after the line restarted well. [At Kineton] Orford and Richardson made good but unsuccessful efforts with their Austins; Buckley, however, gathered speed and got over the top, the difference being that he had a blower on his Seven.

1936 NWLMC Coventry Cup 14ᵗʰ March

Grasshopper Results

H. L. Hadley	33	BOA 60	Best Sunbac
W. H. Scriven	34	BOA 57	
C. D. Buckley	56	BOA 58	Third Class Award
C. L. Goodacre	58	BOA 59	

The course for this 'open-by-invitation' event was held in the Exmoor district, with a start just outside Bridgwater – the Control Point was the Royal Clarence Hotel.

'Buckley was here with the supercharged Austin. There were some more of the new type 'blown' Sevens there, besides Buckley's, and I [C. A. N. May] met his team mates, both Birmingham men, H. L. Hadley and W. H. Scriven. Hadley, of course, went on to do big things in the racing world with the twin-O.H.C., single-seater Austins, and Scriven you will probably remember from his shattering imitations of Pop-eye! The Austin boys evolved the team name of 'The Grasshoppers''. May describes the course:

*'Proceedings opened with a new hill...and the hill was chiefly worthwhile for the beautiful scenery in which it was set...Next came the first special test, accelerating downhill to cross a line, stopping, and reversing back up the hill over the original starting line...Widlake was up to form...A little way up the main road off which Widlake runs, but leading off the opposite side of the road, is a hill, not often used, called West Howeton...About half-way up, the hill doubles back on itself, in an acute left-hand hairpin, with a greasy surface on the corner and mud above. There was a timed climb round the hairpin...The Kershams were quite 'mild' after Widlake (***The Motor*** records Goodacre as being the only failure on Kersham 1), and after lunch at the delightful old 'Luttrell Arms', in Dunster, the route led to familiar Doverhay, outside Porlock...Yet another timed climb was taken here, including both corners...Cloutsham was new to me, although I knew it well by repute, and it looked pretty grim.'* **The Autocar** praised Hadley's success at Cloutsham *'for a very neat and well-driven climb'*.

1936 United Hospitals Trial (Cotswolds) 29ᵗʰ March

Grasshopper Results

W. H. Scriven	BOA 57	First Class Award, Team Award
C. D. Buckley	BOA 58	First Class Award, Team Award
H. L. Hadley	BOA 60	First Class Award, Team Award

A total of 36 starters from 43 entries left the Cotswold Gateway Hotel, Burford, following a 90 mile course. Those fitted with competition tyres and solid rear axles fared well. The climbs began with Stancombe, Bismore and Mackhouse and then the notorious Nailsworth Ladder, which stopped 14 cars, most of which had standard tyres. W. Sewell (blown Austin Ten, solid axle but no comps), showed it could be done and sailed to the top, while the team of blown Austin Sevens – C. D. Buckley, H. L. Hadley and W. Scriven – also made fast climbs with the same equipment. A wooded stretch of sticky mud called the 'Gummah' came after the lunch stop, followed by a special test on Bushcombe, involving reversing down a gradient of one in seven, which saw S. Curry (847 M.G.) overturn, his passenger suffering a nasty cut over her left eye.

Warning sign on Nailsworth Ladder:

 **THE LADDER**

THIS HILL TRACK WITH A GRADIENT OF 1 IN 3

IS VERY DANGEROUS AND

ENTIRELY UNSUITABLE

FOR ALL WHEELED TRAFFIC.

MOTORISTS AND OTHERS USE IT ONLY

AT THEIR OWN RISK.

OWING TO THE NUISANCE CAUSED BY EXCESSIVE NOISE MOTORISTS ARE REQUESTED NOT TO USE THIS HILL TRACK **ON SUNDAYS**.

(Speed Magazine 1938)

102. Unfortunately for the local residents, this was a Sunday event!

58

Grasshopper Results

R. J. Richardson	222	AOX 4	Silver Award
J. G. Orford	223	AOV 343	Premier Award
C. L. Goodacre	274	BOA 59	Premier Award
W. H. Scriven	275	BOA 57	Premier Award
H. L. Hadley	276	BOA 60	Premier Award
C. D. Buckley	286	BOA 58	Premier Award
W. J. Milton	318	AOX 3	Bronze Award

This year there were 308 starters. The Austin Works boosted their original team of Grasshoppers with the four BOA series cars developed for the previous year's 24 Hour Le Mans Race. Milton, Richardson and Orford were joined by drivers Scriven, Goodacre, Hadley and Buckley. For this event there were three Starting Controls: Virginia Water, Penzance and Stratford-on-Avon, all leaving from 11.10pm on the Friday, 10ᵗʰ April. The Breakfast Control at Deller's Cafe, Taunton, was shared by all routes, a distance of approximately 120 miles, from 2.23am with the finish at 5.33pm. There was a change to the observed hills: Lynmouth, Station, Beggars' Roost, Barton Steep (Test), Darracott, Crackington (newly introduced) and the redesigned Bluehills Mine.

The Light Car (17 April 1936) was not sparing in its praise for the Austins' performance; referring to the Beggar's Roost section, Hadley was singled out as giving *'one of the neatest climbs of the day'*. On the later Darracott section *'Everybody was impressed by the Austins, of which C. D. Buckley's made probably the best climb, although J. G. Orford and C. L. Goodacre were also excellent'*. **Motor Sport**'s coverage of this climb (May 1936) described the Austin performance alongside other marques, as *'a usefully polished display'*.

1936 MGCC Abingdon Trial 9ᵗʰ May

Grasshopper Results

C. D. Buckley	49	BOA 58	Premier Award
J. G. Orford	54	AOV 343	Premier Award

Team Award (Inter-team) Runners-up – Sunbac 'B' Team:
W. C. Butler, J. G. Orford, G. L. Boughton

The Trial started with a 'double garaging' test in the grounds of the MG works, one of many varieties of special or tie-deciding tests. The route then led out into the Cotswolds, taking in Bismore (stop-and-go test), the inevitable Nailsworth Ladder, a lunch check at Rodborough Common, Axe Hill and Old Hollow (an acceleration test and braking test was held between these two hills). After a 50-mile run back to Abingdon, competitors were entertained to tea at the works. *The Light Car* (15 May 1936) described the trial as *'easy'*, as the dry weather had *'robbed the four hills of their winter-time potency'*.

1936 MCC Edinburgh Trial 29-30th May   29th Event

Grasshopper Results			
W. J. Milton	95	AOX 3	Silver Award
H. L. Hadley	206	BOA 60	Held Over

Entries numbered 170 with 155 Starters. Wallis Milton with **AOX 3** was joined by H. L. Hadley in **BOA 60** for this year's event. The Starting Controls remained the same as the previous year, London, Stratford-on-Avon and Carlisle, with the London entrants leaving from 8.53pm, 29th May, to reach the Breakfast Control (Granby Hotel) in Harrogate from 3.44am and a Finish from 5.47pm on the Saturday. There were four observed hills: Park Rash (32 miles from Harrogate), Summer Lodge, Wrynose Pass ('to-fro-to' Test) and Hard Knott Pass (restart Test). From Carlisle, rally conditions held sway to Liberton, five miles outside Edinburgh. Conditions were very cold and saw a light snowfall on the bleak moors above Summer Lodge, although showers, steady downpours and intervals of pale sunshine were the common experience. Hadley, alongside numerous other rivals, created a favourable impression on Park Rash, according to *The Light Car*. A bumpy 32 mile stretch, including a descent of Askrigg, brought the competitors to Summer Lodge with its steep first half-mile, which part was observed. Three sharp bends and a formidable long gradient caused radiators to boil, before reaching the exposed top. After leaving Ambleside, Wrynose Pass, with its two passes, was the next destination, reached after a long drive through winding, twisting lanes and by-roads. To dispel any misconception that these events were simply enjoyable jaunts through the countryside, *The Light Car* reported the following incident at this section: *On Wrynose Pass there are two loops, remnants of an old track, and used today only in order to make the climb worth observing. On the lower of these loops, about halfway through the trial, an unfortunate accident occurred to Lieut. R. C. B. Buckley, RN (847 M.G.). Between the two hairpin bends, Buckley placed his car rather too near to the off-side edge of the track from which the ground fell away steeply. The ground being soft at that point, his wheels slipped over and the car rolled sideways downhill. During this the passenger was thrown clear, and she escaped with one or two cuts and some bruises, but the driver was trapped under the car when it came to rest, and he sustained a broken thigh. For the remainder of the entry that lower loop was cut out, but naturally there was considerable delay while an ambulance came from Ambleside and went back there.*

The second Lakeland section, Hard Knott, is a steep hill that is covered by 18 to 20 bends from bottom to top, but is now relatively easy. The stop and restart test was conducted on its gradient, and also a timed section to decide team ties. After the lunch stop at Carlisle *'the weather reformed. The sun shone, and the rain had washed the landscape clear of dust, so that the 'greens' were really green. In fact, the rest of the route was more like a pleasant summer evening's run than a trial.* Not much consolation for Lieutenant Buckley with his freshly-plastered leg!

1936 Lancashire AC Blackpool Rally 12-14th June

Grasshopper Results			
C. D. Buckley	96	BOA 58	Starting Test Prize (Saturday)

There were 222 entries and 200 starters leaving from six starting points, each sharing a run of approximately 250 miles. C. D. Buckley won the Starting Control Prize at Birmingham in a time of 1 minute and 24 seconds.

The Motor, June 16th, 1936

The event started early on Friday morning, when competitors started out from London, Glasgow, Birmingham, Manchester, Leeds or Bristol. There were 22 non-starters, so that exactly 200 took the road, converging on the Trough of Bowland, near Clitheroe, at different times of day...The next morning things began with the starting test...then the most spectacular part of the rally began, two special tests on Middle Walk, on the sea front. The first was essentially a matter of nice handling and driving skill... Excitement was at its height when C. D. Buckley's Austin Seven (supercharged) clipped the best time of the day – so far –'and was heartily cheered for his snappy performance' (Autocar June 19th, 1936) ... only to be beaten by S. G. E. Tett driving his unsupercharged Balilla Fiat. (See picture 153)

1936 MCC July Rally (Torquay) 17-18th July

Grasshopper Results

W. J. Milton	34	AOX 3	Silver Award
J. G. Orford	106	AOV 343	Premier Award
C. D. Buckley	108	BOA 58	Premier Award
R. J. Richardson	109	AOX 4	Non-starter
P. H. J. Barugh	112	BOA 60	Silver Award

Starting Controls for this year's event were based in London, Cardiff, Stratford-on-Avon and Penzance, commencing at 10.31pm on Friday 17th July. There were 96 starters overall, from a list of 106, 4 of which took part in the Rally. Competitors met at Exeter for the Breakfast Control. The competitors for the Trial event began leaving for Torquay at 6.30 am, Rally competitors went straight to Torquay via Newton Abbott, where, on arrival, Final Tests were conducted from 9.30am to 1.30am. For this year's trial route, the observed hills were Windout, Doccombe (where *Motor Sport* praised the performance of '*the supercharged Austins of Orford, Sewell and Buckley*', although Sewell was not competing in a Grasshopper), Pepperdon, Waterworks and Simms. Heavy rain and blustery winds made conditions very uncomfortable for the participants throughout the trial as they tackled the sodden hills. Hadley was taking part in the MAC/Worcester MC sprint with the side-valve Works single seater, so it appears P. H. J. Barugh piloted **BOA 60** in his absence.

1936 MCC Members' Meeting – Brooklands 26th September

R. J. Richardson	50	AOX 4 's'	1 Hour High Speed Trial <850 Premier Award (66.71 mph), & team relay car no. P2
C. D. Buckley	80	BOA 58 's'	1 Hour High Speed Trial; 1 lap handicap <850 Race VI, Comp. No. 47 (2nd) & team relay car no. P3
W. H. Scriven	82	BOA 57 's'	1 Hour High Speed Trial; 1 lap handicap <850 Race VI, Comp. No. 48 (3rd) & team relay car no. P1

In the Team relay event, each competitor completed one lap of 3 total laps. The team had a 1 minute 30 seconds handicap.

Programme for the event

1936 MCC Sporting Trial (Buxton) 7th November   16th Event

Grasshopper Results

W. J. Milton	24	AOX 3	Premier Award
R .J. Richardson	81	AOX 4	Non-starter
J. G. Orford	89	AOV 343	Premier Award
W. H. Scriven	90	BOA 57	Premier Award
C. D. Buckley	91	BOA 58	Premier Award
H. L. Hadley	113	BOA 60	Premier Award

A total of 90 Starters out of a 96 Entry left Buxton at 9.00am, tackling Jenkins Chapel (2 Sections), Taddington Moor, Litton Slack, Bamford Clough and Winnatts Pass.

The Light Car 13th November 1936

Strong wind kept the rain away for some hours last Saturday in the Buxton area, but in the afternoon a light drizzle soon turned into good Derbyshire rain. Quite apart from that, but perhaps in consequence of heavy rain the night before, some of the hills were in difficult form. Bamford Clough in particular saved the M.C.C. much expenditure in the form of awards...Jenkins Chapel was the first obstacle and, as usual, its principal difficulty was the hairpin corner...Amongst the four-wheeled cars the palm for climbing highest up the bank should certainly go to G. Warburton (4,234 Vauxhall), but C. D. Buckley (747 Austin) ran him close, described as a 'high flyer on the hairpin' in The Motor's account, and W. J. Milton making 'one of the neatest climbs'. *The next climb at Taddington Moor and its triple-rutted grass that was just sufficiently moist to be highly objectionable to the motorcycles and three-wheelers...had little or no difficulty for the four-wheelers. The first of them, W. J. Milton's 747 Austin, proceeded steadily to the top and this was followed by a succession of other faultless ascents... On Litton Slack: Car after car romped, or, at any rate, proceeded, to the top... Half a mile of narrow lane with a loose and greasy surface, numerous cross gullies and a final gradient of about 1 in 3, describes a really difficult hill. No wonder, therefore, that Bamford Clough stopped about three-quarters of those competitors who reached it... Generally speaking, non-stop ascents were made by acknowledged experts... Winnats Pass was fairly easy, and thereafter there was only the run to Buxton and the Palace Hotel for feasting and merry-making. The trial formed the final round of the 1936 team championship which was won by the 'Musketeer' team of blown 1,408 M.G. Magnettes.*

1936 Bristol MC & LCC Roy Fedden Trophy Trial 14th November

Grasshopper Results

C. D. Buckley	10	BOA 58	
W. H. Scriven	11	BOA 57	
R. J. Richardson	12	AOX 4	
H. L. Hadley		BOA 60	Anthony Cup

The start was from the Prince of Wales Hotel, Berkeley Road Station and followed a 33 mile route taking in Tramp's Paradise, one mile from the start, Hodgecombe Farm, Middle Drag, Old Hollow and Nailsworth Ladder. There were 43 starters from an entry list of 47. Hodgecombe Hill and Weighbridge were new finds.

The Light Car 20th November 1936

'Tramps Paradise was so deep in glutinous mud' it had to be abandoned and *'the company set sail for the next section',* Hodgecombe Farm Hill, *'and its tree-clad leafy slopes easily justified its claim to be included without causing too heavy mortality. Approximately one driver in four needed the assistance of the horse or backed down and took the by-pass. The route card, by the way, listed a by-pass for each of the six hills.* Nailsworth Ladder claimed a mere five victims... Next on the programme should have been a very difficult section called Weighbridge, but it was here that a quantity of earth fell from its rightful place and blocked the way, so the trial passed on to two tests... a rolling-start brake test and a restart test... Straightforward hill-climbing was resumed with the ascent of Old Hollow...Only one hill remained...Known as Middle Drag, it rises out of the village of Dursley and is an eminently fair hill. Running up a tree-clad slope between high banks, it has a severe gradient to call for power and natural difficulties in the way of surface and bends to put a premium on clever handling.*

H. L. Hadley was numbered among the ten successful drivers to reach the top. **Motor Sport** (December 1936) also singled out Hadley, among others, for his performance up Middle Drag, although **The Autocar** (20 November 1936) lumped Hadley in with the drivers who *'struggled to the top'*!

*There is a video clip of (not too clear) **BOA 57** and **BOA 58** on Nailsworth Ladder on the Wheelspin website and on You Tube. **BOA 58** is the first car to appear, fitted with Le Mans type wings and competition number 10 (1m 06s), so ruling out **BOA 60** which was fitted with full wings. This is immediately followed by **BOA 57** with number 11 (1m 10s), sporting full wings. **AOX 4** was also sporting Le Mans type wings for this event, probably retained since the September Brooklands meeting.

1936 SUNBAC Shell Cup/Vesey Cup 21ˢᵗ November

Grasshopper Results

R. J. Richardson	7	AOX 4	Second Class Award
J. G. Orford		AOV 343	Tankard
W. H. Scriven		BOA 57	Second Class Award/**Team Prize**
C. D. Buckley		BOA 58	Watson-Gwynne Bowl/**Team Prize**
H. L. Hadley		BOA 60	Cup winner/**Team Prize**

This Event took place in the Severn area (West Worcestershire), despite darkness and a heavy fog threatening postponement. There were 29 entries of which one failed to start and three failed to complete the 57 mile course. The start was from Stourport and an ascent made through the deep sandy surface of Droppingwell Hill, followed by a driving test, and another on Beauchamp Hill, quite near to Shelsley Walsh. A dozen miles further on a 'stop and go' test was staged at Sandy Lane. From here the course wound through the Worcestershire lanes and byways for a further seventeen miles to reach the third driving test, after which the trial continued on to the finish at the Talbot Inn, Hartlebury.

Hadley wrote in later years that '*quite a lot of needle existed in the trials crowd...There seemed to be a Gentlemen and Players set-up*' and he singles out the M.G. teams for being '*toffee-nosed*'. It seems the M.G. people's smugness was short-lived when he was announced the winner, with popular support from the Singer team, led by his friend Bill Butler. Hadley attributes the success to his secret weapon, a specially manufactured blower pulley used to increase boost, kept hidden from the rest of the Austin team despite their mutterings and snooping round the car after the announcement. He had anticipated their suspicions by leaving '*brief Anglo-Saxon instructions under the bonnet*' to his great delight.

The Motor, November 24ᵗʰ 1936

Dropping Well Hill, less than two miles from the start, stopped 13 of the 28. The gradient is not severe, but the surface consists of deep, loose sand. H. L. Hadley was amazingly fast here.

Immediately over the top of the hill was the first driving test, with two sharp corners and a long reverse around a bend. C. D. Buckley and H. L. Hadley, with supercharged Austins, shared honours for the fastest performance with 20 1/5 secs.

On Beauchamp Hill, near Shelsley, the chief difficulty was another driving test with two lines a dozen yards apart. After crossing the top one and then reversing over the lower line, competitors had to drive on up the hill. In this test Hadley again shone – his 12 2/3 secs. being three-fifths faster than the next best by C. D. Buckley with a similar car...

Sandy Lane, north of Malvern, was the scene of a restarting test, in which 23 competitors exceeded the allowance of 7 secs. The only successful ones were the Austin team (H. L. Hadley, W. H. Scriven and C. D. Buckley) and N. V. Terry (1,991 Frazer-Nash-BMW), who was fastest .Mill Lane, two miles away, stopped four drivers.

Finally there was the third driving test conducted in the dark. One good corner and a bit of reversing sums it up. Hereabouts occurred the last retirement – G. N. Mansell (1,287 M.G.) with back-axle trouble. Once again Hadley was the fastest, his time being 18 2/5 secs.

Motor Sport, December 1936

[H. L. Hadley] the Austin racing recruit, driving a supercharged Austin Seven, put up the most meritorious performance...

Dropping Wells caused a great deal of trouble, on account of a deep layer of sand on the surface, but R. J. Richardson's Austin Seven nearly got up, and both C. D. Buckley and W. H. Scriven proved that the Austin is a worthy trials car...

In the special tests Hadley and Buckley were the best in the supercharged class... So to the finish, after Mill Lane had stopped four cars and a special test had smashed the rear axle of Mansell's blown M.G. Magnette and Hadley's little Austin had proved faster than Langley's and Bastock's M.G. Magnettes, with Eadon and Wadworth (Singers) outstanding in the unsupercharged class.

1936 SUNBAC/NWLMC London – Gloucester 5th December 26th Event

Grasshopper Results
C. D. Buckley   75   BOA 58   **Team Award**

The Trial saw the introduction of a 'selling plate' clause which effectively ruled out any works entries. As the Grasshoppers were all privately entered, they belonged to the factory, and could have placed the Austin entrants in a questionable position; perhaps this explains why Buckley was the only Grasshopper combatant? Competitors also had to demonstrate 'reliability' and this was achieved through sealing filler caps and bonnets with a penalty for any broken seals or work carried out on the transmission. Of the 88 competitors entered, 69 left the Starting Control at Spider's Web Road House (Watford by-pass), passed through one observed section in the night at Kineton Hill, to arrive at the Plough Hotel, Cheltenham for the Breakfast Control, where the ceremony of breaking the seals was performed and tanks replenished. The finish was at the Bear Inn, Rodborough Common from midday Saturday, after tackling Ferriscourt (Descent – and a Special Test on the opposite slopes of Bismore), Quarhouse, Ham Mill, Old Hollow (which proved unexpectedly troublesome and stopped nearly half the field, including Buckley among the 28 failures), the newly introduced Middle Drag (with its steep, narrow approach, a slight bend where a jutting tree root left no choice in the course to be steered, and then a hard pull up between tree-clad banks on a surface of mud and leaf mould), Hodgecombe (the second of the new hills, like a slightly flattened and elongated edition of Middle Drag), Juniper (where there were only four clean ascents, although Buckley made *'a good attempt'*, according to **The Motor** (8 December 1936), followed by a good stretch of hill-free motoring leading to Ferriscourt (Acceleration Test), Station Lane and finally Nailsworth Ladder which proved to be rough but easy.

C. D. Buckley teamed up with C. A. N. May (MG) and H. K. Crawford (MG 'N' Magnette) to win the Team Award for 'SUNBAC'.

1936 MCC Exeter Trial 1st-2nd January 1937 22nd Event

Grasshopper Results

H. L. Hadley	152	BOA 60	Premier Award
C. D. Buckley	153	BOA 58	Premier Award
W. H. Scriven	154	BOA 57	Silver Award
W. S. Sewell	155	BOA 59	Bronze Award

The 'Exeter' actually took place on New Year's Day and the day following in **1937** and became the third event of the 1936 series to qualify for the Triple Award. There were 191 Starters from an entry list of 215. Stratford-on-Avon and Penzance were introduced as Starting Controls to join Virginia Water. London starters left from the Wheatsheaf Hotel, the Stratford contingent from the Falcon Hotel, where the MCC based their headquarters, and the Western Hotel Garage, Exeter, saw off the Penzance starters. There was only one intermediate control on each of the night routes before the 4.30pm convergance point at Deller's Cafe, the Exeter Breakfast Control. The Final Control was the Crown Hotel, Blandford, finishing after midday, the last man checking in at 9.40pm, just over two hours late. **The Light Car** reported: The usual' *fog, ice, snow, floods, teeming rain, biting winds...that generally form such a tiring part of "Exetering" were absent and only a gentle, if somewhat persistent, drizzle prevented the weather being really kind.'*

The trial saw the introduction of two new hills, Windout and Pin. Windout Hill was reached via Cheriton Bishop, the curtain-raiser for the trial, and only stopped a score or so cars, despite *the runnels of water and slime over the rocky but hard surface*. Windout has five bends including a hairpin and a right-angle turn that stopped most people. Fast climbs were made by many, including the Singer and M.G. teams, but *'H. L. Hadley was the most convincing of the blown Austins'.*

Nine miles further on came Fingle Bridge with its dozen hairpins. *The worst part of the hill, a right and left-hand S-bend, caused the most serious trouble. One of the earliest failures at this point was that of B. E. F. Fielding (old J2 M.G.), who slowly came to a standstill, baulking F. Sturgess's old 12-50 Alvis, which, however, made a fine restart when the hill was clear; a feat which was repeated a little later by H. L. Hadley, of the impressive supercharged Austin Seven team...* who, 'with as healthy a note as ever' in his blown Austin (**The Motor** 5 January 1937), 'made a perfect restart after an out-of-order motorcycle had baulked him... The others of the Austin Seven team were good'...*Miles of narrow, muddy lanes with many sharp corners kept drivers very busy for the next 14 miles. Then came Simms* [where] *the Singers were particularly impressive, as also were several supercharged Austin Sevens... streaking up the hill at amazing speeds... From the summit more muddy lanes awaited competitors, and then some extremely welcome main roads skirting Exeter by way of Countess Weir to Sidford. The second new hill, Pin, between Sidmouth and Honiton – and, incidentally, the old pack-horse and coaching road between the two – did not prove any great terror... as a site for the stop-and-restart test and a timed test.* Here, Buckley was included as sharing one of the best performances. *Only one hill remained and 30 miles – for the most part main roads – gave drivers a breather before they arrived there. The last hill was, of course, Meerhay, which has figured in the "Exeter" longer than any other... The extremely loose surface of small stones, resulted in Meerhay claiming many more scalps than it has for some time past... From the last hill main roads were soon joined and competitors settled down to 30-odd miles of easy motoring to Blandford, where the welcome portals of the Crown Hotel denoted an end of their labours and something in the nature of well-earned food and drink.*

1937 SUNBAC Colmore Trophy Trial 27th February

Grasshopper Results

W. S. Sewell	4	BOA 59	Second Class Award
R. J. Richardson	5	AOX 4	Third Class Award
C. D. Buckley	22	BOA 58	Principal Award, Shell Cup
W. H. Scriven	23	BOA 57	Second Class Award, Trial-to-Trial Trophy
H. L. Hadley	24	BOA 60	First Class Award, Best 750 Performer
J. G. Orford	52	AOV 343	Retired

The Trial followed a different format from the previous year. The 87 mile route followed a 'figure of eight' pattern of two circuits, with one group starting on the top loop and the other group completing the lower loop first. The Start and Finish was the Plough Hotel in Cheltenham, leaving in groups of three from 10.03 and returning from 2.21pm. Six Grasshoppers were entered in a field of 84 Starters from an Entry List of 90. The observed hills were: (Northern Circuit) Stanway (Stop and Restart Test), Kineton, Guiting (Driving Test) and West Down; (Southern Circuit) Leckhampton, Juniper, Stancombe (Test), Station Lane and finally, Syde (Test). The Austin Team were Runners-up for the Committee Team Prize behind MG's Three Musketeers Team. P. H. J. Barugh, the driver who filled in for Hadley in the MCC July Rally, also competed as No. 86, but, curiously, driving a '750s' Austin, according to the Cowbourne listings.

There is some discrepancy between *The Autocar* and *The Light Car* reports regarding which of the **BOA** Austins were blown. Earlier reports show they were all supercharged by this time, but were not all displaying the characteristic 'cottage loaf' bulge on the bonnet:

The Autocar, 5th March 1937

"Only the weather can beat us," claimed a marshal at the beginning of the trial. Coming from an official, that was an ambiguous remark, but, whether you look at it from the point of view of the organisers or the competing driver, it proved true. For the course was well chosen, well marked, and stiff enough yet fair enough to meet all tastes. The hills, especially Leckhampton and Juniper, were real tough nuts for even the modern trials cars to crack. Yet clean sheets by cars as widely divided as an Austin Seven and a Ford V8 showed that it could be done...

The first hill observed as a hill was Kineton. This proved [more] lethal, about one in three failing... Three miles farther on, a tie-deciding driving test was held, competitors having to drive forward over a cross-roads, reverse into one arm, and then accelerate straight ahead to the finishing line, cross it, and stop...Hadley (Austin) was apparently averse to stopping at all...

Westdown, the next observed section, proved quite innocuous, claiming only a single failure...there were many good climbs, one of the best being made by W. S. Sewell's supercharged Austin...failure was no disgrace on Leckhampton, especially in the morning, for only seventeen climbed it altogether (including the Austin Team of Buckley, Scriven and Hadley).. only fifteen drivers managed Juniper (including Buckley, Scriven and Hadley).

Stancombe Hill followed. There was a timed test here, in which Buckley and Hadley, both driving supercharged Austins, jointly recorded the best times – 11 3/5 sec - Buckley being especially noticeable for the magnificent way in which he took the first corner. Station Lane, the next observed section, did not do much execution. Only nine failed here...Thence to the next timed test at Syde, a roughly surfaced but not steep hill with a couple of right and left hand bends leading to a fierce left-hand hairpin, on the loose surface of which many waltzed gaily... Fastest time of all was shared by Allard and Hadley, the small Austin and the large eight cylinder car tieing in 13 1/5 sec... And so back to the Plough in time for a much-needed tea.

The Light Car, 5th March, 1937

Leckhampton Hill, on the southern circuit, was very muddy on its lower section, and bright sunshine gave way to stinging rain on the ascent:

This downpour washed a good deal of the mud off the lower slopes and made things somewhat easier for the earlier numbers in the second group, although that does not in any way detract from some very good performances, particularly on the part of the works Austins with which C. D. Buckley, W. H. Scriven and H. L. Hadley made a most convincing demonstration. Hadley was driving the only blown model of the three and was half-way up before he thought it was time to try bottom gear!... Juniper Hill proved quite as difficult as Leckhampton. Competitors were started from the firm surface of the main road, but, even so, few could make much of the hill in the first half... As on the first hill, the rain made it easier for the second group, but the surface began to cut up rather badly at the very end. The successful drivers were W. S. Sewell (747 Austin, S), E. Lloyd-Jones, P. S. Flower (847 MG), S. Curry (847 MG, S), R. M. Andrews, H. Bolton, T. C. Wise and the Austin Seven and Musketeer MG teams complete.

From Juniper, the southern route led to Stancombe, where there was a timed climb in which Buckley put in some marvellous corner work to tie with Hadley's performance in the blown model of 11 3/5 secs.... Station Lane cost marks to only nine competitors, and the only other observed section on the circuit was Syde Hill, where Allard and Hadley, representing both ends of the scale, tied for best effort in the timed section with 13 1/5 secs.

The Northern Circuit started off with a restarting test on Stanway where about one in ten failed on time...Then came Kineton, approached by a water splash about 14 ins deep. About a third of the entry went down as failures... At a cross-roads at Guiting there was a tie-deciding test so schemed to place a greater premium on the competitor than his car...Only two drivers failed to do what they should, but both Hadley and A. B. Langley were reluctant to stop motoring at the end and accordingly recorded poor times. The final hill was West Down, and here Bolton, inspite of his success on Leckhampton and Juniper, was the only one to fail.

1937 MCC Lands End Trial 26-27th March   25th Event

Grasshopper Results			
C. D. Buckley	275	BOA 58	Premier Award
H. L. Hadley	276	BOA 60	Retired
W. H. Scriven	277	BOA 57	Premier Award
J. G. Orford	278	AOV 343	Premier Award
W. S. Sewell	279	BOA 59	Non-Starter
W. J. Milton	280	AOX 3	Bronze Award
R. J. Richardson	281	AOX 4	Bronze Award

Of the 276 entered, 260 were Starters. The Grasshopper entry matched the previous year's strong contingent, but with the addition of Captain W. S. Sewell, replacing last year's Goodacre, and the only non-starter in the team. This was reported as 'The Toughest Land's End for many Years'. Starting Controls were located from Virginia Water (Sunningdale), Exeter and Stratford-on-Avon. Exeter Starters left from 10.23pm on the Friday, and all routes converged for the Breakfast Stop from 1.08pm, again at Deller's Cafe, Taunton. The Saturday finishing time for cars is not recorded. The observed hills were Station, Beggars' Roost, Barton Steep (Non-stop) and Barton Steep (Test), Darracott, Crackington (Non-stop), Hustyn, Bluehills Mine 1 and Bluehills Mine 2. Hadley had to retire with a blown gasket.

The Autocar 2nd April 1937

Of the formidable group of seven Austins, poor Hadley had a gasket go just after the start and set off back to the works for repair, but, with a supercharger fitted, the job was rather a long one and he gave up. Captain Sewell was a non-starter with his Austin... The group of supercharged Austins pleased everyone by their good climbs. Two were fast, others medium and even quite slow, but all succeeded with the same ease. ..[At Beggars' Roost] the team of supercharged Austin Sevens showed up well, particularly Buckley and Scriven, but Orford got the cheers for it was "touch and go" with him for a long stretch, and the holiday crowd will always encourage competitors in such plight...

As usual there was a stopping and starting test on Barton Steep in the Lyn Valley... Buckley, for instance, leading the contingent of green supercharged Austins, was terrific, giving the car plenty of "gun" and managing to change into second higher up. Scriven and Orford followed successfully with similar cars, to the delight of the holiday crowd who thoroughly appreciated the fine performance of the small cars. The three Austins chose the left hand side of the hill... Among the fastest on the actual restart were Richardson's supercharged Midget (1 1/2 seconds), Orford's supercharged Austin, Potter's M.G. (1 2/5 seconds) and Whittindale's Singer (1 4/5 seconds).

The Light Car and **The Motor** were equally lavish in praise of the team's performance on Crackington.

The Light Car 2nd April 1937
Difficult conditions, mainly owing to the wet surface, accounted for a large number of failures. Only 55 cars succeeded in the restarting test and there were further failures on the higher reaches. These troubles accounted for a delay of over two hours. Several competitors put up really good performances, however, amongst them were C. D. Buckley, W. H. Scriven and J. G. Orford, all driving supercharged Austin Sevens.

The Motor, 30th March 1937
Near Bude, Crackington Hill, scene of the second special test, was approached through a magnificent coastal road, dipping and sweeping from sandy cove to rocky promontory. Starting in a shallow splash, the hill reaches a gradient of about 1 in 5. On nearly the worst part of the climb the test was staged on Barton Steep lines. In other words, cars had to stop astride a line, and then, stationary, and without rolling back, they had to clear the line with the back wheels within 3 secs., continuing non-stop to the top. The hill was wet and difficult: there were 72 failures all told...Many failed on the higher reaches of the hill after making good restarts at the foot. Among the outstanding performances, however, were noted...C. D. Buckley, W. H. Scriven and J. Orford (blown Austin Sevens)... Later, at Hustyn, there were: 'many good M.G. ascents' and 'Austins also were consistently impressive with C. D. Buckley's blown Seven the fastest.'

1937 Liverpool MC Jean's Cup Trial 11th April

Grasshopper Results
R. J. Richardson   AOX 4   Wade Trophy – best performance<1100cc

The trial started and finished at Buxton, fielding 60 cars and 60 motorcycles, divided into sporting and touring classes. The former had eight sections and a route of 68 miles, and the latter covered 73 miles and nine sections. *The Light Car* (16 April 1937) reported: *Jenkins Chapel, Easy Litton, and the Winnats were common to both cards, but whilst the experts had to tackle Hollins Clough, Washgates, Cheeks, Cow Lane and Bamford Clough, there were easier alternatives for the 'tourists'... Cheeks... was a gift for most of the competitors... Jenkins Chapel found a fair proportion of failures, and there was a sensation when G. S. Watson's M.G. Midget turned over on top of him. Fortunately it was righted and he and his passenger came out unhurt. Among the notable climbs were those of J. A. Bastock (M.G. Magnette) and R. J. Richardson (Austin Seven).*

Although A. B. Langley (1,292 Singer), brother to A. H. Langley, won the Jeans Gold Cup, Richardson put up the best performance in the opposite class to win the Wade Cup.

1937 SUNBAC Inter-Club Team Trial 24th April

Grasshopper Results
R. J. Richardson	AOX 4	Worcestershire Austin OC 'B' Team
C. L. Goodacre 38	BOA 59	Worcestershire Austin OC 'B' Team
P. H. J. Barugh		Worcestershire Austin OC 'B' Team
H. L. Hadley	BOA 60	Worcestershire Austin OC 'A' Team?
C. D. Buckley	BOA 58	

Thirteen clubs fought it out in the Sunbac Inter-team Trial and was won by the Lancashire AC. The 67 mile course took place in the Buxton area, starting and finishing at the Spa Hotel, Buxton. It began with a Relay Driving Test on Burbage Edge under the soubriquet 'Pylon Polka'. Washgate Hill followed, a quarter mile in length and not exceptionally steep, but with five corners, two of which were awkward. The surface was bumpy and part consisted of an *'antique style of stone sett which caused a lot of tyre spin, a rough approach and a hummocky water splash at the foot'*. C. D. Buckley's *'excellent judgement showed up on this tricky hill'*.
Barugh, who crops up at the MCC July Rally with **BOA 60**, and at the later Sunbac Colmore with an, as yet, unidentified '750s' Austin, completed the Worcestershire Austin OC 'B' team with a 747 Austin; we are unable to confirm if this was a Grasshopper.

1937 MGCC Abingdon 1st May

Grasshopper Results
C. D. Buckley	59	BOA 58	
H. L. Hadley	60	BOA 60	Watkinson Cup (Best Visitor)
W. H.Scriven	61	BOA 57	Novices' Award

The start for the 1937 Event was moved to 'The Prince of Wales', Berkeley Road, on the main Gloucester to Bristol road. The trial was run in *'delightful weather conditions'*. The start was less than a mile from the terror of the day, the first hill which went under the name of 'Tramp's Paradise', rechristened 'Tin Pan Alley' for this event, rising between high banks from the main Dursley road, and described in *The Autocar* (7 May 1937) as a *'dump-heap-cum-forgotten track'* where Hadley *'caused some alarm by coming to rest with the Austin on its side, half in, half out of a gigantic rut'*. This was followed by Axe, Old Hollow, Hodgecombe, *where* 'the works Austin team, knew just how a gear lever should be used and made supremely neat changes into bottom some two-thirds of the way up the hill', Sandford (Timed Climb) and Ashmeads, and a return to Abingdon but with a stop at Witney aerodrome for two Driving Tests. The first one was a 'triangle doubling' and the second a figure of eight which resulted in a tie for J. E. Orgee (1296 MG) and Hadley in 12 4/5 seconds, although Buckley *'had less luck, landing up concentric with the circumference of one finishing circle after a skid and being quite unable to get into it'*. H. L. Hadley with Twyford and Wise were runners-up to Dickie Green and Jack Bastock.

Grasshopper Results

W. J. Milton	81	AOX 3	Premier Award
W. S. Sewell	201	BOA 59	Non-Starter
C. D. Buckley	202	BOA 58	Premier Award
W. H. Scriven	203	BOA 57	Silver Award
H. L. Hadley	204	BOA 60	Premier Award

The 'Edinburgh' saw 155 Entries with 142 Starters, boosted by a strong Grasshopper presence of four drivers; W. S. Sewell in **BOA 59** was again amongst the non-starters. Reports described this as the 'Easiest Edinburgh for Years'. Carlisle drivers left at 8.58pm to join the Stratford-on-Avon and Wrotham Park (Barnet) drivers in Harrogate for the 3.44am Breakfast Control, finishing in Edinburgh from 4.12pm.

The combined entry left Harrogate for Kettlewell, the jumping- off point for Park Rash and the start of the trials driving, in reasonable weather conditions. Park Rash is a two mile long hill with a stretch or two of 1 in 4 gradients, a fairly hard surface, but strewn with stones. *The Light Car* and *The Motor* both praised *'The M.G., Singer and Austin Teams- specialists all* [for their] *convincing demonstration of how Park Rash should be climbed.'* **The Autocar** (21 May 1937) noted *W. J. Milton's blown Austin Seven was surprisingly quiet and sedate and made a nice climb'.* **The Light Car** continued: *From the top... competitors continued on the rough track over the moors and down Cover Dale to West Witton and Newbiggin, shortly afterwards crossing a stretch of road they were to follow later, as the route at this point made a wide loop to bring drivers to the foot of Summer Lodge, the second hill of the day, which proved to be unexpectedly easy...*

Good climbs noted were by the blown Austin Sevens, the two teams of 1,292 M.G.s and 1½ litre Singers... (**The Motor** *notes the Stratford starters tackled the hill last: The two M.G. T model teams, the two 1½-litre Singer teams and the four 747 supercharged Austins. All these had plenty of power and, even though the hill was fairly rough by now, they were fast.)*

Next came Tan Hill, near Brough, on which a special test was held... Failure to stop on the prescribed line spoiled the chances of D. E. Harris (1,496 Singer) and W. H. Scriven (747 Austin S)...Main roads were soon rejoined, and some 40 miles brought competitors to the lunch stop at Carlisle. From this point to Lauder – a matter of some 67 miles (where there was a distance check) *– free-and easy rally conditions were the rule.*

Sixteen miles beyond the check the first of the two new hills awaited... Costerton is approached by a rocky watersplash (not very deep) and swings sharp right immediately, thereafter winding gently up the hillside with a wall on the left and a sloping bank on the right. (**The Motor** *reported: Everyone... climbed with the greatest of ease.) Humbie Hill, the last, was a bare three miles away... The surface on the upper part of the hill rapidly broke up... into a tacky power-absorbing mass, which brought some 15-20 cars to a standstill. Officials had marked out one of the bends with red flags which competitors took great delight in knocking down! From the top, a mere 20 miles of main roads remained to bring the story of the 30th M.C.C. Edinburgh Trial to a sunny end.*

1937 Bristol MC & LCC Whitchurch Airfield 22nd May

The event took place on the private road on the eastern side of the airport and followed a 750 yard course. Some 33 racing and sporting cars took part on a wet day. Hadley competed with his regular trials car, **BOA 60**, in the Sports Car Class, switching to the single-seat OHC race car for the Racing Car Event, with which he won all four of the racing-car classes. The event itself was a great success, but because of the dismal weather, commercially, it was a financial failure and was not to be repeated.

Peter Stowe's description of the event is quoted here, in part: *The action was due to start at 3 pm, beginning with the timed runs for sports cars. These had to have complete two (or more) seater bodywork and wings, and be equipped with head and sidelamps, although windscreen, hoods and spare wheels could be removed. First to line up under the 'John Bull Tyres' START banner was Hadley in a sports Austin 7, but it was Poore's little 750cc MG that was by far the quickest, his best time of 26.4 seconds, an average speed of 58 mph, allowing him to win all three of the sports car classes (and £15 prize money!)...*

1937 Lancashire AC Blackpool Rally 4-6th June

Grasshopper Results	
C. D. Buckley	BOA 58
W. H. Scriven	BOA 57

Over 200 cars were entered. The road section on the Friday covered approximately 260 miles with 188 cars leaving the six starting points – London, Birmingham, Bristol, Manchester, Leeds and Glasgow, at a scheduled average of 26⅔mph. The Birmingham starters travelled via Chester to Higher Hodder, near Whalley, North-East of Preston, where other starters met to complete a restart test, before travelling to Birdie Brow for a 'stop-go' test. From there the competitors made their way to the Lakes, over a speed control section maintaining the 26⅔mph before doubling back to Blackpool. On the Saturday two special driving tests took place on the lower Promenade. C. D. Buckley in the first 'Scissors' test, *'was very fast in his supercharged Austin Seven, but flicked a pylon and the railings'*. In the second test, the 'Monte-Blackpool Wiggle-Woggle', *'Buckley made no mistakes [this time] and the little Austin rocketed up the course only 1/5 second slower than H. Bolton's SS'*. A Coachwork competition on the Sunday morning saw nearly 50 cars lined up. Buckley merits two mentions in **The Motor** (8 June 1937), but did not pick up any awards. Although none of the usual magazines mention Scriven, Canning-Brown reports that he was there and completed the course. The photograph (No. 202) confirms the presence of another Grasshopper behind Buckley's **BOA 58**.

1937 24 Hour Le Mans 19-20th June

Grasshopper Results				
K. Petre/G. Mangan	55	COA 119	31st (750 Class)	72 Laps DNF
C. L. Goodacre/C. D. Buckley	56	COA 118	37th (750 Class)	32 Laps DNF
C. J. P. Dodson/H. L. Hadley	57	COA 121	30th (750 Class)	74 Laps DNF

COA 118, **119** and **121** were entered for the 1937 Le Mans. These three cars retired, two with fractured copper oil-pipes supplying oil to the centre main bearing and **COA 118** ran out of fuel, only to suffer the same fate after getting going again. Jamieson had specified flexible, braided internal oil pipes, but was overruled by Alf Depper and solid copper pipes were fitted in their place.

This was the race Hadley and Dodson set up their £10 side bet with the other team drivers. They won the bet after lapping their rivals within the first 4 hour stint, each of the losing drivers stumping up £5 apiece! Luckily for them the oil pipes held out longer than the time frame of the bet! There were only 17 finishers from the 48 entrants to the race.

The Works team trip to the 1937 Le Mans 24 Hour Race began with an overnight stay at the London and Paris Hotel, Newhaven on Sunday 13th June, after leaving Longbridge at 11 am with the drivers presumably driving their own cars to Newhaven. The four sports cars (**COA 118, 119, 120? and 121**) and the saloon tender took the passenger ferry to Dieppe on Monday morning, 14th June. The van and the 10hp sports sailed with the cargo ship in the evening. George Coates and Knight were in charge of these two vehicles. The cars were to be driven by road to Le Mans with accommodation arranged at the Continental Hotel. The return journey was on Monday 21st crossing over by the night boat and arriving at the works on Tuesday 22nd June.

Memo reproduced courtesy of Ian Moore

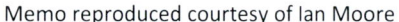

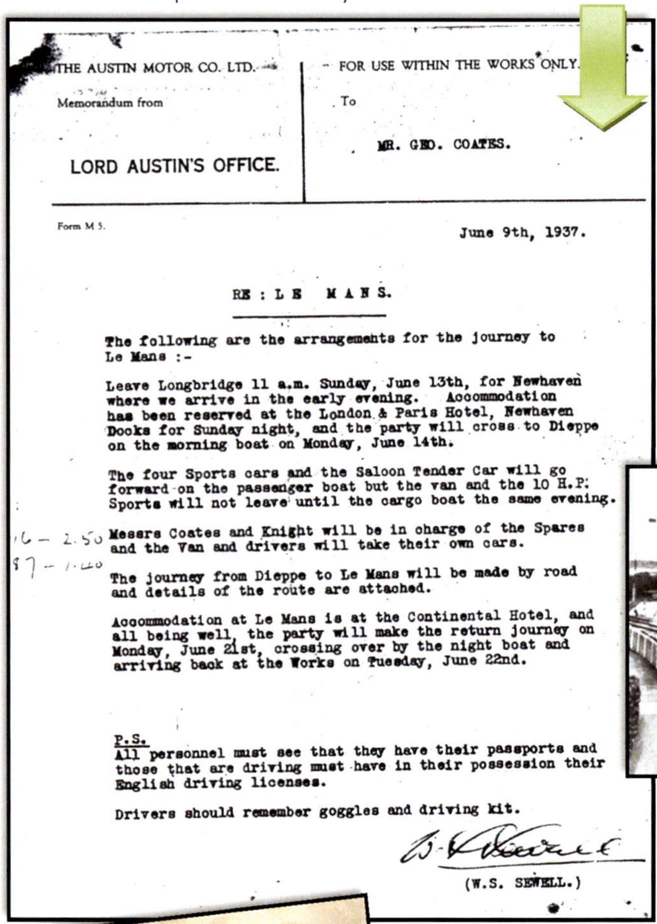

THE AUSTIN MOTOR CO. LTD. — FOR USE WITHIN THE WORKS ONLY.

Memorandum from: LORD AUSTIN'S OFFICE.

To: MR. GEO. COATES.

Form M 5.

June 9th, 1937.

RE : LE MANS.

The following are the arrangements for the journey to Le Mans :-

Leave Longbridge 11 a.m. Sunday, June 13th, for Newhaven where we arrive in the early evening. Accommodation has been reserved at the London & Paris Hotel, Newhaven Docks for Sunday night, and the party will cross to Dieppe on the morning boat on Monday, June 14th.

The four Sports cars and the Saloon Tender Car will go forward on the passenger boat but the van and the 10 H.P. Sports will not leave until the cargo boat the same evening.

Messrs Coates and Knight will be in charge of the Spares and the Van and drivers will take their own cars.

The journey from Dieppe to Le Mans will be made by road and details of the route are attached.

Accommodation at Le Mans is at the Continental Hotel, and all being well, the party will make the return journey on Monday, June 21st, crossing over by the night boat and arriving back at the Works on Tuesday, June 22nd.

P.S.
All personnel must see that they have their passports and those that are driving must have in their possession their English driving licenses.

Drivers should remember goggles and driving kit.

(W.S. SEWELL.)

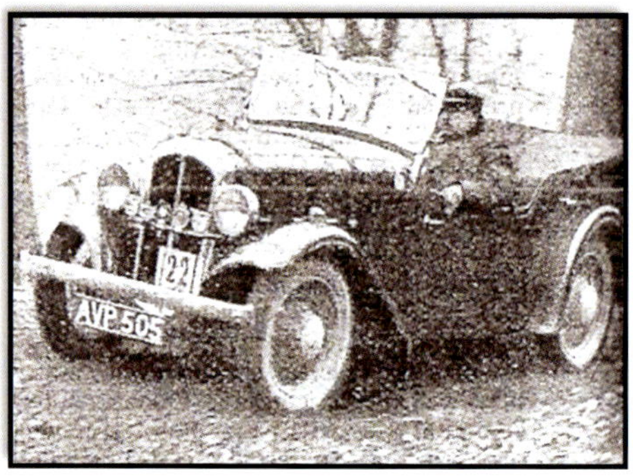

103. W. S. Sewells's 10hp Sports (AVP 505) at the earlier 1936 Colmore Trial *Light Car 28 February 1936*

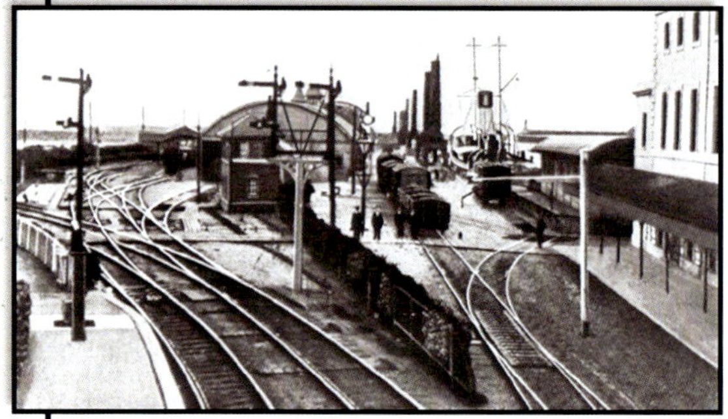

104. London and Paris Hotel and Station, Newhaven

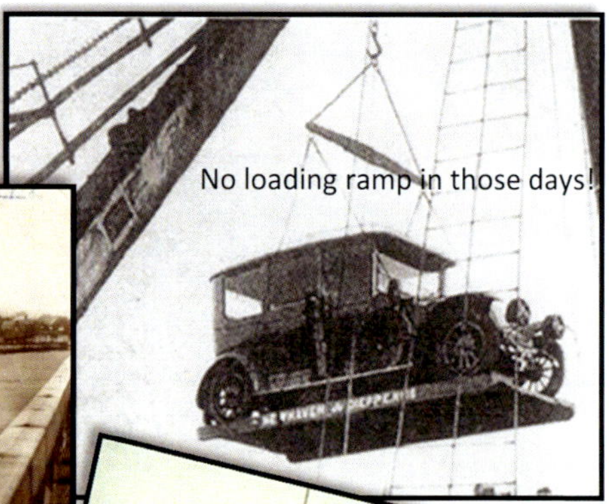
No loading ramp in those days!

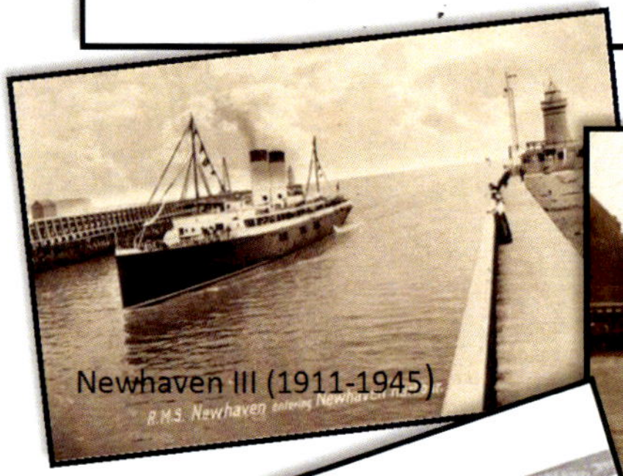
Newhaven III (1911-1945)
R.M.S. Newhaven entering Newhaven

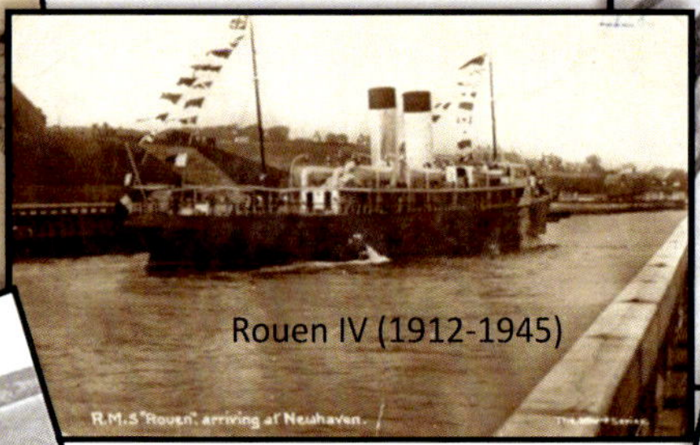
Rouen IV (1912-1945)
R.M.S "Rouen" arriving at Newhaven.

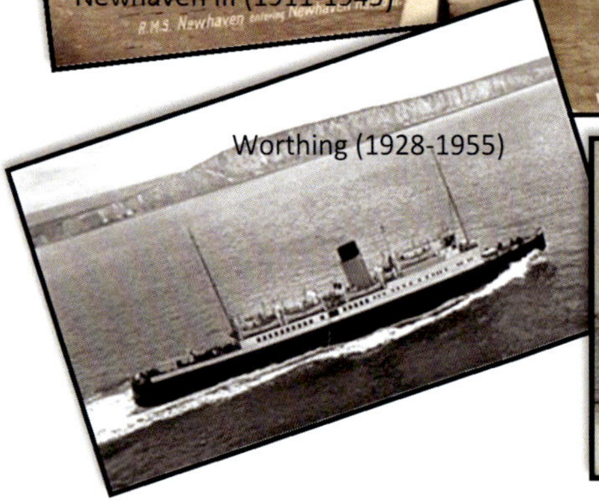
Worthing (1928-1955)

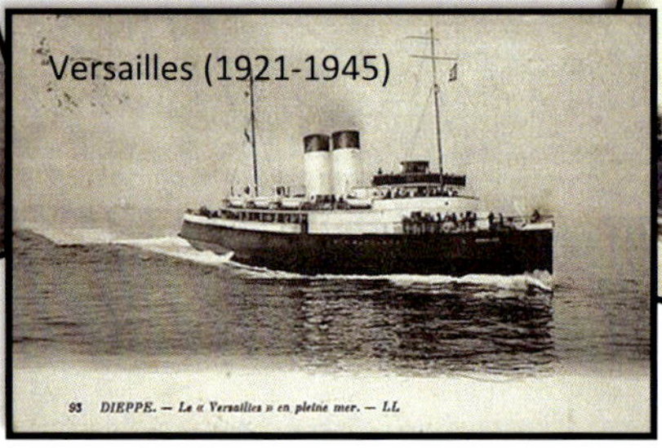
Versailles (1921-1945)
93 DIEPPE. — Le « Versailles » en pleine mer. — LL

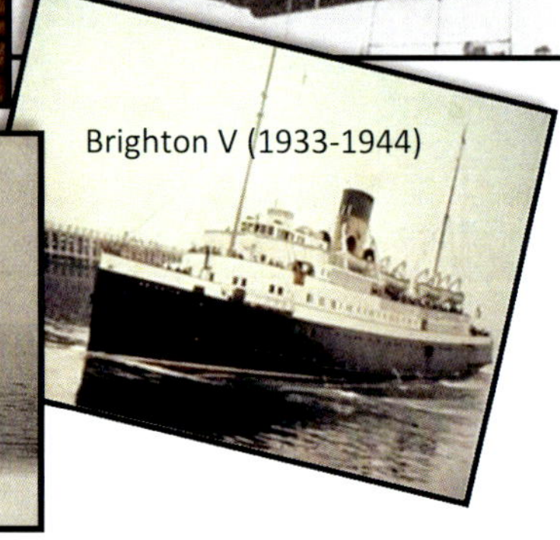
Brighton V (1933-1944)

105 – 110 (Above) The steam passenger ferries in operation between Newhaven and Dieppe at the time.

The Light Car 25th June 1937

The interval of two years that elapsed between the previous Le Mans 24-hour Race and last Saturday's event made little difference to the enthusiasm which surrounds this unique event...

The day had dawned cloudy and cold, but as 4 p.m. (zero hour) approached the wind dropped and the sun was obviously trying to break through, although threatening clouds on the horizon suggested that anything might happen long before what was left of the entry struggled in the next afternoon; but it needed more than a few dark clouds to damp the enthusiasm of the crowds that took up their positions eight deep in the enclosure in front of the huge grandstand facing the long line of permanent two-storey pits gaily decked with flags.

Of the 60 original entries, 49 were drawn up en echelon in front of the pits for the start, their drivers standing impatiently in little circles on the opposite side of the road ready to sprint across, leap into their cars, press the starter button and (if the starter worked) roar off down the road, swirl round the right-hand bend into the new Esses and out on to the undulating three-mile Mulsanne Straight, where the fastest cars reach the 140 m.p.h. mark before braking for Mulsanne corner.

Then to the old Esses and steadily uphill on a curving, narrow road to White House corner, which has to be taken flat out unless revs. are to be lost for the whole stretch that terminates in the slightly curving run down to the stands – that was what faced the drivers ...24 hours of it...

The British contingent numbered 18... Amongst the small cars... three trials-type Austin Sevens (Mrs. Petre and Mangan; Goodacre and Buckley; Dodson and Hadley)... Against them was the very strong foreign entry – 18 French cars... [including] seven Delahayes... three Bugattis...three Peugeots... four Fiats and two baby Simca-cinq models. From Italy... an Alfa-Romeo... and Germany fielded four Adlers and a B.M.W... and then the loud-speakers began to tick off the minutes, then the seconds... and, with a scurry of feet, 49 drivers leapt into their cars, 49 engines burst into snarling life and they were away... Hadley's Austin was the leader of the "seven-fifties"... Then, with the race half an hour old, tragedy, swift and terrible, intervened... Coming down the slight incline some 150 yds, beyond White House, Kippeurt (Bugatti) got into difficulties, grazed the palisading whilst travelling at some 100 m.p.h. and swung round. With a horrible rending of metal, the Bugatti rolled over and over, throwing out poor Kippeurt into the road.

Before anyone could raise a hand in warning, five other cars bore down on the wreckage. In the resulting melee, Roth (B.M.W.) cannoned into the hedge and overturned in a deliberate effort to avoid Kippeurt. Pat Fairfield (Frazer-Nash-B.M.W.), also trying to avoid Kippeurt, was charged from behind and rolled end over end into a field, and Tremulet's Delahaye, Ralph's Talbot and Forestier's Riley followed one another into the wreckage.

Of the drivers involved, Kippeurt was killed outright, Pat Fairfield, who was at first thought to be superficially hurt, was later found to have grave internal injuries, and, after a vain operation, died early on Monday morning. Ralph was seriously hurt, and the rest suffered bruises and concussion ... one of the most terrible accidents in motor racing history, reminiscent of the Bentley crash at White House only a few hundred yards away, but far, far worse... A lap after this the catastrophe the Italian challenge faded out, as Sommer retired... By the end of the first hour... Hadley headed the Austins and the '500' Fiat of Viale and Alin was running round like clockwork some way ahead of its team mate.

With the passing of the Riley, Skeffington, in the privately owned Aston Martin, took the lead in the 1 ½-litre class and the leaders of the smaller categories remained unchanged. These cars, in fact, were still leading their groups when, at 8 p.m., the heavy rain clouds that had been threatening in the distance, came over and dropped their load of stinging rain that lashed down on the drivers, made perilous business and drenched hundreds of spectators... After about an hour the rain ceased, the sky cleared, and darkness came on... And so into the night, the battle went on... In the early morning... from twelve retirements, it had grown to double that number. The three Austins were out. Goodacre's car with petrol-feed trouble after 30 laps and the other two after 72 laps with lubrication problems...

1937 MCC July Rally (Torquay) 16-17th July

Grasshopper Results			
J. G. Orford	44	AOV 343	Premier Award
C. D. Buckley	47	BOA 58	Premier Award
H. L. Hadley	48	BOA 60	Bronze Award
W. H. Scriven	49	BOA 57	Silver Award
W. J. Milton	72	AOX 3	No Award

There was no Trials section offered for this event. Competitors left from London, Stratford-on-Avon and Exeter at 10.01pm, Friday 16th July, arriving at Deller's Cafe, Taunton for the 3.00am Breakfast Control, before continuing to the Final Control at Torquay. Here competitors faced three Eliminating Tests. The five-strong Grasshopper presence must have felt underwhelmed at the level of challenge; no Austins were entered for the 1938 Event, despite offering a 'diluted' Trials section of four observed hills!

The Light Car (23 July 1937) began with: *Fine weather and the absence of a trials section lent quite a holiday atmosphere to this year's Torquay Rally...* and continued: *The run from Taunton to Torquay kept drivers very busy, the winding main roads through Lynton, Simonsbath, Okehampton and Two Bridges making time-keeping a question not to be treated too lightly... Immediately on arrival, competitors were faced with three eliminating tests, the first on the steep Babbacombe Beach Road and the other two on the level in Ilsham Road. The former, as its name suggests, rises from the beach and in its ascent winds round a number of sharp corners and has a gradient of the 1-in-4 order... The road surface... was damp under the trees... Misfiring engines... were common, possibly due to the competitors having to descend the hill before they climbed it... Of the light cars, the T-type M.G.s of Toulmin, Crawford and Jones were driven briskly and capably, the blown Austin Sevens displayed lots of power (H. L. Hadley changed up between the stops)... Orford performed particularly well in the restart test according to* **The Autocar** *report (23 July 1937). For the next (timed) test competitors moved to Ilsham Road...Amongst the cars C. D. Buckley (Austin S) put up the very fine time of 24 2/5 secs., whilst Toulmin was also outstanding with 25 4/5 secs.*

1937 Donington 12 Hours Sports Race 24th July

Grasshopper Results			
C. J. P. Dodson/H. L. Hadley	1	COA 121	finished 2nd (7th overall)
C. L. Goodacre/C. D. Buckley	2	COA 118	finished 3rd (11th overall)
K. Petre/P. Stevenson	3	COA 119	finished 5th (16th overall)
Runners up for the Team Prize			

Following the failure of the 1937 Le Mans 24 Hour Race **COA 118, 119** and **121**'s engines were rebuilt and the cars entered for this 221 lap race, the longest speed event run on British soil since the demise of the Brooklands 'Double-Twelve'. A total of 35 cars started, from an entry of 39. The day was marred by a bad accident, resulting in the death of M. K. Bilney (A.C.), one of the two drivers involved. The other, S. H. Robinson (Riley), escaped with concussion and a broken thigh.

The Light Car (30 July 1937) set the scene for the day: *Grey and sulky skies gave more than a hint of rain to come when the 35 starters lined up at the pits en echelon a few minutes before 7 a.m. Bira, first driver of Prince Chula's Delahaye, occupied the best position in the rank on the strength of his practice times – fastest of the field – but when the starting flag fell the Delahaye stuck fast and the 34 rivals streamed away past the little knot of mechanics who worked feverishly to get the French car under way... At 8.30 a.m. Bira had made up one of the three laps deficit...Meantime, Dobson, first of the three Riley drivers who dominated the 1½-litre class, clung gamely to the tail of the leading Frazer-Nash-B.M.W., whilst a plucky little '750', Bert Hadley's Le Mans type Austin, led the 500-1000c.c. class, with J. D. Barnes (Autosports Singer Nine) second... Then, at the end of the first three hours' spell, a number of cars came in for fuel and a change of drivers, these including the three works Austins... Leadership in the 1000c.c. and 1,500 c.c. classes had meanwhile changed hands. Alf Langley, co-driver to J. D. Barnes, headed the smallest class with Charles Dodson (Hadley's partner) second on the Austin... Then tragedy stalked upon the scene (see above)... The course being temporarily blocked at Holly Wood, the officials halted all cars for 16 minutes whilst the victims were removed by ambulance. Then, by unanimous agreement of the competitors, a second mass start was staged on the spot and the race went on.*

Not long before 2 o'clock the heavens opened and a perfect deluge of rain fell, to be followed throughout the afternoon by alternating bursts of sunshine and further downpours. Speeds were naturally reduced a lot during the storms and lurid skids were frequent... Apart from the leaders of the various classes, Kenneth Crawford ('Musketeer' M.G.), Alan Hess (H.R.G.), Mrs. Petre (works Austin), and E. Winterbottom (T-type M.G.) were impressive on the corners all round the course...

1937 Singer Motor Club, Midland Centre Annual Sporting Trial 7th August

Grasshopper Results

W. H. Scriven   BOA 57   Patrick Challenge Trophy and Replica up to 1100cc

The title for this Cotswold event was changed from 'Trial' to 'Motor Competition'. Instead of a series of observed hills there was only one – Kineton with its watersplash. Four tests, or 'long-distance timed restarts', together with three rally-style tests replaced the observed hills. Of the 40 entries, 38 made it to the start on the Singer Test Track at Birmingham. ***The Light Car*** takes up the report:

The Light Car 13th August 1937

Three tests (on the Test Track) preceded the road section. The first of these took the form of an 'In and Out of the Garage'; no fewer than 18 drivers lost marks for illegal contact with the mark posts, or by exceeding standard time (which, incidentally, was fastest run plus 25 per cent.). On the other hand, D. E. Harris (Singer), T. C. Wise (Ford) and N. H. Grove (M.G.) were noted as spirited performers, although, as in the cases of the other tests, definite times were not available.

In the second test, which was somewhat similar to the first, there were 19 who lost marks, and in the third, which involved driving in complex fashion between a number of pylons and stopping in a restricted area, 14 blotted their copybooks. Leaving the Singer Works, competitors then followed an 85-mile route over main roads to Warwick and Wellesbourne, through the Cotswolds lanes, taking in timed tests on Windmill Hill (1 in 8 with a stony surface), Stanway (a combination of loose stones and grass), Mill Hill (fairly hard) and Down Street (sandy), together with the observed climb of Kineton already mentioned.

1937 XI RAC International Tourist Trophy, Donington 4th September

Grasshopper Results

C. J. P. Dodson   29   COA 121   DNF

Austin only entered one Le Mans car for this event (**COA 121**), with Charlie Dodson driving. The course covered 100 laps, beginning at midday. Dodson started with the third group 1 minute and 27 seconds later, with a 16 lap 52 second advantage, expected to average 55.4 mph if he was to finish alongside the other competitors. With the class to himself, Dodson *'in the sole little Austin'* failed to touch handicap speed, and failed to finish his course after 61 laps (lap 78) owing to engine problems. Earlier in the afternoon, some time before his retirement, ***The Light Car*** (10 September 1937) observed: *'Charles Brackenbury's 4½-litre Lagonda and Charles Dodson's little Austin, became involved in a minor fracas which resulted in both broadsiding hectically at close quarters. Quick wits saved an awkward-looking situation and the two Charlies went on their way rejoicing.'*

Some time before his retirement with engine trouble on lap 78, Charles Dodson, the limit man, had been relieved of his lead on actual road position (as distinct from handicap) by Donald Barnes (972c.c. Singer). Dodson's Fastest Lap time was 55.97mph; he was the only runner-up in the 750 Class and was placed 29th overall.

In the months following the race, **COA 121** was stripped down at Longbridge and converted for use in Trials.

1937 IMRC International Grand Prix, Phoenix Park 11th September

G. A. Mangan, Kay Petre's co-driver for the 1937 Le Mans, is listed in the Official Programme for the Handicap Race, competing in a 'similar Austin Seven... of the new three-bearing crankshaft unsupercharged sports type' most probably **COA 119**. He was entered by Lincoln and Nolan, Ltd. of Dublin and listed as number 42. Unfortunately, the Motoring magazines make no mention of Mangan in their reports of the event, leaving one to consider a 'no show' on the day.

1937 MCC Members' Day Meeting – Brooklands 25th September

Grasshopper Results

T. H. Cole	27	AOV 343	High Speed Trial (1 Hour) 69.46mph Premier Award;
			2 lap handicap car no. 73; 1 lap handicap car no. 68 (Events 6 & 11) 'S'
C. D. Buckley	28	BOA 58	2 lap handicap car no. 45; 1 lap handicap car no. 43 (Events 4 & 9)
W. H. Scriven	29	BOA 57	2 lap handicap car no. 44; 1 lap handicap car no. 42 (Events 4 & 9)

The programme consisted of the usual one-hour trials, one- and two-lap handicaps and one lap trials against the clock, starting at 11am and continuing until after seven in the evening. All 18 events were run on the outer circuit of the track. T. H. Cole, *'sporting an interesting cooling cowl on its bonnet top'* (**Motor Sport** October 1937) won the only Premier Award in the up to 850c.c. group, despite a wet track, with a speed of 69.46 m.p.h. in the First One-Hour Trial.

1937 Wye Valley Automobile Club, Hereford City Trophy 10th October

Grasshopper Results

W. H. Scriven	BOA 57	First Class Award
C. D. Buckley	BOA 58	First Class Award
A. H. Langley	BOA 59	First Class Award

The Grasshopper Austin team attended this event, but with the third car driven by Alfred (Singer) Langley in place of H. L. Hadley, the Singer Team having disbanded. Hadley and Goodacre were competing this weekend at Crystal Palace in the Road Racing Club Imperial Trophy in the twin OHC racers, coinciding with the first BBC outside broadcast of a motor sport event. The trial attracted an entry of 30 competitors. *The Light Car* (22 October 1937) notes: *The hills were all in fairly easy condition owing to the summerlike weather, and five of them, in fact, did not cause a single failure. The most difficult was Pontyweston, which stopped six competitors, whilst Cusop Dingle brought five cars to a standstill.*

1937 MCC Sporting Trial (Buxton) 23rd October   17th Event

Grasshopper Results

W. J. Milton	40	AOX 3	Non-starter
J. G. Orford	41	AOV 343	Premier Award
R. J. Richardson	96	AOX 4	Premier Award

This year's event was not dissimilar to previous years' events with 88 Starters out of 96 leaving the Palace Hotel, Buxton, at 9.31am to finish from noon onwards, after completing the 59½-mile course. The trial took place in heavy rain:

*'The sweeping torrents (**The Light Car** 29 October 1937) tended to wash the surfaces clean so that they were almost as easy as if the dry spell had continued... Competitors made their way by Goyts Bridge to Jenkins Chapel hill....To small sports cars this hill presents no particular difficulty, especially since the wear and tear of trials appears to have widened out the corners a little. They snapped up with great rapidity and the tow-gang's services were useful mainly to extricate the bigger fry that stuck on the turns.... Climbing up past the 'Cat and Fiddle'- England's second highest inn – competitors needed lights and at Taddington Moor, the next section, drifting mist reduced visibility to the point of seriously cramping the style of a portion of the entry. On Litton Slack the surface had been well washed and the hill was easier than usual.*

There are no fearsome turns about the notorious Bamford Clough – just gradients and gullies. However, last Saturday the gullies had been filled in so that only a small minority required the assistance of the tractor that was stationed over the crest.... The final section was Winnats Pass, but although clouds were down on the road when the earlier drivers came through, no one had trouble. Two half-hour breaks in the succession of starting times reduced the possibility of cumulative delays...In the evening there was the usual very successful dinner, dance and film show at the Palace Hotel, Buxton.

This Trial marked the final round for the MCC Team Championship, the cumulative performance from Lands End, Edinburgh, Exeter, Torquay and the One Day Sporting Event.

1937 Mid-Surrey A. C. Experts' Trial – Exmoor 30th October

Grasshopper Results

W. H. Scriven		BOA 57	Retired (blown gasket)
C. D. Buckley	21	BOA 58	Runner-up in Timed Tests (Tied)
A. H. Langley		BOA 59	Class Winner (750cc)
H. L. Hadley	31	BOA 60	

The trial took place in the Exmoor region. Of the 31 invited drivers, there were 30 Starters and 22 Finishers.

The start was at Dunster and went by way of Kersham to the first observed hill, Colly (*long and steep with two sharp corners and great rock slabs between high banks*), just outside the village of Luxborough, four miles due south of Dunster (abandoned after S. H. Allard overturned); Widlake (*long, steep, rocky and very difficult; Buckley and Langley managed this climb 'with great skill', but Hadley failed*); Cloutsham (*a difficult proposition with its loose rocks, which saw 12 failures including the 'Musketeers' team of M.G.s*); Downscombe, where Scriven suffered a blown gasket, (*easy, but after a few miles of moorland tracks the route dipped into the Barle valley for the ascent of Cowcastle*); Cowcastle (*steep track up a grassy hillside; Buckley mounted the bank on the top corner*). A short but hectic scramble across the moor led to Picked Stones (*the first part is a short, deep watersplash with a steep approach, and a stiff climb out – most people stuffed their radiators with newspaper and rugs to keep out the water.* **The Light Car** reported '*The little Austins were at a disadvantage but Buckley, Hadley and Langley all manipulated their Investments with cunning and completed the climb*'; *the second part of the hill is a narrow track with a sharp hairpin where two reverses were permitted,* where Hadley '*scorned a reverse and got away with it*' (**The Autocar** 5 November 1937)); Mannacott tunnel (*deep mud but not very difficult*); Trentishoe (*Brake Test. Here the 'Cream Cracker' Midgets managed to take the club team trophy from the Sunbac Austins (Langley, Buckley and Scriven) by the very narrow margin of 2/5 secs.*), and finally, shortly after dark, Blackmoor Gate.

Alongside Colly, both Kersham and Yealscombe were also cancelled. C. D. Buckley was Runner-up in the Timed Tests. Two pesky MG 'T's driven by A. G Imhof and J. M. Toulmin were tied winners. Hadley lost marks through missing his route and by-passing one hill.

1937 SUNBAC Vesey Cup 6th November

Grasshopper Results

W. H. Scriven		BOA 57	Premier Award
C. D. Buckley	25	BOA 58	Watson-Gwynne Bowl & Ixion Cup (most consistent performance by SUNBAC member during 1937)
H. L. Hadley	26	BOA 60	
C. L. Goodacre		COA 121	Premier Award

The trial shared the Black Mountains area used in the Wye Valley Club's Hereford City Trophy Trial: Cusop Dingle, Pont-y-Weston and a timed driving test towards the end. Forty entrants participated, running under extremely bad weather conditions. This event signalled Goodacre's return to road trials and the first outing of **COA 121** following conversion to trials specification.

The Light Car, 12th November 1937

The real business of the day began eight miles from the start with a stop-and-go test near Brentwardine. A 7 second limit was set, which was managed by C. Goodacre in 4 4/5 secs. Pont-y-Weston, the second obstruction, was also the worst in the trial. It brought 13 cars to a standstill. This is a long hill, with its worst part near the bottom. A firm but grass-grown surface with sharpish corners here and there describe it... Cusop Dingle, near Hay, ought to have caused more trouble than it did. Starting with a water splash and a steep bank out of it, the hill has a fair selection of rocks, with a nice film of mud over them. Yet only four failures occurred. Shaw's Farm Hill, however, caused none at all and only one car stopped on Lower Cefn Hill.

Near Rowlstoen a stop-and-go test was to have been staged on Hill Lane, but conditions were so bad that it was decided to convert this section into a plain observed hill. Paved with cobble stones or setts and covered with mud of an extreme oiliness, Hill Lane needed no corners to make it tricky. Nine cars failed there. One, it is true, H. L. Hadley's 747 Austin S, was less a victim of the hill than of some other misfortune. In some peculiar way its brakes locked on and refused to release their grip until long after there was any doubt about the number of marks that Hadley had lost in consequence of this occurrence!

A mile further on there was the phenomenon or visitation without which no Sunbac trial could be complete. A hairpin, Lines A, B etc., and a broad hint to designers that reverse stops should be easy to operate. In short, a driving test.

Here poor Hadley, now apparently with no brakes at all, was at a disadvantage, but C. D. Buckley (747 Austin S) showed what the model could do, clocking 16 4/5 secs. and thereby winning the 1100cc award as things turned out (Watson Gwynne Bowl for best performance under 1100cc).

1937 Bristol MC & LCC Roy Fedden Trophy Trial (Cotswolds) 13th November

Grasshopper Results

W. H. Scriven		BOA 57	Third Class Award
C. D. Buckley		BOA 58	Winner Roy Fedden Trophy
A. H. Langley		BOA 59	Second Class Award
H. L. Hadley		BOA 60	Clutch problems
C. L. Goodacre	48	COA 121	First Class Award

The following hills appeared on the 45 mile route card: Narkover, Tor, Cow Kllcott, Hodgecombe, Nailsworth and Old Hollow. **The Autocar's** headline (19 November 1937) reported dry weather making the new hills of Narkover, Cow Kilcott and Tor, easy. There were 57 entries and 49 starters who left the Prince of Wales Hotel, Berkeley Road Station for a twelve sharp start to Hodgecombe, where Buckley's Austin was amongst the best, alongside the Three Musketeer's Macdermid, Imhof's M.G. and Flower's M.G. Narkover, the first of the new hills, according to **The Autocar** report, *'provided good lessons in wheelspin control...C. A. N. May (having failed at Hodgecombe) was the first failure...The Cream Crackers and the Three Musketeers all made perfect climbs in formation. The Austin 'Grasshoppers' were all good, although Hadley was rather slow.*

Later, on the third new hill of Tor, Hadley was one of four failures *' who seemed to have a nasty time with his clutch.'* The final stop and restart test on Old Hollow caused failure after failure due to wheelspin where *'screaming engines, howling tyres...smoke from burning tyres mingled with the steam from boiling engines as car after car tried in vain... Buckley, who let nearly all the air out of his rear tyres ... made a fine climb.'*

The Light Car (19 November 1937) attributes *'poor Hadley's'* failure on the Tor Hill section to a sheared hub key, limiting him to one-wheel drive since the earlier Nailsworth Ladder section, but agrees that C. D. Buckley was *'the best performer of the day'* for which he was awarded the Roy Fedden Trophy. Goodacre's second outing in **COA 121** was captured by the motor sport photographer E. S. Tompkins and the resulting picture appears in his book, Speed Camera.

1937 Torbay and Totnes MC Third Annual English Riviera Trial 20th November

Grasshopper Results

W. H. Scriven	BOA 57	
C. D. Buckley	BOA 58	Winner, Premier Award
A. H. Langley	BOA 59	Best Visitor
H. L. Hadley	BOA 60	Runner-up
C. L. Goodacre	COA 121	

Team Award: Buckley, Scriven, Langley

The Light Car describes the 95 mile course as exceptionally difficult, starting and finishing at Torquay and covering 15 sections of which there were 12 observed hills and a final test in Ilsham Road, Torquay. The Grasshoppers were among 40 starters.

According to C. A. N. May's account in *Wheelspin*, the Grasshoppers competed well against teams such as the MG's 'Musketeers'. There were two difficult hills called Snails Castle and 'S.O.B'. Another 'horror' rejoiced in the name of 'Autobahn'. *The Light Car* (26 November 1937) gave a more descriptive account of the Grasshoppers' performance in its 'Club Items' section: *On Snail's Hill H. L. Hadley did actually overturn, but both he and his passenger crawled out unhurt and continued...After this matters became really difficult, and on Nuckwell, the next section, a right hand bend, deep in heavy mud, caused car after car to come to standstill. All sorts of tactics were tried without success until C. D. Buckley showed that it could be done, and H. L. Hadley, now going strong again, gave further proof that it was possible. These two were the only successful drivers, although C. L. Goodacre, in a third Austin, almost managed it and reached the highest point of those who failed...and on the next section not a single driver reached the top. Best attempt was made by C. L. Goodacre and W. P. Uglow (HRG) was the next highest... There only remained Coarsewell, where all were clean, and Autobahn, where 11 failed. Owing to delays the final test had to be carried out in the dark, and here the Austins again gave an exceptionally good account of themselves.*

In later years Hadley records the accident as happening on 'S.O.B' after negotiating a tight left hander followed quickly by a right: *'I used a large flat slab of rock like a banking. I climbed and would have got away with it, but the nearside (front) hit a rock and we went, completely upside down...The engine was still ticking over and I found the key and switched off. The spectators lifted the car off us, and I didn't have a scratch but Bob (Simpson) was badly shaken, having had difficulty breathing. I offered to retire, but he was unwilling. We were towed to the top by tractor; then we looked the car over. Filler caps, petrol and water were pushed in, but no leaks. Lost some oil, but we replaced that.'*

1937 SUNBAC/NWLMC London-Gloucester Trial 4th December   27th Event

Grasshopper Results

A. H. Langley	62	BOA 59	Bronze Medal, Third Class Award
C. D. Buckley	63	BOA 58	Silver Medal, Second Class Award
W. H. Scriven	64	BOA 57	Bronze Medal, Third Class Award
C. L. Goodacre	75	COA 121	Silver Medal, Second Class Award
H. L. Hadley	76	BOA 60	Silver Medal, Second Class Award

Some 77 Starters out of 85 left the Starting Control at the 'Thatched Barn' Road House (Barnet by-pass) from 12.15am. Main roads were followed via Aylesbury, Bicester and Chipping Norton to Broadway, shortly after which the route branched off via Old Stanway Hill to Kineton Hill, which was observed. The Breakfast Control was once again the Plough Hotel in Cheltenham with the Final Control remaining at the Bear Inn, Rodborough Common from midday onwards. The observed hills were Kineton, Ferriscourt (Descent- Special Test), Bismore (Special Test), Ham Mill, Old Hollow, Fort, Breakheart, Hodgecombe, Juniper, Ferriscourt (Special Test), Station Lane and Nailsworth Ladder. It seems the 'selling-plate' restriction must have been lifted for this year as Austin fielded five Grasshoppers in contrast to the previous year, and scooped three Silver Medals (Second Class Awards) and two Bronze Medals (Third Class Awards). The best one-make performance was achieved on Breakheart.

The Light Car 10th December 1937

*...the [**Gloucester**] event was marred by a fatal accident during the night, when C. J. Turner (1,493 Singer) found himself approaching a corner a few miles beyond Kineton on a main road that suddenly became a sheet of ice. In the inevitable skid that followed, the car overturned partly on the road and partly in the ditch, with fatal results to the passenger. Turner himself was flung on to the soft ground at the side of the road and escaped with a few bruises. [After the Breakfast stop at the Plough Hotel, Cheltenham] drivers had to get down to things in earnest, starting with an acceleration and braking test on the descent of Ferriscourt. Here H. K. Crawford (1,292 MG) and J. W. Mills (1,287 MG) both put up the excellent time of 12.4 seconds, H. L. Hadley (747 Austin) and B. Dyke Ackland (1,408 MG) came along a little later and improved the figure to 12.2 seconds ... [Old Hollow] has a vicious S-corner on a gradient of about 1 in 3 and a rocky surface. The corners come within 100 yards or so of the start and are followed by a long climb between high banks – quite difficult, but of interest only to the tow gang, because anyone who managed the corners was quite equal to what followed. Driver after driver hurled his car at the corners, charged the bank and stopped – or missed the banks and stopped just the same...failure after failure was wearing down the poor towing gang (there was no room for horses), but they stuck manfully at it and even found the energy to hoist a venturesome Austin Seven tourer right off the ground at the command "One...two...three...Heave."*

Of the three 'Musketeers' MG team, only R. A. Macdermid was successful ... only J. M. Toulmin of the 'Cream Cracker' MG team was successful...The Grasshopper Austins were more successful with two clean performances – by A. H. Langley and C. D. Buckley – and an 'all-but' by the third member of the team, W. H. Scriven. Of the remainder the only ones to save the towing gang a job were E. B. Booth (ex-Autosports 1 ½ litre Singer), W. A. Goodall (Morgan 4/4), M. H. Lawson (H.R.G.), J. F. A. Clough (1,496 Riley) and C. Goodacre (Austin)...The new loop on Station Lane came as a surprise to most drivers...faced with climbing a bank about 10 yards long with a gradient of something like 1 in 2 1/2 and an evil surface. A mere 11 managed it (including H. L. Hadley).

Motor Sport December 1937

On Breakheart, *'Three of the five trials Austins were among the thirteen who eventually provided the total of clean climbs. The drivers were A. H. Langley, who earned particular applause, C. D. Buckley, and C. L. Goodacre. It was a remarkable feature of the event that success on various hills was so evenly divided. This was particularly the case with the Austin team. A. H. Langley, after his good climb of Breakheart, stopped on Hodgcombe, which also claimed a notable failure in S. H. Allard's Allard Special... To continue the tale of the Austins, H. L. Hadley, who had not climbed Breakheart, was the only one of the five to climb Station Lane. Then all five cars covered themselves in glory by a series of successful climbs on Juniper, when the rain had made the hill so slippery that failures were becoming general...Juniper was not in its worst form at the beginning, when a number of cars climbed, but grew steadily more slippery as the rain fell, and had it not been for the successful Austin onslaught at the end, the total of twenty-one successes would have been considerably smaller.*

1937 MGCC South West Boxing Day Trial, Kimber Trophy 26th December

Grasshopper Results

C. D. Buckley	BOA 58	First Class Award
A. H. Langley	BOA 59	First Class Award, Spencer Trophy

Motor Sport (January 1938) covered this trial in which thirty starters left the Weston Hotel, Bath, on a dull day, to tackle Gipsy Lane (unobserved) and Uplands, with its deep gully and steep left-hand bend on a stony and thick clay surface. There were 23 failures but there were *'well-judged climbs by W. J. Green, J. E. S. Jones and members of the Austin and Musketeer teams. The Austins jumping through the gully was a most exhilarating spectacle... Timsbury Hill, a continuation of the old Roman Fosseway, followed by Douglas Hill both accounted for few failures, and as Castle Hill was unobserved competitors had comparative breathing space before the Special Test at Doynton Lane. The experienced E. H. Goodenough was in charge of this test...and in this and the brake test which followed at Christmas Harry E. J. Haesendonck showed his superiority... Then came that freak of nature consisting of about one hundred twisting yards of narrow, steep and very muddy lane, called Puddlebrook...divided into two sections... Haesendonck, Gilson, Macdermid, Buckley (Austin) and A.[B.] Langley (Austin) managed to use about ten yards of the second section, but were still far from the top. They were assisted the rest of the way by tractor, with the exception of Langley who was more or less lifted to firmer ground.'* The trial finished at the White Hart Hotel, Ford.

1937 MCC Exeter Trial 7-8th January 1938   23rd Event

Grasshopper Results

W. H. Scriven	182	BOA 57	Premier Award
A. H. Langley	183	BOA 59	Premier Award
C. D. Buckley	184	BOA 58	Premier Award
T. H. Cole	193	AOV 343/AOX 3	Premier Award
C. L. Goodacre	212	COA 121	Premier Award
H. L. Hadley	213	BOA 60	Premier Award

This final event of the 1937 Triple Award series saw 181 Starters out of 201. The three Starting Controls continued from The Wheatsheaf Hotel, Virginia Water, The Falcon Hotel, Stratford-on-Avon and Gallows Service Station, Exeter, the latter leaving from 12.42am. The Exeter Breakfast Control was to be reached by 4.30am with the Final Control now moved to the Grand Hotel, Bournemouth for a 12.21am finish. The observed hills also saw changes starting with Windout, Fingle Bridge (2 sections), Simms, Higher Rill (Non-stop), and Higher Rill (Test), the newly introduced Woodhaynes and Ryall and the final Knowle Lane, both near Bridport. This event marked the end of the Grasshopper participation in the 'Exeter', replaced by a team of Austin Big 7s for the 1939 event. It also marked Hadley's last trials appearance for a few months whilst he underwent back surgery, and also his final outing with the trusty **BOA 60**.

The Light Car 14th January 1938

...Windout has the makings of a really stiff hill, with a watersplash at the foot, a steep hairpin followed by a couple of sharp corners, loosely surfaced and covered with dead leaves...All the works Austins made light of the gradient...There was a timed section [Fingle Bridge], including the hairpin, for settling team ties, and the best figure of the day went to the credit of W. S. Perkins (H.R.G.) with 8.2 seconds... A figure of 8.6 seconds went to the credit of...T. H. Cole (747 Austin S)...

The Autocar (January 14th 1938) reported that at Fingle, *'the Austin Grasshopper team for once was not outstandingly fast, though Cole's supercharged car of the same type was very good.'*

...After the terrors of Fingle, the long procession – spread out now and the order broken up – wended its way by devious routes and winding roads through typical Devon sideroads to Ilsington, in the middle of Exmoor. There, by the little church around which the cottages clustered, the route bore left down a muddy lane between high hedges to the muddy foot of muddy Simms Hill...Simms seemed to have lost its terrors, and the light cars, on the whole, made the hill look as if there were no gradient (which is, in reality, about 1 in 3), but merely a lot of bumps and mud...the Austin team shot up as in a speed event, even going so far as to change up and down – and even up again... Among hosts of very good climbs we noted the following as being better than most: D. W. Biddle (T Midget) – first car up – all the special Austins, including C. L. Goodacre: J. E. West (H.R.G.) etc...

Avoiding Exeter by the use of the Countess Weir bridge, competitors made their way from the top of Simms to the next hill, Higher Rill. Here was staged a restart test...In so far as the majority of the competitors found little difficulty in restarting in the allotted time (3 seconds)...many made the whole thing look rather like the restart after a traffic light hold-up, using little throttle and getting away gently, although none the less quickly (A. H. Langley was picked out for his performance here, alongside many others).

1938 MGCC Ludlow Midland Sporting Trial 13th February

Grasshopper Results

W. H. Depper	20	COA 121	Grasshopper Cup & First Class Award
C. D. Buckley	22	BOA 58	Ludlow Cup
A. H. Langley	23	BOA 59	Bryant Cup Winner
W. H. Scriven	24	BOA 57	First Class Award
T. H. Cole	30	AOX 3	

Kimber Team Trophy: Buckley, Langley, Scriven

The event was the first organised by the MGCC Midland Centre and took place in the district north of Ludlow, in the Welsh Marches. It was a triumph for the Grasshopper Austins. The 63 mile course included six hills and a couple of driving tests. Strong winds and a cold, bright spell made the surfaces pretty easy, making the trial *'more like a pleasant ramble through the countryside'*.

The Light Car 18th February 1938

The start was at 10.30 a.m. from Burway Bridge, Ludlow, and 47 of the 50 entrants duly departed. Titterhill, the first observed section, stopped none of them, but a stop-and-go test staged on it caused no end of trouble... only four completed the test within the stipulated 7 seconds (two being A. H. Langley, 6 3/5 seconds and C. D. Buckley, 6 4/5 seconds). [This was followed by the Yeld which has] a grass surface with a sharp right, a gentle left and another sharp right turn in its moderate length. Stanway, 18 miles from the start, was the site of Driving Test 'A' with two stops and a 20 yard reverse. A. H. Langley made the best performance, his time of 17 2/5 seconds being a fifth better than that of N. H. Grove (1,292 MG), who in turn was a fifth quicker than W. H. Depper (747 Austin), son of Alf Depper, well known to all Austin enthusiasts.

A couple of miles further on, Lutwyche Lane, put a new complexion on things. It has steepness and a hairpin with a grease-coated hard surface on the inside of the bend. Moreover, this corner is right at the foot so that the standing start made it more difficult... A short lunch stop at Church Stretton gave a chance for competitors and passengers to show that they were enjoying themselves. Then Rattinghope stopped a couple... 'Alley Oop' (Long Mynd) was another matter.

This was simply a track up a steep hillside. It led nowhere and competitors had to turn round and descend again from the top – if they got that far... Horderley Hill, the last observed section, was not a very serious proposition and the trial really concluded at Goat Hill, on which a hairpin was the principal feature of Driving Test 'B', which was timed from a standing start to a standing finish... C. D. Buckley and A. H. Langley tied for best time with 9 seconds dead, and Team-mate W. H. Scriven was the next best with 9 1/5 seconds... Very promptly indeed the provisional results were announced at tea time in the Angel Hotel, Ludlow...

1938 SUNBAC Colmore Trophy Trial 26th February

Grasshopper Results

T. H. Cole	10	AOX 3	Second Class Award, Trial-to-Trial Trophy
R. J. Richardson	11	AOX 4	Retired
W. H. Depper	12	COA 121	Third Class Award
W. H. Scriven	28	BOA 57	Principal Award, Special Award
C. D. Buckley	29	BOA 58	Principal Award, Shell Cup
W. S. Sewell	30	BOA 60	Third Class Award

From the Entry List of 79, there were 75 Starters. The 'figure of eight' pattern was continued, both circuits leaving the Plough Hotel in Cheltenham at 10.00am and returning on completion of the Trial. The Northern Circuit took in Leckhampton, Gipsy Hill (Stop and Restart Test), Warren, Kineton, Guiting (Test) and West Down, whilst the Southern Circuit tackled Juniper, Stancombe (Test), Nailsworth Ladder, Station Lane and Lypiatt (Test). Courses changed at Seven Springs.

Sewell covered for Hadley's absence in this trial, and it turned out to be the last appearance of **BOA 60**; Hadley used **COA 119** on his return to trials. Buckley, Scriven and Sewell were runners-up for the Committee Team Prize.

The Autocar 4th March 1938

Autocar described this trial as not too arduous or too easy, in fact a *'perfect combination'* and a deluge on the Friday night ended seven dry days to add to the interest. More interestingly is a reference to an event outside the subject of the report: *'...the Northern circuit was the most arduous, the first hill being the well-known Leckhampton. The entrance to this hill is almost opposite the grim-looking, police-guarded house where the recent "Torso" crime is supposed to have been committed, and the hill itself is steep and straight with a sticky approach',* perhaps an unfortunate choice of adjective given the location! T. S. [H] Cole seems to have captured the attention of the writer at this event, earning himself four favourable mentions. *'Of the first ten to attempt [Leckhampton], nine failed, amongst them being F. D. Gilson's Allard Special, R. J. Richardson and W. H. Depper in their blown 747 c.c. Austins, and the complete H.R.G. team... Cole's supercharged Austin Seven was the first success... Buckley and Scriven, of the supercharged 747 c.c. Austin "Grasshopper" team, were particularly good, as were P. S. Flower (847 M.G.) and Symmons in his big L.M.B. Special ...'*

After Leckhampton and Gypsy Hill came Warren, which was a hill new to cars, *'situated in a wooded district and has the reputation of being wet in all weathers. It was certainly wet on Saturday, and failed all but three of the entry, these being the two Allard Specials of Warburton and Allard, and the tiny Austin of T. S. [H] Cole, the only driver who managed to keep going after the steep corner at the end of the section, in the morning. As all had attempted Warren, this meant that Allard and Warburton were the only two left with clean sheets, Cole, in the other section, having already failed on Juniper. There is little to be said about Warren. On it Warburton – as was reported everywhere else on the course – was magnificent, his pedal control appearing to be perfect. Allard and Cole were good, too, and Flowers (M.G.) and Buckley (Austin) and J. Terras (939 M.G.) were perhaps the best failures.'* By the time the trial reached West Down Hill, *'the last on the Northern section, the Trial became mixed up with the local Hunt, and the conglomeration of huntsman, hounds, horses and cars made an unusual scene.'*

'In the Southern section the worst hill was the first, Juniper. Only fourteen succeeded, amongst them three complete teams of "Grasshopper" Austins (Scriven, Buckley and Sewell), "Cream Cracker" M.G.s and the Allards...' *'W. H. Depper's Austin (**Motor Sport** March 1938) also made the climb, but T. H. Cole, the hero of Warren, spoilt his clean sheet'.*

In the Stancombe test which followed, *'Warburton recorded the fastest time (14 3/5 sec.) and Buckley's Austin was best of the small cars.'* Nailsworth Ladder followed, *'stopping some sixty per cent. W. H. Depper (747 supercharged Austin) was amongst the successful...'*

'Except for Warburton and Allard, there were no clean sheets, and therefore, no first-class awards. Because of the special circumstances of the trial, however, the Sunbac decided to give awards for the best performance in each class.'

Richardson's retirement in the trial notwithstanding, this dramatic picture of **AOX 4** at the Colmore provided useful publicity for the Richardson family business!

1938 MGCC South West Skurray's Scramble Trial 13th March

Grasshopper Results

W. H. Scriven	BOA 57	Second Class Award
C. D. Buckley	BOA 58	First Class Award
A. H. Langley	BOA 59	First Class Award

Motor Sport April 1938

The Trial attracted twenty-nine entries... *The day was so brilliant that the marshals more or less sprawled in the sunshine performing their clerical requirements. Proceedings commenced at the Market Square, Swindon, and there were two hills encountered before the luncheon stop. The first – 'Breakheart' – was a grassy track, climbing between a valley, the steepest part (about 1 in 3) being at the end of the section. Only about half-a-dozen competitors failed. They appeared to suffer from insufficient power at the starting line. H. V. Slade (M.G.), the first man to try, failed for this reason, but there followed a long succession of fast ascents. R. A. Macdermid (M.G.,S.) and A. H. Langley (Austin, S.) both used their second gears to good advantage... Over tracks across the Marlborough Downs, the course led to 'Mount Everest' which, whilst similar to the previous hill, abounded with rocks and chalk. Here again there was a succession of clean climbs, the most outstanding ones being perhaps the Austin team of 'Grasshoppers' and the M.G. team of 'Musketeers'... After lunch at the Swindon Golf Club, 'Wyds Mount', another chalk hill, was the order of the day, or rather afternoon, and the refreshed competitors took it in their stride... Carrying on over the Downs, and following old coaching roads, 'Stromboli' was reached. This hill only caused trouble to a few... 'Heckler' was a twin type to the previous hill and most competitors treated it with comparative scorn...With more than half the entry maintaining clean sheets, competition was stern in the acceleration and brake test... A. B. Langley (M.G., S.) and R.A. Macdermid (M.G., S.) proved the champions... A 'figure of eight' test was to have been held but owing to the large number of spectators who had congregated, it was determined wiser to abandon this. The final result of the trial rested on the brake test.*

1938 West of England Motor Club Trial 19th March — 6th Annual Spring Trial

Grasshopper Results

W. H. Scriven	BOA 57	First Class Award
C. D. Buckley	BOA 58	MCC Cup winner – Best non-member
A. H. Langley	BOA 59	Class Cup winner (under 1000cc)

Team Award - Knill Memorial Trophy: Buckley, Langley, Scriven

The Autocar March 25th 1938

The trial took place in *'bone dryness and consequent easiness of most of the hills'. Of the twelve who obtained clean sheets, nine constituted those three famous teams – the "Grasshopper" Austins, the "Three Musketeer" M.G.s, and the "Tail-wagger" Allard Specials. In the two timed tests they had a fine three-cornered fight for the team prize.* The starting point was from the Great Western Hotel, Exeter, *and without passing through a single village, the course led to Pack Horse Lane, a hill which had never before been used by cars... The next hill, Hollacombe, was entirely new, and, although not very formidable on Saturday, is of the kind which would be really stiff in wet weather... the "Grasshoppers" made what might be described as perfect climbs – not too fast but completely effortless.*

Pilemoor came next, and succeeded in failing a goodly number... On this hill a local policeman, who was enjoying things as a spectator, dropped his helmet on to the course, where its usually impressive appearance was somewhat marred by an ascending car.

Hatherland Hill was next and failed six. Here C. D. Buckley, of the "Grasshopper" team, made an excellent climb, followed in quick succession by his team-mates, A. H. Langley and W. H. Scriven... The other three hills – Bickleigh, Lee and Wellcoombe – were very easy, although Wellcoombe has the reputation of being almost impossible in wet weather... Because of the comparative easiness of the hills, particular interest was centred round the brake and restart tests. In the brake test seven failed altogether, which left twelve cars with clean sheets, and a battle royal was waged for the team prize. The three teams still in the running – the Allards, the Three Musketeers, and the Grasshopper Austins – totalled respectively 36 4/5 sec., 36 3/5 sec., and 36 sec. Thus the Grasshoppers carried off the team award.

1938 Liverpool Jeans Cup Trial 10th April

Grasshopper Results

R. J. Richardson	AOX 4

R. J. Richardson, according to C. A. N. May's account of this trial, competed with a Grasshopper-type Austin Seven (Wheelspin p139), although May won the Wade Challenge Cup this year. Summer conditions prevailed, and the dry conditions made the hills an easier proposition than anticipated by the organisers.

The Light Car, 15th April 1938

An entry limit of 120 included 53 cars divided into touring and sporting classes, each section competing for its own particular awards: *27 Sporting car competitors covered a 70-mile course, which included Flash Bottom, Ludburn Ford, Church Hill, Eyam Bank, Station Hill, Taddington Moor, Pilsbury, Dow Low, the smoother of the two Hollinsclough ascents, and Washgates. Other car competitors who were in the touring class, had a distance of 72 ½-miles and bypassed Flash Bottom, Dow Low and Washgates.*

In reaching the start, competitors had to penetrate right into the hills, and over the first six miles of the course, conditions were such that an average of only 15 m.p.h. was demanded, although thereafter progress was quickened to 20 m.p.h. First section which came at six miles, was Flash Bottom, which was on private grounds. Divided into three subsections... the middle section was particularly muddy.

Both classes of drivers took in the rather steep-sided Ludburn Ford, and it needed a certain amount of confidence to plunge in with sufficient power to pull out on the far side. Only three or four unlucky ones failed and the lighter machines generally made easy work of this rather insignificant obstacle. From here there was a run of 17 miles in an eastward direction to Church Hill, at Stony Middleton, which was another 'so-so' section. Eyam Bank was reached soon after, but this, too, was simple and there was not a single mark lost... competitors rolled into the time-check at Foolow with almost monotonous regularity. Pilsbury Hill found a few victims among the less-expert. Dow Lane's rocky outcrop is normally wet, but last Sunday, of course, things were otherwise... Numerous spectators who turned into the narrow lane that leads to Washgates were responsible for a traffic block that might have paralysed the trial, but prompt action by a marshal, who diverted them into a handy field, saved the day and the competitors went on to deal with Washgates as they had dealt with the other hills before it.

1938 MCC Lands End Trial 15-16th April   26th Event

Grasshopper Results

R. J. Richardson	428	AOX 4	Premier Award
C. D. Buckley	435	BOA 58	Premier Award
A. H. Langley	436	BOA 59	Premier Award
W. H. Scriven	437	BOA 57	Premier Award
W. C. Butler	438	AOX 3	Retired
H. L. Hadley	448	BOA 60	Non-Starter
W. H. Depper	449	COA 121	Premier Award
T. H. Cole	450	AOV 343	Premier Award
Team Award (Team 38) Buckley, Scriven, Langley			

This was to be the last MCC Classic Trial in which the Grasshopper cars competed. A total of 234 entrants yielded 216 starters, Hadley, not yet ready to resume trialling following his back operation in (presumably) **BOA 60**, being one of the non-Starters. Interestingly, *The Autocar* reports W. C. Butler, a close friend of Hadley's, as driving an Austin, although his usual mount was a 1½ litre Singer with which he was reunited for the following week's SUNBAC Inter-Club Team Trial. He appears on the Entries List with an Austin and teamed with Depper and Cole (Team 39). The results in *The Light Car* (29 April 1938) list him under the Singer entries as 'Retired'. He was listed as 438, consecutive to the Grasshopper team numbers. If it was an Austin, it could have been **AOX 3** or perhaps Hadley's unused **BOA 60**? Nevertheless, it was a very impressive turnout for the little Austins and one that was never to be repeated! Of the 79 Premier Awards claimed, six of these went to Grasshoppers, starting from Stratford. The Exeter start was at 10.20pm, others leaving from Virginia Water (Sunningdale) and Stratford-on-Avon, and all converging on Deller's Cafe, Taunton, from 1.08pm for the Breakfast Control. No Finishing Time is recorded for the drivers. The observed hills were Station, Beggars' Roost, Barton Steep (Non-stop), Barton Steep (Test), Darracott (Non-stop) and Darracott (Test), Crackington (Non-stop), the newly introduced New Mill, Hustyn, Bluehills 1 and Bluehills 2. Team No. 38 comprising Buckley, Langley and Scriven won the Team Prize.

The Autocar 22nd April 1938

*The sub-heading for this event read: Classic Trial Easier Than Last Year: Interest as Great as Ever: Glorious Sunshine: Beggar's Roost and Bluehills Again Difficult: Surprise at Darracott and Hustyn. A number of the Austin drivers merited a mention for their performance on Beggar's Roost: Buckley's supercharged Austin Seven demonstrated that little cars can do big things, and three others repeated the performance when A. H. Langley, Scriven **and Butler** took their neat little two-seater Austin Sevens over the crest.*

*A trio of Riley Sprites was impressive, but whereas Fairclough and Hill did well, Boardman had finally to give in. The tail-enders of this long procession provided another Austin Seven success, but W. H. [Deeper] simply streaked over... Hustyn was in a fairly difficult condition, the lower part being dry and loose and the upper part muddy and rough. The main difficulty was a rocky outcrop about half way up: if a car succeeded in passing over this, a clean climb usually followed... The two Austin teams were all fast and sure, particularly the Grasshopper team, Scriven, Buckley and Langley. **The Motor** (19 April) singles out the Grasshopper Austins for their performance on the restart section on the steepest part of the hill at Bluehills Mine: A series of Austin "Grasshopper" Austins in the hands of C. D. Buckley, A. H. Langley, W. H. Scriven, W. H. Depper and T. H. Cole was particularly impressive and they all grasshopped away at great speed', equal praise echoed in both **The Light Car's** report, being 'particularly good', and **Motor Sport** (May 1938) which commented: ' The team award...went to the "Grasshopper" Austins of C. D. Buckley, A. H. Langley, and W. H. Scriven, who thus and by their subsequent victory in the "Sunbac" Team Trial proved themselves an outstanding combination. The Austin performance in the Land's End was indeed the best of any, with seven premier awards out of nine starters.'*

1938 SUNBAC Inter-Club Team Trial Worcestershire Austin Owners Club 23rd April

Grasshopper Results

W. H. Scriven	BOA 57	**Team Winner** WAOC	
C. D. Buckley	BOA 58	**Team Winner** WAOC	
A. H. Langley	COA 121	**Team Winner** WAOC	
T. H. Cole	AOX 3	Sunbac 'B' Team	

This took place in the Herefordshire area, a move away from the previously held Buxton events, and had gone right into the foothills of the Black Mountains, on the Welsh border, taking in Pont-y-Weston, Nany-y-Bar, Bullen's Bank, Turnant and the challenging Red Daren, divided into six sections, a few miles west of Hereford and about half way round the 60 mile course. There were two stop-and-go tests at Trewern and Hill Lane and two driving tests: a timed climb at Llanveynore and a relay driving test. The trial started at 2 o'clock from the King's Acre Halt Garage, two miles from Hereford and finished to the west of the city. Despite a drought which had oppressed the country for weeks beforehand the course offered quite enough of a challenge.

The Autocar 29th April 1938

'At the beginning of the trial the weather was brilliant, with a hot sun and very little wind. Towards the latter part, however, heavy clouds swept across the hills, rain fell, and these bleak mountains [Black Mountains] became grim and foreboding.' The report noted that C. D. Buckley stopped his engine four times during the relay driving test, and goes on to mention what could have been T. H. Cole's climb of Red Daren: *'A spirited but not very effectual climb as far as Section C was made by J. A. Bastock (M.G.), and soon afterwards a Grasshopper Austin, not mentioned in the programme, went right into section D in grand style'.* The Grasshopper Team represented the Worcestershire Austin Owners' Club and proved to be winners on Red Daren: *'when Buckley was only able to persuade his car into section 'D' it looked as though Red Daren was not going to be conquered, but Bill Scriven got round the second hairpin and through the rough stuff with sufficient urge left to carry him about half-way through the last section – a magnificent effort...Alf Langley's was the last attempt of the day, and taking the right-hand hairpin rather slower than most, he kept on motoring until he passed the 'Observed Sections Ends' notice. A truly remarkable climb and one that was loudly acclaimed by his team-mates and other spectators on his return to the foot of the hill.'*

T. H. Cole of the SUNBAC 'B' Team was teamed with C. A. N. May and Goodenough for the Hill Lane event; W. J. Green (939 MG) joined up with E. John Haesendonck (939 MG) and Dave E. Harris (1,292 MG), for the NWLMC 'No.2' team, eventually securing third place, but C.A.N. May was forced to retire when his crown wheel stripped and Goodenough withdrew from the trial to tow him back to Birmingham. **The Light Car's** report of the trial was covered under the heading *'Austin Conquers Sunbac's Find in Hereford District'* The Grasshopper Team of C. D. Buckley, A. H. Langley and W. H. Scriven representing the Worcestershire Austin Owners' MC took First to win the Team Award.

The Light Car 29th April 1938

For marking purposes, Red Daren Hill was divided into six sections, and it was there that the trial was won. Section A stopped nobody, it is true, and B caused only one failure, but two-thirds of the field came to rest in Section C. Nine of the remainder got one peg higher, but only two did better than that. One was W. H. Scriven (747 Austin), who reached Square Five with the aid of a good car and very considerable driving skill. He was surpassed only by his team mate Alf Langley, who seems to know pretty well every trick that can coax a car to continue. One he demonstrated on this occasion was that by hitting a suitable hump so as to bring the wheels off the ground you can let the revs. scream up and also secure good wheel grip when the outfit lands again with the effect of more than the most concerted bouncing. There may have been a couple of yards of track left when Langley and the Austin finally gave it best, but there certainly was no more. If any doubt still remained as to his ability it must have been removed by his control of the car during the subsequent descent.

The Motor (26 April) also singled out this performance: *W. H. Scriven (747 Austin) reached Section "E" and A. H. Langley in another Austin, went right on to the limit of the track, which petered out thereabouts.*

The Autocar was equally impressed with the team's performance on the final sections of Red Daren: *Cheers greeted C. D. Buckley when he drove his tiny Austin well into the fourth section, but W. H. Scriven went creeping up well past this point to the great joy of the crowd (four men and a boy). Lastly came Alf Langley and **his** Austin stopped only when it reached the perpendicular part of the mountain. It was a great climb, well deserving the full marks it earned.* The introduction to **The Motor's** report comments: *As in some recent trials the Austin "Grasshopper" team covered itself with glory and won the Trophy – by the comfortable margin of seven marks, losing only 13 marks as against 20 lost by the runners-up...the M.G.C.C. second team.*

At about this time the surplus Grasshoppers (**AOV 343, AOX 4** and **BOA 59**) were withdrawn from English trials and prepared for sale to Scotland. It is most likely Langley switched to **COA 121** for this event, and Cole took on **AOX 3** for, what could have been, the final pre-sale appearance, and this, Cole's last Grasshopper partnership.

Less than a month before these three ex-Works Grasshoppers began competing north of the border under the banner of 'The Tartan Grasshoppers', the following lines were published in the **Glasgow Herald** (Monday 16 May 1938). It appears to express the unease and suspicion some private entrants harboured against those competing with connections to the motor trade and their perceived advantage:

'For many reasons it has been found impracticable to limit rally entries to private owners without any connection to the trade, and it is just as difficult to ban specially prepared cars. In the first case a driver is not necessarily an expert because he is engaged in selling cars. In our Scottish rallies many traders take part who have never driven in any other form of competition, and many have not the experience or the skill in competition driving that some of their customers have.

Again, how to distinguish the trade assisted driver from the genuine amateur is a problem which has never been solved, and it may be just as difficult to recognise a standard type of car which has been specially prepared for rally tests...'

All three new owners were connected to Austin dealerships; family-run and well-established (Carlaw in Glasgow, Valentine in Perth and Blyth, Dundee). It would be wrong to think of these as small concerns. The description of Carlaw and Sons' new Glasgow facilities the following November clearly illustrates the point. If notice had been served on the trialling and rallying community that a successful batch of specially developed ex-Works Austins were about to compete against them in the hands of drivers with full trade assistance, perhaps they were right to be worried. Their expected arrival may well have provided the motivation for the article. As it turned out, they were very successful in Scottish trials, but not spectacularly so!

Glasgow Herald, Monday 7th November 1938

111. Valentine's, Perth *Austin Magazine January 1938*

This latest edition to Glasgow's growing number of modern automobile service stations is a striking illustration of the tremendous development that sections of the industry has made in recent years.

The old, dirty, muddled-looking workshop, with bits and pieces of this, that and everything lying around has passed almost entirely from the knowledge of motorists, and in its place has come the up-to-date service station which can undertake every job a car can require from the repair of a humble puncture to a complete rebuilding of body or chassis. "We can do anything to a car here," Messrs Carlaw claim, "We can even build you a car if you wish."

And one can realise the potentialities of such a place the moment one passes behind the attractive brick facade with its two decorative pylons, and, by crossing a pad at the entrance, automatically summon an attendant.

Latest Equipment

That is the first noteworthy feature of the new station. The motorist requiring service of any kind has not to go chasing round the place looking for attention. He receives it immediately he enters the building.

To this attendant he makes known his wants, and the car is driven to whatever department has to deal with it. If the car requires washing, for example, four of the very latest plants are available for the job, each self-contained, with high-pressure hoses led from the roof. The floor of each washing chamber is covered with an iron grating giving complete freedom from the pools of muddy water that are usual accompaniments of car cleaning.

If it be greasing that is required, again the mst efficient and up-to-date plant is available with which the car is raised on easily controlled ramps, and to give the mechanic every chance to do the job thoroughly he has the assistance of sunk lighting from the floor which shows up clearly every point under the car.

The whole layout of the new station is, in fact, based upon the principle of giving the employees the best possible working conditions, the argument being that the better the conditions the better the work turned out.

Best Working Conditions

In this respect, perhaps, the greatest improvement upon the old days is the new system of pits which has been designed for the station. Instead of the old-fashioned 'holes in the ground' into which mechanics had to climb laboriously and out of which they had to scramble if they wanted to do any bench work, Carlaws have incorporated benches and pits in one unit.

A car is now run on the ramps over these tiled pits and the job can be examined with the assistance of four powerful lights incorporated in the structure of the pit. At the back, but on the same level as the floor of the pit, is the mechanic's bench, each with its individual light. Every one of the old discomforts of doing this kind of work is removed, even special ventilators being provided through which exhaust fumes are drawn away.

On Grand Scale

Close to the pits is the section devoted to the tinsmiths, blacksmiths, welders, panel beaters, and the like, and here also is where the bigger engine jobs, such as reboring, are carried out by the latest machinery. The station also possesses one of the few crankshaft grinding machines in the West of Scotland.

Coachwork treatment in all its branches has its full equipment available, including specially constructed cellulose shops and paint-shops capable of holding eight cars. Here warm and cleaned air is constantly circulated.

The whole concept of the building is on a grand scale. Of the single-storey type, it is spanned by a glass roof, and although there is an area of 7000 square yards there are no pillars rising from the floor, which is both oilproof and waterproof to ensure cleanliness.

For the comfort of the employees, who number about 80, retiring-rooms and a canteen have been provided, and for the customer who may desire to wait while a job is being done to his car there is a comfortable waiting-room contained in the office block.

1938 MGCC Abingdon Trial Challenge Trophy 14th May

7th Event

Grasshopper Results

A. H. Langley	77	COA 121	First Class Award
W. H. Scriven	78	BOA 57	First Class Award
C. D. Buckley	79	BOA 58	Watkinson Cup for Best Visitor

The course of approximately 100 miles started at the MG Works at Abingdon, finishing at the Plough Hotel, Cheltenham. Of the 88 who had signed up for the trial, 77 duly appeared on the day.

All non-MGCC entrants were eligible to compete in teams of three for the Inter-club Team Trophy and were invited from members of the Brighton and Hove JCC, SUNBAC, NWLMC and the Harrow Car Club. Invited members were charged an entry fee of 10 shillings and Team entry fees were 7s 6d which the newly slimmed-down Grasshopper team would have gladly extracted from Lord Austin's deep pockets, the results clearly justifying the expense!

The Light Car, 20th May 1938

What should have been a very difficult and interesting Abingdon Trial was turned into a distinctly easy event, owing to the drought and one or two things that did not pan out entirely according to schedule. Fortunately the special tests were far more intricate and entertaining than average and that saved the situation somewhat... [The first test was held at the M.G. Works test track] For this purpose the roughly oval track was divided into three sections. For the first part drivers had to average 15 m.p.h., then for a stretch including a horseshoe corner at one end, they had to motor as rapidly as possible and finally come down to a sedate 15 m.p.h. for the remainder of the lap...

After this, competitors made for Witney Aerodrome, where on a large area of tarred surface, two tests were marked out. In the first, two concentric circles provided a path to be followed by drivers, who had to reverse into apertures at intervals. Good judgement was needed to do all that was required rapidly without running over the 'kerbs'... Several competitors motored over kerbs, including such old hands as D. E. Harris (1,292 M.G.) and J. E. S. Jones (1,548 M.G.)... Easily the best of all... was C. D. Buckley in one of the 747c.c. "Grasshopper" Austins with 24.8 secs...

The third test consisted of describing a figure of eight round some posts and coming to rest in a finishing circle... W. J. Green (939 M.G., S) was outstanding and his time of 12.8 secs. remained unbeaten almost to the end. Then in rapid succession, A. H. Langley equalled it and C. D. Buckley improved it to 12.6 secs. – both in "Grasshopper" Austins.

After this, luck began to go against the organizers. The next obstacle should have been a watersplash, but there wasn't any water, the first hill, Breakheart, should have failed a high percentage, but was so awkward that it eventually had to be by-passed, and the next section, Tin Pan Alley, was blocked by a deep trench.

Breakheart, actually, was tried by some 16 competitors of which Green once again was outstanding. Running well up the bank on the vicious S corner, and slithering and sliding the rest of the way, he got to the top non-stop. He was the only one to do so... The rest, however, never looked like getting up...K. C. Delingpole (939 M.G., S) essayed a rapid ascent, climbed high up the bank and slowly toppled right over. The driver was unhurt, but his passenger suffered a broken collar bone... After that the hill was eliminated.

The remaining sections in Saturday's comparatively dry state, were neither difficult nor interesting. Hodgecombe stopped exactly a dozen, Nailsworth Ladder brought precisely the same number to rest. Ashmeads went one better with 13, and even Juniper could not better a dozen.

1938 Scottish S. C. C., Royal Scottish AC Trophy and Scottish Team Trophy 11th June

Grasshopper Results

G. Valentine   AOV 343

J. H. Blyth   AOX 4   Winner of RSAC Trophy and **Team Award**

Caledonian MC 'A' Team: J. E. Playfair, Frazer-Nash-BMW; J .P. Millar, Ford V8; J. H. Blyth, Austin Seven S

This event saw the reappearance of two ex-Works Grasshoppers with their new, Scottish owners. Fourteen teams from both Scotland and England competed. A difficult sporting event was made more so by rain. The 55 mile route started at Castlecary near Glasgow to finish at Stirling after tackling five observed sections and a driving test. From Castlecary came a few miles over good roads to the driving test which was staged in the spacious grounds of a bus station; twelve miles further on came Polmont Brae (*unconquerable*); Slate Brae, near Culross; Black Bottom; main road work through Dollar, Tillicoutry and Alva to Menstrie (*stopping entire entry*); finally to Craigormis (*too dangerous and was abandoned*).

The Motor 14th June 1938

The driving test, a complicated affair of swerving round pylons and over lines, was run in relay form, first man of the team pressing the time switch and last man switching off. **The Light Car** *(17 June 1938) commented; probably the best individual performances while negotiating a bewildering maze of pylons were those of J. H. Blyth (Austin Seven S) and George Murray Frame (M.G. 'T'). Best time was recorded by the Falkirk and District team in 146 secs, but Haugh was penalized for a fault. Thus the Scottish S.C.C. 'A' team made best correct performance in 156.7 secs.*

The first hill was Polmont Brae, a short 1-in-2½grassy slope, reached through a stream. It proved unclimbable, but **Valentine's new Grasshopper Austin** *got furthest up, while N. W. Gibson (M.G. and D. P. Laird (Ford Eight Saloon) both made very good attempts.*

*Slate Brae stopped all but 14 cars with its difficult second corner, and the Caledonian M.C.'s 'A' team was the only team to climb it intact. (***The Light Car*** praised Blyth for a good climb here, alongside D. P. Laird (Ford Ten), Leslie Bissett (M.G.), J. S. Alexander (Ford Ten) and others.) Menstrie Hill was a 1-in-3½ macadam start, leading to a steep grass-covered track with two very stiff hairpins. Actually no-one got beyond the first corner before stopping but valiant attempts were made by Valentine and Blyth (Austins) and J. R. Millar's shortened K.3 Magnette.*

Craigorms, nearby, has endless hairpins up a steep grassy hillside. I. A. Dickson (Singer) made a fine climb and later T. L. Macdonald (Singer) and Valentine succeeded at the second attempt. Then the rain came down. Cars travelling fast enough to defeat wheelspin were in danger of hurtling over the edge and the hill was abandoned. Toulmin, however, obtained permission to try and took his M.G. up in a fine climb, controlling slides on the edge of a precipice.

1938 Caledonian Motor Club Summer Half-Day Trial 18th June

Grasshopper Results

G. Valentine	AOV 343
J. H. Blyth	AOX 4
B. L. Carlaw	BOA 59

The third ex-Works Grasshopper (**BOA 59**) flew the Saltire here for the first time since its sale to Carlaw.

The Light Car, 24th June 1938

The start [of this standard tyre trial] was from Milngavie, near Bardowie, observed as a Stop-Go test... Gipsies Path, near Strathblane, proved too simple for words, but Drumtian, surprisingly enough, caught [some drivers] unawares.

Kepperculloch was climbed by all, but the organizers saved some silverware on Drumerchan, where 12 failures were recorded. On Aranmore Keith Elliot and Murray Frame (M.G. Ts) were easily the most outstanding performers, while Watson's handling of his adapted Ford V8 also deserved much praise. R. Mickel (M.G. T) was neat and confident, and the same can be noted of J. L. R. Miller (Magnette), E. R. Herrald (M.G.) and B. L. Carlaw (Austin Seven).

Next an excursion was made to Leckie, a section that last year caused quite a crop of failures, but this time only docked marks from [three drivers]... A few miles farther on towards the finish, near Stirling, came the driving test in which B. L. Carlaw (Austin Seven) clocked the best time of 19.2 secs. Next best was shared by T. W. Stewart and J. R. Carmichael, both on T-model M.G.s who returned 19.8 secs., while Leslie Bissett (M.G.) had an excellent 21.4 secs.

1938 Paris-Nice Rally, Automobile Club de Nice 31st July to 5th August

Grasshopper Results

K. Petre/A. C. Itier	72	COA 119	26th out of 29 Finishers

Cars entered for the Rally had to be genuine standard catalogued chassis, made since 1934, and they had to carry full equipment, hood, lights, windscreen wiper, self-starter and horn, and all had to be in full working order at the finish. The chassis frame, back axle, engine and cylinder head were all marked with special paint to prevent their being changed during the trial. Bodies had to meet minimum dimensions and the driver and passenger had to weigh more than 60 kilogrammes.

On the **31st July and the 1st of August 1938** at the Montlhéry track, cars were weighed and marked, gear ratios and body dimensions checked, before attempting the timed flying laps of the circuit. Mrs. Petre and her passenger, Mme. Itier fell foul of the weight regulation with the unblown trials Austin, weighing less than 60 kilogrammes each. The difference was made up with ballast. Then the body dimensions of the little Austin were found to be too small, but after some discussion the difficulties were overcome.

Following an official reception of the competitors by the A.C.F., at 10.15pm on the night of Tuesday 2nd August, the road section started from Boissy St. Leger, just outside Paris. The road section stretched for 500 miles and included the Col de la Croix Haute and the Col de Leques! Cars under 1,500cc were sent off first, the larger cars an hour later. All open cars had to run with their hoods up until the Breakfast Control at Pont-de-Claix just beyond Grenoble, open from 7.15 to 8.45am, the route passing through Troyes, Dijon, Beaune and Bourg. '*Mrs Petre and Mme. Itier only paused at the control long enough to have their route cards stamped*', foregoing the breakfast offered courtesy of la Société Dunlop. '*That they managed to get their little Austin along over the very sinuous hilly roads between Grenoble and Nice at anything like the required average speed* (40 mph) *reflects great credit on them.*'

After Pont-de-Claix competitors were faced climbing the Col de la Croix Haute and over the Col du Pas de la Faye. The cars continued to Grasse and Cagnes before going into the control at Pont-du-Var on the outskirts of Nice and the final tests. From here the cars were driven to the Quai des Etats-Unis where they were examined and the equipment tested, before facing two special tests. The first test was a slow running test taken in third gear over 100 metres, followed by acceleration in the same gear over a similar distance. An official sat with the driver during these tests. The second test was a 200 metre acceleration test from a standing start, immediately followed by a braking test. The final stage involved la Turbie Hill Climb.

Kay Petre's recorded results are conflicting; *Motor Sport* (September 1938) places her as first in the 500-750 c.c. class for La Turbie Hill Climb with a time of 6 minutes and 48 seconds. They are recorded on the 'teamdan' website as second in class with a time of 6 minutes and 12 seconds, being placed 36th out of 37 finishers. Her overall placing in the Rally is recorded as 26th, beating the last placed Peugeot (La Rue – 27th), Jaguar (Pycroft – 28th) and Simca (Madame Largeot- 29th).

Although no colour photographs have been discovered of **COA 119** in this event, it is generally felt that that Kay Petre had the car prepared in the mid-blue livery she so favoured, just as it is presented today following 'Jock' Wilson's 1990s renovation.

1938 Kirkcaldy & District MC Club Trial 27th August

Grasshopper Results				
G. Valentine		AOV 343	First Class Award	
W. K. Stewart	7	AOX 4	First Class Award	**2nd in Team Prize**
B. L. Carlaw		BOA 59	First Class Award	

J. H. Blyth's car, **AOX 4**, was presumably loaned to W. K. Stewart for this event, which saw the 'Tartan Grasshopper' team pitched against MG's 'Highlanders' but with the Team Prize going to the Highlanders. The close rivalry which had developed between the marques in earlier English trials seems to have extended across national borders!

The Light Car, 2 September 1938

Heavy rain at the start did little to impress the course of last Saturday's trial. Twenty cars came to the line at Beveridge Park, Kirkcaldy, including the "Highlanders" team of M.G.s and the "Grasshoppers" team of Austins which were in close competition throughout.

First on the route card was Pond Hill, where the slippery grass failed eight. H. Dewar's Singer Nine made a very impressive climb. Then came Grassy twist, with its three hairpins; here the entire entry came to rest. Frog's Delight claimed two, and Queen Mary's Road, which consisted of boggy grass failed three. R. Gardiner (M.G.) and A. Clarkson (Ford V8) retired at this point. Three more failed on Lover's Lane and G. V. Simpson's Ford V8 slammed a large boulder, but he was able to carry on.

Falkland Hill stopped two, but caused W. S. Millar (Ford V8 Special) no anxiety, for he made an exceptionally fast climb. In the special test, Millar was again extraordinarily rapid: his time was 19 secs., while W. K. Elliot (M.G.), who was next fastest, could not do better than 24 3/5 secs.

1938 Lanarkshire MC and CC Shersbie-Harvie Trophy 29th October

Grasshopper Results

G. Valentine	AOV 343	Second Class Award
J. H. Blyth	AOX 4	
B. L. Carlaw	BOA 59	First Class Award

On the Saturday 26 drivers started from Bothwell Bridge to tackle Sydes, followed by Calder Glen, Darngaber, Thinacre, Canderside and the driving test which took the form of a three-corner acceleration and braking manoeuvre. Probably the most interesting hill of the afternoon was Auchenglen, observed in three sections. The Grasshoppers, Blyth, Carlaw and Valentine performed well and retained full marks. The final check was at Carluke. First Class Awards went to B. L. Carlaw and many others, and G. Valentine received a Second Class Award. The Caledonian MC Team comprised: J. P. Miller (Ford V8), Elliott Playfair (1½-litre Frazer-Nash-BMW), J. H. Blyth (Austin Grasshopper), and won the 1938 Club Championship.

The Light Car 4th November 1938

Newly formed is the car section of the Lanarkshire M.C. and C.C., and Saturday's event was the first step in real competition work. Guided by the master hand of Drew MacQueen, a thoroughly good testing course was planned, a course too, that boasted plenty of mud but no section whereon the models might suffer damage.

Starting from Bothwell Bridge the 26 drivers were sent to tackle Sydes, which proved easy, as did Calder Glen, but on Darngaber a different tale is to be told. Every competitor lost marks. Thanks to a rather tight hairpin and a slippery surface, failure after failure was recorded, and the only drivers who looked as though they might be successful were George Simpson (Ford V8) and T. L. MacDonald (Singer).

After this Thinacre provided a good pick-me-up, while Canderside, despite the crossing of a railway line, gave little trouble. Next came the driving test which took the form of a three-corner acceleration and braking manoeuvre... Probably the most interesting hill of the afternoon was Auchterglen, which was observed in three sections. Goodall (Singer) led the way with a fine effort and completed a trouble-free run, while his team mate, Leslie MacDonald, was clean on the lower portion but found plenty of trouble on the second section. The Highlanders, Elliot, Murray Frame and Norman Gibson, performed well and retained full marks, while the same can be recorded of the Austin Grasshoppers, Blyth, Carlaw and Valentine.

People at Carluke, the final check, rubbed their eyes at seeing such a bedraggled and mud-strewn collection of cars and drivers, but, despite all this, this was one of the best organized and most enjoyable trials of the Scottish season.

1938 Mid-Surrey Automobile Club Experts' Trial (Exmoor) 29th October

Grasshopper Results

C. D. Buckley	15	BOA 58	Class Award Runner-up 1100cc
A. H. Langley	17	COA 121	Winner, Gliksten Trophy, Best Performance
W. H. Scriven	19	BOA 57	Third in Class
H. L. Hadley	29	COA 119	**Runners-up in Team Award: Ballards Trophy**

Twenty-six starters met at Dunster Market, the trial opening with a non-stop climb of Cloutsham, arriving at Ditch Lane (a pseudonym for Colly!), Widlake, a break at Exford, and then on to the moor for Cowcastle and Picked Stones, followed by a new hill, Stoke Mill, Yeo Vale and back to Blackmoor Gate. A Timed Test took place at Pennycombe. A total of 22 drivers completed the event. A. H. Langley won Best Performance with C. D. Buckley as Runner-up in the 1000cc class. The Grasshopper Team, Buckley, Langley and Scriven, took second place behind the winning Allard 'Tailwaggers' for the Team Award. The event marked Hadley's return to trialling with the newly supercharged **COA 119**, last seen in August with Kay Petre. Whether or not it retained Petre's blue livery is impossible to tell from the black and white pictures of the day.

The Light Car 4th November 1938

Unquestionably the worst hill of the day was Stoke Mill, used for the first time in the Experts' Trial, and probably for the last, since a clean climb would seem to be an impossibility without the assistance of 'comps' [competition tyres]. On Saturday, only S. H. Allard and K. Hutchison (Allard Specials) reached the top...There were, however, some gallant failures, notably those of M. H. Lawson (1,497 H.R.G.) and the team of Grasshopper Austins (C. D. Buckley, A. H. Langley and W. H. Scriven)...Most spectacular of the hills was Ditch Lane, previously known as Colly Hill...First man up was M. H. Lawson (H.R.G.)...Then came a succession of failures... until the arrival of the Grasshoppers put a stop to the rot which seemed to have set in. Both Buckley and Langley made clean, well-judged climbs, and only wretched luck robbed Scriven of the same pleasure.

Particularly neat were U. P. Uglow (1,497 H.R.G.) and H. L. Hadley (Austin): the latter's short-chassis motor showed astonishing grip...Then came Widlake, straight, steep, but with a slippery, rocky surface. Again, almost the entire entry failed, with the exception of Lawson, Flower, Imhof, Toulmin, Buckley, Langley and Scriven... Guy Warburton (Allard) was fastest in the Pennycombe special test by a big margin. His time of 16 ½ seconds was only approached by Hutchison (Allard) and Frost (B.M.W.), who tied with 17 seconds. A. H. Langley (Austin) was only .1 second slower...Cowcastle was easy, but Picked Stones, which followed, was not. There were two snags about the last named: (a) the watersplash at the bottom and (b) the hairpin, on which one reverse was allowed...T. W. Dargue (Frazer-Nash-BMW) made the mistake of attempting the hairpin in one, as did Hadley, who got the nose of his Austin well up the bank in the process...It was a very weary contingent which checked in at the finish in the early hours of darkness. A gruelling trial, which only the experts could have tackled!

1938 SUNBAC Vesey Cup 5th November

Grasshopper Results

W. H. Scriven	BOA 57	Watson Gwynne Bowl (under 1100cc)
C. D. Buckley	BOA 58	Ashtray
H. L. Hadley	COA 119	
A. H. Langley	COA 121	Vesey Cup Winner

Team Prize: Langley, Scriven, Buckley

The start was placed at Bridgnorth and the route card included Eaton Hill, the proper name for 'Hunt's Horror' of earlier trials. The next hill was at Dunstan's Lane before tackling The Yeld.

The Light Car 8th November 1938

A. H. Langley followed up his win in the Experts' Trial the previous weekend by winning the Sunbac Vesey Cup on Saturday. He was driving his supercharged Austin Seven. Those "Grasshopper" Austins are hopping to great effect at the moment and Langley, Buckley and Scriven won the team award.

Sunbac broke new ground with this event, which was held over a compact course near Bridgnorth, Shropshire. All hills but the last were new to car trials of any importance, and although difficult they were very fair and in no wise injurious to the health of the average vehicle...

Proceedings commenced with a driving test demanding smart swerves and reverses at a T-road... C. D. Buckley (Austin) skidded his rear wheels off the road... Stop-watches clicked again on Longville, which was a timed climb. Two sharp corners, mud and leaves, made it quite tricky, and five cars failed to climb it at all, including Gilson's Allard V8, which eventually retired with a broken axle. The small supercharged Austins were particularly good, and Hadley and Langley tied for best time in 20 secs., which was very good indeed.

Eaton Hill is quite a discovery and was taken in two sections. Deep, slimy mud and ruts at the start make it difficult to gather speed for the long, steep climb which follows, and the tractor and hawser were kept busy. Half the entry failed on that first section. Those who managed to climb it were Flathey (Bugatti Special), Lloyd-Jones (Triangle V8 Special), Hutchison and Warburton with Allards, the four blown Austins, Frost (BMW), and the Cream Crackers M.G.s. ... The second section only accounted for three failures, but was immediately followed by a stop-and-go test, where Imhof and Hutchison tied for best performance in 5 2/5 secs. Next best were A. H. Langley and Bastock, who took 5 4/5 secs.

Dunstan Lane is another new obstacle, not steep, but sticky. Cars were started in a stream and had to negotiate a difficult section of ruts and mud. Most of them didn't. Applause, therefore, for those who did; E. B. Wadsworth (2-litre BMW), Lloyd-Jones, Langley and Scriven, Warburton and Hutchison.
Yell Lane is another long climb with sandy stretches, where wheelspin trapped the unwary. It was divided into two sections and only eight competitors climbed both successfully. They were Imhof, Hutchison, the Cream Crackers, Langley, Scriven and Lloyd-Jones.

1938 Scottish Sporting Car Club Anniversary Trial, 5th November

Grasshopper Results

B. L. Carlaw	BOA 59

This trial marked the final event of the season and attracted an entry of 41. Cars were restricted to standard tyres for this short-route event that commenced at Kirkintilloch and concluded at Drymen. The **Glasgow Herald** (7 November 1938) reported: *'Observed sections and three tests were not difficult, but weather had made the surface treacherous on the hills, so that there were seven failures on Bardowie and three on Blairstaith; but contrary to expectation all competitors made clean ascents of Milndavie.'* The report's only 'Grasshopper' reference was to B. L. Carlaw's performance in the first test, near Blanefield, making equal time of 5.8 seconds as I. O. K. Stewart (S.S.) and J. L. R. H. Miller (M.G. Magnette). The Chairman's Cup for Best Performance went to J. E. Playfair (B.M.W.).

1938 Bristol MC & LCC Roy Fedden Trophy Trial 12th November

Grasshopper Results

H. L. Hadley	3	COA 119	Second Class Award
C. D. Buckley	19	BOA 58	
W. H. Scriven		BOA 57	
A. H. Langley	20	COA 121	Alexander Duckham Cup

The start was from the Prince of Wales Hotel, Berkeley and followed a route taking in Tin Pan Alley (Tramp's Paradise), Narkover, Old Hollow, Hodgecombe, Nailsworth Ladder, Juniper, Stancombe and Ferriscourt (cancelled by the police).

The Light Car, 18th November 1938

First of the hills, shortly after the start at Berkeley, Glos., was Tin Pan Alley, a long narrow climb, which is usually rendered impossible by a spring half way up. On Saturday, the water was not forthcoming, and car after car sailed up without difficulty... All the Frazer-Nash-B.M.W.s were fast, as were the Grasshopper Austins and the Musketeer M.G.s.

A stop-and-restart test was held on Old Hollow, the times of which materially affected the final results. Fastest was A. H. Langley (747 Austin) with 23.6 secs.; Guy Warburton (Allard) clocked 23.8secs., and V. S. A. Biggs (1,911 Frazer-Nash-B.M.W.) 1/5 sec. longer. Hodgecombe, which followed, was in difficult mood, and claimed 18 failures, including such veterans as K. C. Delingpole and R. M. Andrews (M.G.s), H. L. Hadley (Austin) and A. W. Jones (1,496 Singer).

Then came Narkover, very narrow and long, with lots of leafy mud. Of the entire entry, only seven made clean climbs, earning bonus marks... Nailsworth Ladder was rather easier than usual, and there were 21 clean climbs. Police intervention ruled out the special test on Ferriscourt, but there was an acceleration test on Stancombe to make up for it... The stop-go-reverse test on the same hill produced some interesting times...

By the time Juniper, the last hill, was reached, it was quite dark for the greater part of the entry. This section is long, steep at the start, and gets steeper towards the summit, where there is an unexpected hump which needs every ounce of remaining power... only 11 were successful. C. D. Buckley (Austin) had clutch trouble and stopped near the top; A. G. Imhof (M.G.) was another surprising failure. Macdermid changed his passenger and made a fast climb, and the Austins of Hadley, Scriven and Langley showed astonishing power, as they had all round the course.

1938 Hagley & District LCC Autumn Trial 21st November

Grasshopper Results

W. H. Scriven	BOA 57
C. D. Buckley	BOA 58

An entry of 58 cars was received for this closed invitation trial, divided into sports and touring classes; competition tyres were permitted. The course started from Bridgnorth, leading to Lye Hill (a mud and clay covered timber-hauling track), then to Lutwyche (where heavy rain had washed away the mud to make it unexpectedly easy); here the touring class entrants had to manoeuvre between posts. ***The Light Car*** (2 December 1938) reported: *H. L. Hadley (900cc Austin saloon) was outstandingly efficient. The stop-and-restart test at Farlow Bank produced some fairly phenomenal times. W. H. Scriven, C. D. Buckley (Grasshopper Austins), Warburton and Guest (Allards) all clocked 4.8 secs., whereas standard time was 6 secs.* There followed an 85-yard acceleration test, made treacherous by rain and two acute corners; Station Hill failed 15 who tackled it too cautiously. Altiora Peto was last on the cards, consisting of three hills for the sports class entries, and two for the touring cars, '*but the course was so cut up that the sports cars were obliged to by-pass their portion and try the others*'. Hadley secured a second-class award with his Austin Big 7 saloon (**DOV 768**).

1938 SUNBAC/NWLMC London-Gloucester 3rd December   28th Event

Grasshopper Results
C. D. Buckley   BOA 58   Silver Medal, Second Class Award

The Gloucester was an invitation test using standard tyres, which caused difficulty for some expert drivers who were usually so successful with such cars as Ford V8s, M.G. Midget, H.R.G., Austin and Frazer Nash-BMW, and saw 61 Starters from an Entry List of 67 leave the Anchor Hotel, Shepperton, at 12.15am on 3rd December. They headed to the Breakfast Control at the Plough Hotel, Cheltenham for 5.00am, finishing at the Bear Inn, Rodborough Common after a 197 mile run. This year's observed hills commenced with Flagstaff Hill (opposite Red Roads at Camberley), Maidens Grove (Restart Test), Kineton (a stop for coffee at Moreton-in-the-Marsh at about 4am), Mackhouse, Knapp Hill (Stop-Go Test), Ham Mill, Old Hollow, Fort Hill, Axe Lane (Speed Test), Juniper (last minute substitution for Sandfords Hill), Bussage, Station Lane, Iles Lane, Nailsworth Ladder and Bownham. This was to be the final London to Gloucester Event held before the outbreak of war in 1939.

The Light Car, 9th December 1938

One of the most unsporting acts in the history of motor sport caused havoc in the London-Gloucester Trial on Saturday last. The entire route marking for the day section of the course was systematically altered during Friday night and chaos reigned throughout the Cotswold section on Saturday... Normal programme order was broken... hills were tackled in the wrong order, some competitors missed certain sections entirely and, instead of the trial ending before 1 p.m., the last arrivals at the finish did not turn up until between five and six o'clock in the evening... The whole thing was deliberately, thoroughly and maliciously done. That was conclusively proved by the fact that false trails, sometimes leading three or four miles in the wrong direction, were laid, and the people responsible had even gone to the extent of using blue dye (the colour used by the trial organizers) to mislead competitors. Another point obviously suggesting malice was a false trail terminating at the drive gates of a prominent local resident.

1938 Ford Enthusiasts Trial 27th December

Grasshopper Results
H. L. Hadley   COA 119   Winner of Super-sports up to 1100cc

The Light Car, 30th December 1938

Last Tuesday's trial in the Bagshot Heath area was originally planned to be held over two circuits with 10 hills and a special test in each. Appalling conditions of snow and mud, however, made delays inevitable, and it was decided to abandon the second lap. A very cunning timing device was used in the special test, of the figure of eight variety... Quite one of the most surprising features of the test was the performance of a non-competing Jowett saloon which, with a full complement of passengers, recorded 26 secs. after the entrants had passed on! [The tied winning time was 25.4 secs!]

First of the hills was Water Tower. Of the standard saloons, only D. G. Silcock (Ford V8) made a clean climb, but 17 of the sports car classes managed it. Kilimanjaro failed the saloons, although 15 got up on competition tyres. Kilimanjaro II was divided into five sections, three of which Silcock conquered on 'standards'. Of the remainder, 16 struggled into the fourth section, before the gradient and surface stopped them. Particularly good efforts were made by H. L. Hadley (Austin), J. L. Dyer (Riley) and A. L. S. Denyer (Lea-Francis).

Sections 4 and 5 had to be abandoned, but the sixth was relatively easy... Next came a hill near Red Roads, which nearly all the sports cars climbed... Little Red Roads was reasonably easy, causing no trouble to the sports cars, and the standard cars reached the third of the five sections.

Last on the route card was Red Roads which, as usual, took heavy toll. There were six sections, three of which Silcock struggled through on standard tyres. Clean climbs on 'comps' were made by [many]. Gallant failures were those of Hadley (Austin), Dyer (Riley) and L. W. Adams (T-type M.G.).

1939 Lanarkshire M. C. & C. C. Half-Day Trial 4th February

Grasshopper Results

G. Valentine		AOV 343	
J. H. Blyth		AOX 4	Second-class Award
B. L. Carlaw	6	BOA 59	Premier Award for Best Performance

This was the first Scottish trial of 1939 and one of the most difficult ever held north of the border, according to *The Light Car* (4 February 1939). 25 competitors, including the Tartan Grasshopper team, and Leslie Bissett in an Austin Seven, left Lanark to tackle Southbrae, Whiteford and Shady Lane initially, followed by Hazelbank: '*A nasty cart track that snaked its way from the level of the Clyde at Kirkfieldbank and appeared to lose itself in a forest of decayed tree trunks. J.W. Parr (M.G.) led the way with a brilliant effort, an example that was followed by the Grasshopper team of Austin Sevens...*' At Nethanford competitors drove through the fast-flowing River Nethan and then tackled a bed of sticky, glutinous mud. Tillietudlum was also difficult, but Tower Hill failed the entire entry, wheelspin being the downfall for all. The trial finished with a driving test.

1939 NWLMC Coventry Cup Trial 11th February

Grasshopper Results

H. L. Hadley	12	COA 119	Runner-up, Whittingham Trophy
			First Class Award

The year's trial was described as 'easy'. It utilised the 'dry' Kentish hills and saw 20 starters from an entry list of 21. Whitehorse, Beechy Lees Acceleration and Knatt's Valley were included in the route. H. L. Hadley, driving **COA 119** with its high-chassis conversion, was the runner-up in this event and was awarded the Whittingham Trophy.

The Light Car 17th February 1939

Brilliant sunshine over the hills of Kent robbed them of much of their stopping power in the Coventry Cup trial on Saturday last. The North West London MC is to be congratulated on attracting an entry which, if not as large as in previous years, at least was composed almost entirely of acknowledged experts.

Twenty cars left Wrotham on a short course, which included observed climbs of Hognore, Cotman's Ash and Beechy Lees, none of which produced a failure. Whitehorse was slightly more troublesome, and Knatt's Valley, a bonus hill, caused quite a lot of excitement.
*Whitehorse is a long, tiring hill, but on Saturday was fairly dry... It was the acceleration test on Beechy Lees which decided the destination of the awards. Best time was shared by L. G. Johnson (1,971 BMW) and G. L. Burroughs (Ford V8) in 7.8 secs. Fastest of the "under eleven hundreds" was D. Murkett (1939 M.G. S), who clocked 8.4 secs. **The Motor** mentions Hadley's impressive speed on this climb.*

Last on the cards was Knatt's Valley, where a new course was used, running parallel to the original track. In addition to the usual combination of mud and gradient, a new hazard was in evidence, in the form of a tremendous bump shortly after the start. Car after car hit it at high speed and bounced with all four wheels off the ground. Very few managed to reach the top after such a rough start, although among those who did were Dargue and Johnson (BMWs), Lawson (HRG) and the Allard exponents. H. L. Hadley (Grasshopper Austin) found second gear was too high and C. R. Y. King (Frazer-Nash) attempted to steer a less muddy course, but stopped half way. The finish was at Farningham.

1939 MGCC Midland Centre Ludlow Trial 12th February

Grasshopper Results

W. H. Scriven	37	BOA 57	Best under 1100cc, Ludlow Cup
C. D. Buckley		BOA 58	Second Class Award
A. H. Langley		COA 121	First Class Award

The Trial exploited the Habberley Wood area, south-west of Shrewsbury, using a metalled-surfaced approach lane before branching off through the woods. A number of sections in Habberley Wood were tackled before 'Allez-Oop' (Long Mynd), where C. A. N. May records seeing *'Alf Langley, wearing headgear exactly resembling an ordinary schoolboy's cap, literally fling the little 'Grasshopper' Austin at the hill. Although he had two or three attempts, only one 'official', of course, enjoying himself hugely, he could not emulate [L. G. Johnson's] splendid climb (T.T. replica Frazer-Nash-BMW)'*.

The Light Car 17th February 1939

Good weather, a happy course and smart organization combined to make a strong success of the Midland Sporting Trial run by the Midland Centre of the M. G. Car Club last Sunday (February 12) in Shropshire. Of the 43 entrants, 39 duly started from the Lion Hotel Garage, Shrewsbury, in the morning, and all but two of these completed the 47 ½ mile course.

Ten miles from the start there were three observed hills in quick succession. Two of them were alongside one another, a loop being used to bring competitors back from the top of the first hill to the foot of the second. The fact that a good deal of timber hauling has evidently occurred in that little area gives a good idea of the nature of Castle Hill, Eastridge and Snail Hill...

Castle Hill was followed by Ratlinghope, starting from an awkward water-splash, and is so long that it was divided into three good sections with dead areas between them...

On Alley 'Oop, the order should be reversed. This is a steep and wheel-spinny track with no way out at the top. Five successive sections were marked in a total length much less than 100 yards. Marks were lost according to the number of sections you did not reach. Very few drivers reached the fourth section... This was much the most difficult hill in the trial. By way of a sort of bonus for the spectators there were a couple of gliders performing overhead, presumably from the Midland Gliding Club, on the Long Mynd.

Horderly Hill was the next observed point... To complete this recipe for a good course there were two driving tests and a stop-and-go test, this last being staged on one of the sections of Ratlinghope Hill. So far as times go, there were three equally good performances, W. C. Butler (3,622 Butler Special), C. D. Buckley (747 Austin) and W. H. Scriven (747 Austin) all took 5 secs. apiece.

In the first driving test, Buckley was fastest with 12 1/5 secs., the next best being K. C. H. Rawlings (847 M.G.), with 12 3/5 secs. Fastest time in the second driving test was 19 2/5 secs. to the credit of Johnson (Frazer-Nash), Scriven being next with 21 2/5 secs.

1939 SUNBAC Colmore Trophy Trial 25ᵗʰ February (Saturday)

Grasshopper Results

H. L. Hadley	67	COA 119	Second Class Award
C. D. Buckley	70	BOA 58	Second Class Award
W. H. Scriven	72	BOA 57	Third Class award
A. H. Langley		COA 121	Third Class Award

The Colmore saw 44 starters out of an Entry List of 50 compete for the 'Trophy', and 20 starters from a list of 21 compete for the 'Goblet', starting and finishing at the Plough Hotel in Cheltenham. Entrants competed for two awards, the 'Colmore Goblet' for the less experienced drivers of more standard cars, and the 'Colmore Trophy' for Sports cars and the more experienced drivers. Both routes followed the established 'figure of eight' pattern, but the 'Goblet' competitors were spared some of the more severe climbs. The observed hills were as follows: (Northern Circuit) Hewletts Hill (Stop and Restart Test), Puckham, Langley (Stop and Restart Test), Stanway, New Guiting, Old and New Kineton; (Southern Circuit) Coombe End (Stop and Restart Test), Stancombe (Test), Battlescombe, Station Lane, Nailsworth Ladder, Bownham. *Motor Sport's* (December 1939) account of the Trial confined its attention to the action around Kineton. Hadley was using Dunlop Freighter covers let down to a very low pressure. Old Kineton saw many failures but Hadley *'got up clean'*. On New Kineton, *Langley's Austin Seven and Buckley's Austin Seven [were] both excellent with revs. much in evidence, and Scriven's Austin Seven, not quite so rapid as its team-mates, but excellent for all that.* This was to be Langley's Grasshopper 'swan song', and (possibly) the last appearance of Scriven's **BOA 57**.

1939 Southsea Club President's Trophy Trial 26ᵗʰ February (Sunday)

Grasshopper Results

H. L. Hadley	COA 119	1,500 Cup and NWLMC Tankard

This event was held on the same weekend as Saturday's 1939 SUNBAC Colmore Trophy Trial. It was a combined trial sharing the course with Harrow Car Club. From the trial report appearing in **The Light Car** (3 March 1939) H. L. Hadley was the only Austin Grasshopper entrant mentioned, driving the supercharged **COA 119**, and would seem to have been representing the North-West London Motor Club with some success. On the day, Hadley's car was still shod with Dunlop Freighters. The previous day's rain had made the course particularly tricky:

The Light Car 3ʳᵈ March 1939

The first hill was Stubbs with a track on the hillside that degenerated into a mixture of heather and sand. There were only nine clean climbs of the 38 starters... including H. L. Hadley's Grasshopper Austin (living up to its name).
Bedford (Redford?), the next hill, was slightly easier for all its deep mud on the lower slopes and its sharp right-hand bend. There were 16 successful ascents, the second easiest of the day. Oxreeds (Oakreeds?) was different – the approach was so muddy that competitors could scarcely reach the starting line – the hill was cut out.

After lunch the course led to WD land at Longmoor, two sections: Holly (longish, steep and peaty) and The Hump (short, very, very steep). No-one climbed Holly. Only J. W. Dyer and H. L. Hadley managed to reach the third of the five sub-sections into which it was divided. Much the same story was that of The Hump, although the small cars were comparatively successful.

There was an Acceleration Test on Old Stoner – (fastest 1,100cc – R. Emmins, MG, 9.2 seconds; fastest 1,500cc – H. L. Hadley, supercharged Austin, 9.6 seconds; fastest unlimited – S. H. Allard, Allard Special, 7.8 seconds) and a Brake Test on the lower slopes of Lythe Farm Right, led to the foot of Lythe Farm Left, which was in practically unclimbable condition. Best times in the Brake Test which involved coasting with 'dead' engine over about 12 yards and stopping thereafter were as follows: 1,100cc J. W. Dyer (1,089 Riley), 7 seconds; 1,500cc H. L. Hadley (747 Austin S), 7.2 seconds... Supercharged cars ran in the next higher class.

Lythe Farm Left (also known as Steep) was very difficult. Hadley made a good effort but failed to reach the summit. Barrow, the easiest hill in the trial saw only 18 reach the top. Nearly everyone had to be pushed through the glutinous mud at the foot to reach the Start Line. The last hill, Salt, lacked marshals to observe performances.

1939 Scottish Sporting Car Club Winter Half-day Trial 4ᵗʰ March

Grasshopper Results

L. Bissett	AOV 343	First Class Award, Team Prize (B Team)
J. H. Blyth	AOX 4	First Class Award, Team Prize (B Team)
B. L. Carlaw	BOA 59⚘	Premier Award in Opposite Class, Under 1500cc Cup, First Class Award, Team Prize (B Team)

The Light Car 10ᵗʰ March 1939

The Light Car offered a brief account of the trial: *The half-day trial was situated in the hilly area of Campsies.* 22 competitors followed a 40 mile course: *From the start at Whins of Milton, on the outskirts of Stirling, first of all came the driving test, which decidedly favoured the smaller models...* (Carlaw and J. H. W. Brown were only .3 secs behind the first-placed Anderson). *The first hill was Carron Bridge, and despite its muddy and boulder-strewn surface little difficulty was experienced... Next came Overton, a long bottom-gear grind that boasted several awkward bends and a surface that was atrocious, to say the least of it...*

Kepculloch and Dumgoyne proved easy, and at the finish at Milngavie provisional results were announced.

Leslie Bissett, who normally competed in an M.G., seems to have 'crossed the floor' (using House of Commons parlance) to join the 'Tartan Grasshoppers' for this event, in place of George Valentine, presumably in his car, since no other Grasshoppers were based in Scotland at the time.

1939 West of England MC Spring Trial 4ᵗʰ March   7ᵗʰ

Grasshopper Results

W. H. Scriven	BOA 57/COA 121	MCC Cup for Best Visitor

The result of this event was seized upon by the writers of **The Austin Magazine** in the May 1939 issue, following a number of successful events under the banner *'More Grasshopping – Austin Successes in England, Scotland and Ireland'*, although the Irish event was not one involving a Grasshopper car. The Scottish event listed above, which took place on the same day, and the later Edinburgh and District MC Challenge Tropy Trial, earned a mention for the Tartan Grasshopper team members. The Grasshopper used by Scriven in this event is not recorded – the trial could mark his brief transition from an 'elderly' **BOA 57** to a more sprightly **COA 121**.

The Light Car 10ᵗʰ March 1939

Heavy rain throughout the morning of Saturday last played havoc with many of the hills in the spring trial. One of the most difficult hills of the day was also the first, Wellcoombe, the top section of which failed the entire entry. Good attempts were made by W. J. Green (M.G.), W. P. Uglow (H.R.G.), W. H. Scriven (Austin) and F. G. Cornish (M.G.), all of whom cleared the second section before stopping. The mud and stones of Brooke I stopped the entire entry, except Uglow, Green, Scriven, Cornish and A. F. Small (M.G.), and Brooke II, which followed, was equally difficult. On Hatherland there were only three clean climbs, by Green, Uglow and Scriven, although C. S. L. Burleigh (918 Morris) and E. G. Smith (Austin) did well to reach the second section. Pilemore was, if anything, even stickier, and only Uglow managed to struggle through three sections. By contrast, Cotton was easy, for there were only two failures, one of whom was L. R. E. Crute, whose Austin jumped out of gear. North Creedy caused no trouble, and Hollacombe only claimed six.

1939 Caledonian MC Invitation Trial 11ᵗʰ March

Grasshopper Results

J. H. Blyth	AOX 4	First Class award
B. L. Carlaw	BOA 59	Premier Award (Opposite Class), First Class award

The trial was staged in Renfrewshire, checking out from Johnstone, near Paisley, on a blustery day.

The Light Car 17ᵗʰ March 1939

The short, snappy Hors D'Ouevres (sic) was the first hill to be tackled. Here, *'The Grasshopper Austins of Blyth and Carlaw acquitted themselves nobly'*, despite 50 percent of the field coming unstuck. A few miles of tarred road led to Longun and Shortun, *'two mud-strewn lanes that also took heavy toll'*.

The Paddock, near Kilmacolm looked worse than it really was, but was not easy. The Snap followed, but was not too formidable, *'but the Twister, on the Old Largs road, boasted sufficient gradient and mud to fail nine drivers. Here the best efforts came from Carlaw, Blyth (Grasshoppers), Diack (Morris Minor), Watson and Clarkson (Rintoul Special)...*

The driving test was staged at the municipal ground at Largs, where the local police willingly co-operated with the officials of C.M.C. It was an intricate manoeuvre that was demanded, and so placed were the pylons that more than one driver got lost in the maze. J. H. Blyth (Austin Seven) was easily best with a time of 32 secs... And so the survivors checked in at the Hollywood Hotel...'

1939 Edinburgh & District MC Challenge Trophy 25ᵗʰ March

Grasshopper Results

G. Valentine	AOV 343	Second Class Award
J. H. Blyth	AOX 4	Premier Award, Challenge Trophy
B. L. Carlaw	BOA 59	**Team Prize:** Blyth, Valentine, Carlaw

This half-day trial followed a 40 mile course so gruelling not one car completed without losing a mark. The **Glasgow Herald** (27 March 1939) described Blyth as being *'The most outstanding driver of the day'*.

102

The Light Car, 31st March 1939

From the start at Millar's Garage, Falkirk, came Meadow's Hill, a trifling gradient that was scaled by all. Nearer the Polmont end of the Glasgow-Edinburgh road was 'Jacob's Ladder', a fairly long section that stopped only W. K. Stewart (M.G. S) and R. K. N. Clarkson (Ford V8) – and only because a flock of sheep wandered on to the track.

The two sections of Balderstone proved equally easy, and perhaps helped to lull the competitors into a false sense of security... At Rumford a narrow lane led to Wallacestane, which proved nothing more than a short excursion on second gear, and then the fun began in earnest.

At Avonbridge was located Prince's (sic) Street and Waterloo Place, two gruelling sections that threatened to turn the trial into a debacle. The former consisted of a brief run to a splash, the sides of which were of V formation and a veritable trap for low sumps. If the surface had not been of 12-inch deep, slushy mire, well, more than a mere handful of drivers might have got through... Here two really splendid efforts came from J. H. Blyth on the Grasshopper Austin Seven and J. G. R. Watson on his McCulloch Special. The former simply hurtled his mount at the ditch, from where it ricocheted on to an embankment, rebounded from this into the morass, and ploughed its weary way, axle-deep in mud, to the top...

At Waterloo Place Blyth and Watson again distinguished themselves, but 80 per cent lost full marks. But the worst hill was still to come! This was Beam, where failures were more or less taken for granted. And so to the finish at Falkirk Ice Rink...

1939 Highland 2 Day Trial 8-10th April

Grasshopper Results

G. Valentine	AOV 343	
J. H. Blyth	AOX 4	Premier Award for Best <1500cc
B. L. Carlaw	BOA 59	

The Highland Two-Day Trial set out from Stirling on the Saturday morning to follow a 165 mile journey northwards with Fort William as its destination and facing the challenge of four observed hills. Honours went to J. H. Blyth who won the Best under 1500cc in his Grasshopper. George Valentine and B. L. Carlaw made up the rest of the Scottish Tartan Grasshopper Team.

The Light Car 14th April 1939

Competitors were sent to Logie Kirk for a timed driving test. Fornought followed a few miles further on, and next the ascent of Sma' Glen to Amulree, where a timed and observed climb was staged. The route led through Kenmore and Aberfeldy to Hudson Hill, which, like Fornought, was in perfect condition and provided no failures. Following a lunch stop, the bumpy road to Trinafour was tackled, where another driving test was staged. After this came a delightful run round Loch Lagga-side and down Glen Spean to the Glen, an old favourite that has been used in more than one 'Highland'... Most of the competitors romped up gleefully... Probably the best effort came from George Valentine driving a Grasshopper Austin Seven, whilst his team mates, Blyth and Carlaw, were equally as good... So tired and bedraggled after motoring over some of the worst roads in the West Highlands, the survivors checked in this evening at Fort William.

(Monday) Whilst the first day might have been termed somewhat easy, no such idea could be connected with the run from Fort William to Glen Devon. Six miles from the start came a real terror, the new hill Muirsherlach, where failure after failure was recorded. The only successful people were James Anderson, S. H. Allard, Guy Warburton and Jack Blyth (Austin Grasshopper S).

Croft David was equally difficult; only Anderson, Warburton and Hutchison maintaining clean sheets, whilst about 60 per cent of the entry came unstuck on Stony Brae, near Ballinluig. Guay, on the other hand, was tackled successfully by the entire field.

1939 NWLMC Lawrence Cup 20th May

Grasshopper Results

C. D. Buckley	51	BOA 58	Special Test Tankard
W. H. Scriven	52	COA 121	

The trial took place on WD land at Bagshot, with sections on Bagshot Hill, Pirbright Common and the optional 'Red Road'. **The Light Car** reports there were eleven sections in total, all hills characterised by loose, sandy surfaces causing plenty of wheelspin. *In addition, there were two special tests. The first immediately followed after the start and was extremely simple. Competitors started from a line and motored some 40 feet, circled round a pylon and returned to stop astride the same starting line, between posts 11 feet apart. Chalk marks were made on the rear wheels of each car before it started the test and checked afterwards; if they were still in line, there was at least a strong suspicion that the axle was 'diff-less'. Fastest in this test was a "Grasshopper" Austin, driven by C. D. Buckley, who performed the desired evolution in 10.8 seconds. The second test was a downhill reverse, once again stopping astride a line.* Buckley won a special test tankard for the most meritorious performance in the special tests. A photograph captures Scriven driving **COA 121** in this event, possibly a one-off partnership, and marks the final pre-war trials appearance for both drivers. **COA 121** was placed in storage until its sale in 1940, and sadly, **BOA 58** was to keep an appointment with the scrapman, never again to turn a wheel in competition.

1939 Plymouth MC '200' Reliabilty Trial 29th May

Grasshopper Results

H. L. Hadley		COA 119 Best Performance (Disqualified)

A spell of dry weather made this Plymouth-based trial easier than usual, with its 15 observed hills, although local enthusiasts doused some sections with water to *'create the desired effect'.*

The Light Car reported: *H. L. Hadley (blown Grasshopper Austin) and E. A. Goodeve (972 Singer) had bad luck to miss Stoney Lane altogether: everybody else toured up. Pencreber had been 'doped' and stopped several cars, including I. K. Dyer's Austin, Goodeve's Singer and D. T. P. Normington's Standard Ten. Lover's Lane was another hill which had received artificial treatment, and soon became really difficult. Hadley made a spectacular ascent, and J. B. Burt at the wheel of an elderly Morris Minor, chose the right course and got up without trouble...*

After the lunch check at Wainhouse Corner came Treworgie, which beat everybody except K. J. Hart (1,292 M.G.) and W. P. Uglow (1,497 H.R.G.). More amateur engineering transformed the the stream at Treveria into a little lake, 2 ft. deep. After the crossing, competitors were faced with a hairpin corner on a gradient of 1 in 2. Only Hadley and Uglow were able to keep going, and the horse team had plenty of work.

The finish was at Glen Holt Holiday Camp, where more than 100 competitors and officials enjoyed a supper dance to the band of the 2nd Battalion The Gloucestershire Regiment. A number of protests, arising out of a time-keeping error, were lodged and the results [were amended].

Hadley's was the best performance of the day, but he was apparently disqualified for late arrival, held up by an accident along the route. It is not recorded whether Hadley was one of those who appealed the decision.

1939 Caledonian MC Summer Rally 10th June

Grasshopper Results

G. Valentine   10   AOV 343   Second Class Award, **Team Prize**:
G. Valentine (Austin Seven), J. Anderson (Anderson Special), W. K. Stewart (H.R.G.)

The Light Car 16th June 1939

A fast driving section heralded the start at Kirkintilloch, followed by the not-so-formidable Quarry. The arid Velvet Path, near Fintry, came next, providing no obstacle to the drivers, but next on the cards was Burnbrae, where competitors had to follow the bed of a boulder-strewn stream that failed only one driver, J. C. Pollock (Singer).

Drumerchan, at Kippen, was also easy, '*but Drumtian Ford at Killearn demanded a fair amount of skill and cunning. Here the drivers had to travel for about 70 yards against the current of the River Endrick before emerging at a spot which was evidently the playground of a herd of Highland cattle. The ground was deeply rutted, sodden and guaranteed to cause excessive wheelspin. Withall the water was over a foot deep. Kennedy, Pollock and Patrick took it slowly in contrast to M. R. Chassells, whose Frazer-Nash sent up a pretty bow wave...Immediately followed a crafty acceleration and brake test, and, with drenched linings it was thought that few drivers would make a good showing. However, Robert Mickel (M.G.) drove like one inspired and his time of 22.4 secs. more than earned his right to have his name inscribed on the trophy presented by Lieut. Gregor J. Grant.*

The End of an Era

The week prior to this final listing of a pre-war trial in which an Austin Grasshopper competed, the Royal Scottish A.C. had held their prestigious five-day Rally and Coachwork competition (29th May to 2nd June). Although none of the Scottish Tartan Grasshoppers or the remaining Works Grasshoppers competed in this event, there were some familiar Grasshopper names present with other cars, perhaps signalling the end of the road for this indomitable little Austin: George Valentine, on this occasion, was here with an Austin Ten saloon, before dusting off **AOV 343** for the event described above; Carlaw competed with an Austin 10 tourer, Kay Petre in a Ford, 'Charles' Buckley with an Alvis, and could Miss K. S. Blyth in her Aston Martin be related in any way to J. H. Blyth? The decline of the Grasshopper had begun well before this. By way of consolidation, the process was as follows:

From 1938, and perhaps earlier, the Austin Works' interest in the Grasshoppers began to wain. The culling process commenced with **COA 120** being broken up for parts and **AOV 343, AOX 4, BOA 59** sold to Scotland to soldier on in the more rugged Northern trials, as presented above; **AOX 3** was exported to Portugal; **BOA 60** was dismantled or scrapped. The two **COA** cars (**121** and later **119**) were converted for trials and by 1938, alongside **BOA 57** and **BOA 58**, were all that remained of a Works team. **BOA 57** and **BOA 58** were summarily acquainted with the scrapman in the final 1939 season. It is of no surprise, really, that with the emergence of a new range of models and the 747cc side-valve engine showing its limitations in the modern motoring environment, the Grasshoppers had outlived their promotional value. The Big Seven, Ten and Twelve saloons, and later the Eight, were used to showcase Austin's catalogue in a number of high profile rallies and trials, piloted by familiar named drivers. Some of these events are listed below, illustrating how the Grasshoppers were gently drawn away into the shadows.

TRIALS – NON-GRASSHOPPER

1937 Welsh Rally

Goodacre/Scriven	10	COP 469	Austin Goodwood 14hp	

1938 Blackpool RAC Rally 25-29 April

Hadley & Dodson	44	DOV 768	Austin Big 7 'Forlite'	
Buckley	247	DOX 22	Austin Goodwood 14hp	
Sewell	246	DOX 31	Austin Norfolk 18hp	

1938 Scottish Rally 6-10 May

Scriven		DOB 306	Austin Ruby's'	
Langley			Austin Cambridge	
Buckley			Austin Goodwood 14hp	

1938 SUNBAC Spring Evening Trial 19 June

Scriven		DOB 306	Austin Ruby's'	
Langley			Austin Cambridge	

1938 Welsh Rally 20-23 July

Hadley		DOV 768	Austin Big 7	

1938 Hagley and District LCC Autumn Trial 21 November

Hadley		DOV 768	Austin Big 7	

1939 MCC Exeter Trial 6-7 January

Hadley	262	DOV 768	Austin Big 7	
Scriven	268	EOM 104	Austin Big 7	
Langley	269		Austin Big 7	
Buckley	276	XG 4673	Austin Big 7	

1939 MCC Lands End Trial 7-8 April

Scriven	327	DOB 306	Austin Ruby's'	Premier Award
Langley	328	FOB 348	Austin 8	

1939 RAC 8th Rally 25-28 April

Sewell/Scriven		EDV 671	Austin 8 Tourer	
Buckley/Valentine		EOV 672	Austin 8 2 door Saloon	
Hadley		EOV 763	Austin 8 4 doorSaloon	

1939 MCC Edinburgh Trial 26-27 May

Scriven	198	DOB 306	Austin Ruby's'	Retired

The final nail in their coffin was soon to be struck. Preparations were well underway for the war that would blight Europe over the following years, and had been for some time. Indeed, the Army had been using MCC events as training exercises for their motor-cycle riders for a while, many of them holding commissioned and non-commissioned ranks! Longbridge had been preparing for war since the mid-thirties with its complex of tunnels, shelters and the construction of the 'shadow' aircraft factory, and they were not alone. Suffice to say, the impending conflict loomed large in the public's consciousness. *The Light Car* (2nd June 1939) had prefaced its account of the Scottish Rally with the following:

'Although the doings of Hitler, Mussolini and their merry men nearly caused the cancellation of this event, an excellent entry of 138 cars was received, of which only 12 failed to materialize at the start...'

Earlier stirrings had been noted in *The Light Car* report of the Caledonian MC Spring Rally (5th May 1939) held on Saturday 29th April, in which, incidentally, no Grasshopper entries or performances were recorded. It began: *Despite the fact that several members were taking part in National Service work no fewer than 30 competitors took part...'*

With the announcement of war, production at Longbridge was turned over to wartime manufacture. The Competition Department was cleared, its contents placed in storage in the North Works and the remaining Grasshoppers were eventually disposed of: Scriven bought **COA 118** (although we don't know when exactly), and Buckley's father, the Austin Sales Manager, allegedly tucked **COA 119** and **COA 121** away for his son in an act of nepotism, begrudgingly having to sell both to two Austin dealers in 1940 - **COA 121** going to Lloyd Evans of Carmarthon, and **COA 119** to Wilson's of Dunoon.

112. Longbridge underground air-raid shelter *Austin Magazine June 1939*

It would be interesting to discover how many of the drivers, passengers and other participants involved in the Grasshopper story were directly involved in war activities, and to learn about their experiences. Some we know about: J. H. Blyth, became a Lieutenant and was wounded getting away from Dunkirk in June 1940; C. L. Goodacre served as Engineer Officer in the RAF during the war; H. L. Hadley, turned down as a fighter pilot because of his age (29), was seconded to the Ministry of Labour to co-ordinate the production facilities of Midlands engineering firms, towards the war effort; W. S. Sewell (Captain) and Arthur Waite (Captain and, later, Colonel) held military rank from the Great War. Some familiar names re-emerged after the war to continue in motor sport, others did not. Of the surviving Grasshoppers that escaped the pre-war cull, and suffered a somewhat perilous passage throughout the forties, fifties and early sixties, their future now seems assured with the current clutch of owners. But there is still a lot we don't know about the early history of the cars.

Therein lies the problem: the people who were directly involved are no longer with us, and many details have gone unrecorded, lost, forgotten, never known in the first place, simply mis-reported, misquoted, misplaced or plain mis-remembered, leading inevitably to myth and speculation. Here's one for starters:

KAY PETRE BORROWED **AOX 3** FOR THE CRYSTAL PALACE SPORTS CAR RACE!

113. Freddie Henry, draped across the bonnet of **AOX 3** which he shared with W. J. Milton, makes this claim in the book Austin from the Inside. All the contemporary accounts refer only to Kay Petre's performance with the single seat side-valve racer at the Crystal Palace events (17th July and 14th August 1937). Glamorous as she was, she either failed to capture the attention of the motoring press behind the wheel of a Grasshopper, or Freddie's got it wrong!

Grasshopper Myth and Speculation

THE ROOT TO MUCH MYTH AND SPECULATION SEEMS TO STEM FROM THE PERIOD SURROUNDING **COA 120**'s DISAPPEARANCE. No photographs of this car have emerged to date, and there is definitely no recorded competition history. The myth attached to this car is that it was written off by an Austin apprentice and broken up for spares very early in its life. Although the **COA** series cars were developed initially for the **1936 Le Mans**, with its cancellation, they were mothballed for an entire year, not appearing in public until the June **1937 Le Mans.** Only three cars competed, **COA 118, 119** and **121**. Captain Sewell's memo (page 70) arranged for *four sports cars* and a tender to be shipped together. The *fourth*, perhaps spare car, was never used, or even photographed. One would expect it to have been **COA 120**. Perhaps it was written off shortly before the Le Mans?

Geoff Roe's 'Bert Hadley Tribute' refers to Scriven having bought one of the later Grasshoppers, *'possibly COA 120, but it was destroyed by fire at Scriven's parents' home in Alvechurch'*. It has already been established Scriven bought **COA 118**, passing it on to George Symonds after it was *'destroyed by fire'*, so unlikely to have been **COA 120**.

UI 3345 is also the victim of speculation, with its later production date, and a suggestion that it might be constructed from a written-off **COA 120**. A persuasive case formulated by Ian Moore utilising production chassis and engine numbers, supports this. **UI 3345** appears not to have any trials history for the pre-war years.

Following the TT in September 1937, **COA 121** was converted to trials specification; **COA 119** underwent a slower metamorphosis during the course of the following year, and **COA 118** disappeared from the pre-war record.

The withdrawal of **BOA 60** from the trials scene has yet to be convincingly explained. Its final appearance was with W. S. Sewell in the **1938 Colmore Trophy Trial** of 26th February, whilst Hadley was undergoing back surgery. Canning-Brown records that **BOA 60**, *'was destroyed by fire'* sometime after this event, but she is unable to recall where the information originated. Coincident to this, Scriven's Ruby (**DOB 306**), purchased from the factory in 1936, was fitted with a Grasshopper engine and supercharger for the May 1938 Scottish Rally; was this salvaged from a dismantled **BOA 60**? Whatever befell **BOA 60** during Hadley's convalescence, the engine survives to this day with the Graeme Steinfort Grasshopper copy, now bearing the same registration number.

Returning to **COA 118**, following its brief track history and conversion of its siblings to trials form, there appears to be no further involvement in pre-war competitions, although it was said to have been used in short Speed Events by Scriven, *after* leaving the Austin company, whenever that was. The claim that the car was damaged in an air raid is given some consideration on the following page. In short, we have three *different* sources claiming that three *different* Grasshoppers were potentially damaged by fire: **BOA 60**, **COA 118** and now **COA 120**, providing fertile ground for the growth of myth and speculation!

Post-war mysteries still mar the record of both **AOX 3** and **AOX 4**. There is now little doubt that **AOX 3** is the car that went to Portugal in 1938, but why was its body changed so significantly? With regard to **AOX 4** in the guise of the ugly 'Ausfod' Special, petrol restrictions reintroduced in December 1947 effectively cut short its fledgling trials career with J. M. Findlay and even though Mike Eyre wrote that it was still registered in 1968, what has become of it since?

Answers to these questions, summarised below, could provide a relatively complete account of the Grasshopper cars. The history of seven cars: **AOV 343**, possibly **AOX 3, BOA 57, BOA 58, BOA 59, COA 119 and COA 121** may have steered skilfully through a boggy morass of myth and speculation; but even after all these years, seven out of twelve is not so bad!

1. In the 1937 Le Mans was **COA 120** the spare car or had it already been written off?
2. In 1938 was **BOA 60** simply broken up, or was it destroyed by fire?
3. What is the story behind **UI 3345**, its construction and pre-war history?
4. Where, when and how was **COA 118** damaged during the war?
5. What happened to the 'Ausfod' special (**AOX 4**) after 1968?
6. What led to the change to **AOX 3**'s (**TM-10-49**) body?

Austin Works, the Birmingham Blitz and COA 118

The Birmingham Blitz commenced 9th August 1940 and ended 23rd April 1943. Two thousand tons of explosives were dropped, countless incendiary bombs and parachute mines. Birmingham was the third most heavily bombed city in the UK during the Second World War, unsurprising since it was an important industrial and manufacturing centre making a significant contribution to the war effort through the production of aircraft, munitions, vehicles and equipment. It suffered the worst bombing between August 1940 and May 1941, although much of the damage was censored at the time. The Austin Works was a key target with the establishment of its aircraft 'shadow' factory. What is surprising, considering the scale of its wartime role, is that the Austin Works was not as heavily targeted as other industrial sites, possibly due to the countryside location, south-west of Birmingham and away from the main manufacturing concentrations to the north and east.

The Longbridge complex was well prepared and defended; in addition to its own Home Guard Company, fire fighting unit, medical centre and network of underground tunnels and shelters, the factory was protected by five barrage balloons (which were sent up to around 5,000 feet to force enemy aircraft higher and so hinder low flying and strafing over the target) and at least two anti-aircraft batteries, one located close to the railway line on Cofton Common to the east of the Works and manned by members of the Auxiliary Airforce and W.A.A.F. personnel.

All very interesting, but how does this relate to our Grasshopper? Well, apparently, there was only *one successful bombing raid* at Longbridge – a lone plane dropped bombs in a daylight attack on 13th November 1940 damaging the engineering works (North Works, by the railway line), killing three (one eye-witness account reports a couple, another nine and another thirty-two!) and injuring several. If this was so, then the suggestion that **COA 118** was severely damaged during an air raid *at the Longbridge Works* would lead one to believe this was the cause.

COA 118 was apparently purchased by Bill Scriven *after* he left Austin, possibly 1939-1940. Harold Biggs wrote in 1947 that he was able to look at the ex-Scriven car's three-bearing engine, then in the hands of George Symonds, *after* it had been destroyed by fire. Symonds had purchased the car from Scriven sometime in the early to mid-40s but we don't know what condition it was in – one presumes the car would have been removed from Longbridge once it had been sold, as happened to **COA 119** and **COA 121**, and, if not already damaged, the damage was sustained elsewhere. It is still possible **COA 118** was in storage close to the North Works Engineering Shop at the time of the bombing raid.

With the outbreak of war the Experimental building was cleared of all race-related equipment, parts and vehicles and these were secured within the North Works. This may have included, according to Bert Hadley, one or two trials cars, although he qualifies this by saying most were out 'on loan'. Certainly, **COA 119** and **COA 121** were on site until their sale and removal in September 1940. Who is left to deny that a lone Grasshopper, **COA 118**, remained hidden in the North Works, beneath a dusty, spidery tarpaulin sheet, when the Luftwaffe struck? There again, perhaps the unfortunate victim of fire at Scriven's parents' home in Alvechurch was actually **COA 118**, and there were no Grasshoppers remaining at Longbridge after 1940? Scriven kept mounted photographs of most of his cars. After his death the collection was sold at auction in 2003. Should these photographs ever reappear, they could, perhaps, shed light on **COA 118**'s early history?

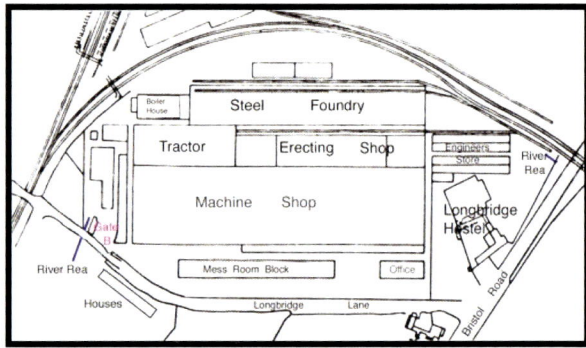

114. North Works (1920) *Austin Memories website*

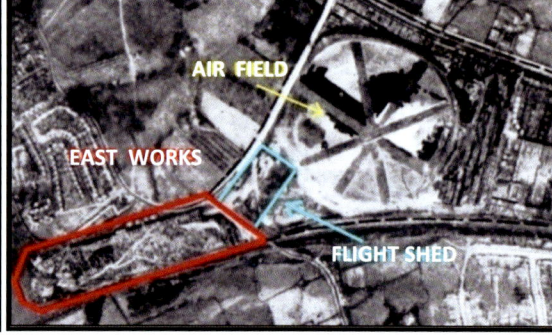

115. Austin 'Shadow Factory', outlined *Austin Memories Website*

Awards by Car

AOV 343

1935

Date	Event	Driver	No.	Award	
19-20 April	MCC Easter Lands End Trial	J. G. Orford	269	Premier Award	⊛
26-28 July	MCC July Rally (Torquay)	J. G. Orford	139	Premier Award	
			16	Coachwork Competition	⊛
5 October	MCC Sporting Trial (Buxton)	J. G. Orford	79	No Award	V

1936

Date	Event	Driver	No.	Award	
22 February	SUNBAC Colmore Trophy Trial	J. G. Orford	42	Second Class Award	⊛
10-11 April	MCC Lands End Trial	J. G. Orford	223	Premier Award	⊛
9 May	MGCC Abingdon Trial	J. G. Orford	54	Premier Award, Team Award Runners-up Sunbac 'B' Team	⊛
17-18 July	MCC July Rally (Torquay)	J. G. Orford	106	Premier Award	⊛
7 November	MCC Sporting Trial (Buxton)	J. G. Orford	89	Premier Award	⊛
21 November	SUNBAC Shell/Vesey Cup	J. G. Orford		Tankard	

1937

Date	Event	Driver	No.	Award	
27 February	SUNBAC Colmore Trophy Trial	J. G. Orford	52	Retired	⊛
26-27 March	MCC Lands End Trial	J. G. Orford	278	Premier Award	⊛
16-17 July	MCC July Rally (Torquay)	J. G. Orford	44	Premier Award	⊛
25 September	MCC Members' Day Brooklands	T. H. Cole	27	Premier Award	
23 October	MCC Sporting Trial (Buxton)	J. G. Orford	41	Premier Award	

1938

Date	Event	Driver	No.	Award	
7-8 January	MCC Exeter Trial	T. H. Cole	193	Premier Award	
12 March	Hagley & District L.C.C.	T. H. Cole			
15-16 April	MCC Lands End Trial	T. H. Cole	450	Premier Award	⊛
11 June	SSCC –Scottish Team Trophy	G. Valentine			
18 June	Caledonian MC Half-Day Trial	G. Valentine			
27 August	Kirkcaldy & District MC Club Trial	G. Valentine		First Class Award, Team (2nd)	
29 October	Lanarkshire MC Shersbie-Harvie Trophy	G. Valentine		Second Class Award	

1939

Date	Event	Driver	No.	Award	
4 February	Lanarkshire CC Half-day Trial	G. Valentine			
4 March	Scottish SCC Winter Half-Day Trial	L. Bissett		First Class Award, Team Prize	
25 March	Edinburgh & District MC Trial	G. Valentine		Second Class Award, Team Prize	⊛
8-10 April	Highland Two-Day Trial	G. Valentine			
10 June	Caledonian MC Summer Trial	G. Valentine	10	Second-Class Award, Team Prize	⊛

AOX 3

1935

Date	Event	Driver	No.	Award	
19-20 April	MCC Easter Lands End Trial	W. J. Milton	268	Silver Award	V
7-8 June	MCC Edinburgh Trial	W. J. Milton	115	Retired	
26-28 July	MCC July Rally (Torquay)	W. J. Milton	20	Silver Award	⊛
5 October	MCC Sporting Trial (Buxton)	W. J. Milton	81	No Award	V
27-28 December	MCC Exeter Trial	W. J. Milton	214	Bronze Award	

1936

Date	Event	Driver	No.	Award	
10-11 April	MCC Lands End Trial	W. J. Milton	318	Bronze Award	⊛
29-30 May	MCC Edinburgh Trial	W. J. Milton	95	Silver Award	
17-18 July	MCC July Rally (Torquay)	W. J. Milton	34	Silver Award	
7 November	MCC Sporting Trial (Buxton)	W. J. Milton	24	Premier Award	⊛

1937

Date	Event	Driver	No.	Award	
26-27 March	MCC Lands End Trial	W. J. Milton	280	Bronze Award	⊛
14-15 May	MCC Edinburgh Trial	W. J. Milton	81	Premier Award	⊛
16-17 July	MCC July Rally (Torquay)	W. J. Milton	72	No Award	⊛
23 October	MCC Sporting Trial (Buxton)	W. J. Milton	40	Non-starter	

1938

Date	Event	Driver	No.	Award	
13 February	MGCC Midland Centre Trial	T. H. Cole	30		⊛
26 February	Sunbac Colmore Trophy Trial	T. H. Cole	10	Second Class Award, Trial-to-Trial Trophy	⊛
15-16 April	MCC Lands End Trial	W. C. Butler	438	Retired	
23 April	SUNBAC Inter-Club Team Trial	T. H. Cole		Winner	

AOX 4

1935

Date	Event	Driver	No.	Award	
19-20 April	MCC Easter Lands End Trial	R. J. Richardson	270	No Award	✿
26-28 July	MCC July Rally (Torquay)	R. J. Richardson	140	Premier Award	✿
14 September	MCC Members' Meeting Brooklands	R. J. Richardson	47	Silver Medal	✿
5 October	MCC Sporting Trial (Buxton)	R. J. Richardson	80	Premier Award	
27-28 December	MCC Exeter Trial	R. J. Richardson	215	Non-starter	

1936

Date	Event	Driver	No.	Award	
22 February	SUNBAC Colmore Trophy	R. J. Richardson	43	Third Class Award	✿
10-11 April	MCC Lands End Trial	R. J. Richardson	222	Silver Award	✿
17-18 July	MCC July Rally (Torquay)	R. J. Richardson	109	Non-starter	
26 September	MCC Members' Meeting Brooklands	R. J. Richardson	50		
7 November	MCC Sporting Trial (Buxton)	R. J. Richardson	81	Non-starter	
14 November	Bristol MC & LCC Fedden Trophy Trial	R. J. Richardson	12		✿
21 November	Sunbac Vesey Cup Trial	R. J. Richardson	7	Second Class Award	✿

1937

Date	Event	Driver	No.	Award	
27 February	SUNBAC Colmore Trophy	R. J. Richardson	5	Third Class Award	
26-27 March	MCC Lands End Trial	R. J. Richardson	281	Bronze Award	✿
11 April	Liverpool MC Jeans Cup Trial	R. J. Richardson		Wade Challenge Cup	
24 April	Sunbac Inter-Club Team Trial	R. J. Richardson			
23 October	MCC Sporting Trial (Buxton)	R. J. Richardson	96	Premier Award	

1938

Date	Event	Driver	No.	Award	
26 February	SUNBAC Colmore Trophy	R. J. Richardson	11	Retired	✿
10 April	Liverpool MC Jean's Cup Trial	R. J. Richardson		First Class Award	
15-16 April	MCC Lands End Trial	R. J. Richardson	428	Premier Award	✿
11 June	Scottish Sporting Car Club, Royal Scottish AC Trophy & Scottish Team Championship	J. H. Blyth		Won by the Caledonian MC Team	
18 June	Caledonian MC Half-Day Trial	J. H. Blyth			
27 August	Kirkcaldy & District MC Club Trial	W. K. Stewart		First Class Award, Team runner-up	✿
29 October	Lanarkshire MC Shersbie-Harvie Trophy	J. H. Blyth		No Award	

1939

Date	Event	Driver	Award
4 February	Lanarkshire CC Half-Day Trial	J. H. Blyth	Second Class Award
4 March	Scottish SCC Winter Half-Day Trial	J. H. Blyth	First Class Award, Team Prize
11 March	Caledonian MC Invitation Trial	J. H. Blyth	First Class Award
25 March	Edinburgh & District MC Trial	J. H. Blyth	Challenge Trophy, Team Prize, 1st Class
8-10 April	Highland 2 Day Trial	J. H. Blyth	Premier Award (<1500)

1946

Date	Event	Driver	Award
January	Enthusiasts' Car Club 'Maiden' Trial	R. K. N. Clarkson	
9 March	SUNBAC Colmore Trophy Trial	H. L. Hadley	Retired – Broken crank
5 May	Yorkshire Sports Car Club, Cowling	R. K. N. Clarkson	First Class Award
26 May	Liverpool MC Jeans Gold Cup	R. K. N. Clarkson	Best Performance

1947

Date	Event	Driver	Award
5-7 April	Scottish SCC Highland 3 Day	R. K. N. Clarkson	Retired – Big end failure
May	Liverpool MC Jeans Gold Cup	R. K. N. Clarkson	Third Class Award (<1500)
25 October	Scottish SCC Autumn Half-Day Trial	J. M. Findlay (Ausfod Special)	Premier Award (<1500)

BOA 57

1935

Date	Event	Driver	No.	Award	
15-16 June	Le Mans 24 Hour Race	P. Driscoll/C. D. Parish	59	DNF	✿
27-28 December	MCC Exeter Trial	W. H. Scriven	282	Silver Award	

1936

Date	Event	Driver	No.	Award	
22 February	SUNBAC Colmore Trophy	W. H. Scriven	25	Second Class Award	✿
14 March	NWLMC Coventry Cup	W. H. Scriven	34	No Award	✿
29 March	United Hospitals Trial	W. H. Scriven		First Class Award, Team Award	
10-11 April	MCC Lands End Trial	W. H. Scriven	275	Premier Award	✿
26 September	MCC Members' Meeting Brooklands	W. H. Scriven	82		
7 November	MCC Sporting Trial (Buxton)	W. H. Scriven	90	Premier Award	✿
14 November	Bristol MC & LCC Fedden Trophy Trial	W. H. Scriven	11		✿V
21 November	Sunbac Vesey Cup Trial	W. H. Scriven		Second Class Award, Team Prize	

1937

Date	Event	Driver	No.	Award	
1-2 January	MCC Exeter Trial	W. H. Scriven	154	Silver Award	✿

Date	Event	Driver	No.	Award	
27 February	SUNBAC Colmore Trophy	W. H. Scriven	23	Second Class Award, Best 750 performer	✿
26-27 March	MCC Lands End Trial	W. H. Scriven	277	Premier Award	✿
1 May	MGCC Abingdon Trial	W. H. Scriven	61		✿
14-15 May	MCC Edinburgh Trial	W. H. Scriven	203	Silver Award	✿
4-6 June	Lancashire AC Blackpool Rally	W. H. Scriven			✿
16-17 July	MCC July Rally (Torquay)	W. H. Scriven	49	Silver Award	✿
7 August	Singer MC Midland Sporting Trial	W. H. Scriven		Patrick Challenge Trophy & Replica < 1100cc	
25 September	MCC Members' Meeting Brooklands	W. H. Scriven	29		
10 October	Hereford City Trophy, Wye Valley Club	W. H. Scriven		First Class Award	
6 November	SUNBAC Vesey Cup	W. H. Scriven		Premier Award	
13 November	Bristol MC & LCC Fedden Trophy Trial	W. H. Scriven		Third Class Award	
20 November	Torbay & Totnes MC Riviera Trial	W. H. Scriven		Team Award	
4 December	SUNBAC/NWLMC London-Gloucester Trial	W. H. Scriven	64	Bronze Medal Third Class	✿

1938

Date	Event	Driver	No.	Award	
7-8 January	MCC Exeter Trial	W. H. Scriven	182	Premier Award	✿
13 February	MGCC Ludlow Midland Centre Trial	W. H. Scriven	24		✿
26 February	SUNBAC Colmore Trophy	W. H. Scriven	28	Principal Award, Special Award	✿
13 March	MGCC South West Skurray's Scramble Trial	W.H. Scriven		Second Class Award	
19 March	West of England MC Trial	W.H. Scriven		First Class Award, Team Award	
15-16 April	MCC Lands End Trial	W. H. Scriven	437	Premier Award	✿
23 April	SUNBAC Inter-Club Team Trial	W. H. Scriven		Team Winner	
14 May	MGCC Abingdon Trial	W. H. Scriven	78	First Class Award	✿
29 October	Mid-Surrey AC Experts Trial	W. H. Scriven	19	Second in Team Award	✿
5 November	SUNBAC Vesey Cup	W. H. Scriven		Watson Gwynne Bowl	
12 November	Bristol MC & LCC Fedden Trophy Trial	W. H. Scriven			

1939

Date	Event	Driver	No.	Award	
12 February	MGCC Ludlow Midland Centre Trial	W. H. Scriven	37	Best <1100cc, Ludlow Cup	✿
25 February	SUNBAC Colmore Trophy	W. H. Scriven	72	Third Class Award	✿
4 March	Hagley and District MC Spring Trial	W. H. Scriven		MCC Cup – Best Visitor	

BOA 58

1935

Date	Event	Driver	No.	Award	
15-16 June	Le Mans 24 Hour Race	C. J. P. Dodson/R. J. Richardson	60	28th	✿
27-28 Dec	MCC Exeter Trial	C. L. Goodacre	280	Silver Award	✿

1936

Date	Event	Driver	No.	Award	
22 February	SUNBAC Colmore Trophy	C. D. Buckley	44	First Class Award, Club Team Prize	✿
14 March	NWLMC Coventry Cup	C. D. Buckley	56	Third Class Award	✿
29 March	United Hospitals Trial	C. D. Buckley	30	First Class Award, Team Award	✿
10-11 April	MCC Lands End Trial	C. D. Buckley	286	Premier Award	✿
9 May	MGCC Abingdon Trial	C. D. Buckley	49	Premier Award	✿
12-14 June	Lancashire AC Blackpool Rally	C. D. Buckley	96	Starting Test Prize	✿
17-18 July	MCC July Rally (Torquay)	C. D. Buckley	108	Premier Award	✿
26 September	MCC Members' Meeting Brooklands	C. D. Buckley	80		
7 November	MCC Sporting Trial (Buxton)	C. D. Buckley	91	Premier Award	
14 November	Bristol MC & LCC Fedden Trophy Trial	C. D. Buckley	10		✿V
21 November	SUNBAC Shell/Vesey Cup	C. D. Buckley		Watson Gwynne Bowl – Team Prize	
5 December	NWLMC/SUNBAC Gloucester	C. D. Buckley	75	Team Award	✿

1937

Date	Event	Driver	No.	Award	
1-2 January	MCC Exeter Trial	C. D. Buckley	153	Premier Award	✿
27 February	SUNBAC Colmore Trophy	C. D. Buckley	22	Principal Award/Shell Cup	✿
26-27 March	MCC Lands End Trial	C. D. Buckley	275	Premier Award	✿
24 April	Sunbac Inter-Club Team Trial	C. D. Buckley			
1 May	MGCC Abingdon Trial	C. D. Buckley	59		✿
14-15 May	MCC Edinburgh Trial	C. D. Buckley	202	Premier Award	✿
4-6 June	Lancashire AC Blackpool Rally	C. D. Buckley			✿
16-17 July	MCC July Rally (Torquay)	C. D. Buckley	47	Premier Award	✿
25 September	MCC Members' Meeting Brooklands	C. D. Buckley	28		
10 October	Hereford City Trophy, Wye Valley Club	C. D. Buckley		First Class Award	
30 October	Mid-Surrey AC Experts Trial	C. D. Buckley		Runner-up Timed Tests	✿
6 November	SUNBAC Vesey Cup	C. D. Buckley	25	Watson Gwynne Bowl/Ixion Cup	✿
13 November	Bristol MC Fedden Trophy	C. D. Buckley		Winner Fedden Trophy	
20 November	Torbay & Totnes MC Riviera Trial	C. D. Buckley		Winner	
4 December	SUNBAC/NWLMC London-Gloucester	C. D. Buckley	63	Silver Medal, Second Class Award	✿
26 December	MGCC South West Kimber Trophy	C. D. Buckley		First Class Award	

1938

7-8 January	MCC Exeter Trial	C. D. Buckley	184	Premier Award	✲
13 February	MGCC Ludlow Midland Centre Trial	C. D. Buckley	22	Ludlow Cup	✲
26 February	SUNBAC Colmore Trophy	C. D. Buckley	29	Principal Award, Shell Cup	✲
13 March	MGCC South West Skurray's Scramble Trial	C. D. Buckley		First Class Award	✲
19 March	West of England MC Trial	C. D. Buckley		Cup Winner – Team Award	
15-16 April	MCC Lands End Trial	C. D. Buckley	435	Premier Award	✲
23 April	SUNBAC Inter-Club Team Trial	C. D. Buckley		Winner	
14 May	MGCC Abingdon Trial	C. D. Buckley	79	Watkinson Cup for Best Visitor	✲
29 October	Mid-Surrey AC Experts Trial	C. D. Buckley	15	Runner-up 1000cc	✲
5 November	SUNBAC Vesey Cup	C. D. Buckley			
12 November	Bristol MC & LCC Fedden Trophy Trial	C. D. Buckley	19		✲
3 December	SUNBAC/NWLMC London-Gloucester	C. D. Buckley		Silver Medal, Second Class Award	

1939

12 February	MGCC Ludlow Midland Centre Trial	C. D. Buckley		Second Class Award	
25 February	SUNBAC Colmore Trophy	C. D. Buckley	70	Second Class Award	✲
20 May	NWLMC Lawrence Cup	C. D. Buckley	51	Special Test Tankard	✲

BOA 59

1935

15-16 June	Le Mans 24 Hour Race	C. L. Goodacre/R. F. Turner	61	DNF	✲
27-28 December	MCC Exeter Trial	W. S. Sewell	281	Bronze Award	

1936

22 February	SUNBAC Colmore Trophy	C. L. Goodacre	23	First Class Award	✲
14 March	NWLMC Coventry Cup	C. L. Goodacre	58		✲
10-11 April	MCC Lands End Trial	C. L. Goodacre	274	Premier Award	✲

1937

1-2 January	MCC Exeter trial	W. S. Sewell	155	Bronze Award	✲
27 February	SUNBAC Colmore Trophy	W. S. Sewell	4	Second Class Award	✲
26-27 March	MCC Lands End Trial	W. S. Sewell	279	Non-starter	
24 April	Sunbac Inter-Club Team Trial	C. L. Goodacre	38		✲
14-15 May	MCC Edinburgh Trial	W. S. Sewell	201	Non-starter	
10 October	Hereford City Trophy, Wye Valley Club	A. H. Langley		First Class Award	
30 October	Mid-Surrey AC Experts Trial	A. H. Langley		Class Winner	✲
13 November	Bristol MC & LCC Fedden Trophy Trial	A. H. Langley		Second Class Award	
20 November	Torbay & Totnes MC Riviera Trial	A. H. Langley		Best Visitor	
4 December	SUNBAC/NWLMC London-Gloucester Trial	A. H. Langley	62	Bronze Medal, Third Class Award	✲
26 December	MGCC South West Kimber Trophy	A. H. Langley		First Class Award, Spencer Trophy	

1938

7-8 January	MCC Exeter trial	A. H. Langley	183	Premier Award	✲
13 February	MGCC Ludlow Midland Sporting Trial	A. H. Langley	23	Bryant Cup Winner	✲
13 March	MGCC South West Skurray's Scramble Trial	A. H. Langley		First Class Award	
19 March	West of England MC Trial	A. H. Langley		Cup Winner, Team Award	
15-16 April	MCC Lands End Trial	A. H. Langley	436	Premier Award, Team Award	✲
18 June	Caledonian MC Half-Day Trial	B. L. Carlaw			
27 August	Kirkcaldy & District MC Club Trial	B. L. Carlaw		First Class Award, Team (2nd)	
29 October	Lanarkshire MC Shersbie-Harvie Trophy	B. L. Carlaw		First Class Award	
5 November	Scottish SCC Anniversary Trial	B. L. Carlaw			

1939

4 February	Lanarkshire CC Half-Day Trial	B. L. Carlaw	6	Premier Award (Best Performance)	✲
4 March	Scottish SCC Winter Half-Day trial	B. L. Carlaw		Premier Award, under 1500cc Cup, First Class Award, Team Prize	✲
11 March	Caledonian MC Invitation Trial	B. L. Carlaw		Premier Award (Opposite Class), First Class Award	
25 March	Edinburgh & District MC Trial	B. L. Carlaw		Team Prize	
8-10 April	Highland 2 Day Trial	B. L. Carlaw			✲

1952

30-31 May	MCC Edinburgh Trial	R. Morley			
4 October	Lancashire AC Davis Trophy Trial	R. Morley		Finishers Award	

1953

2-3 January	MCC Exeter Trial	R. Morley	220	Retired (seized blower)	
3-4 April	MCC Lands End Trial	R. Morley	375		

Date	Event	Driver	No.	Result	
22-23 May	MCC Edinburgh Trial	R. Morley			

1954

16 April	MCC Lands End Trial	R. Morley	323	Silver Award	
21-22 May	MCC Edinburgh Trial	R. Morley	86		
4-5 June	MCC Whitsun Trial	R. Morley			
7-8 October	MCC Derbyshire Autumn Touring Trial	R. Morley	32	Second Class Award	

1955

7-8 January	MCC Exeter Trial	R. Morley	294	Silver Award	✿
8-9 April	MCC Lands End Trial	R. Morley	285	Silver Award	
November	MCC Derbyshire Autumn Touring Trial	R. Morley	120		

1956

6-7 January	MCC Exeter Trial	R. Morley		Abandoned	
19-20 April	MCC Lands End Trial	R. Morley		Gold Award	

1957

Easter	MCC Lands End Trial	R. Morley	130	Gold Award	

BOA 60

1935

27-28 December	MCC Exeter Trial	H. L. Hadley	283	Silver, Simms Hill Trophy	

1936

22 February	SUNBAC Colmore Trophy	H. L. Hadley	24	Second Class Award	✿
14 March	NWLMC Coventry Cup	H. L. Hadley	33	Best SUNBAC	✿
29 March	United Hospitals Trial	H. L. Hadley		First Class Award, Team Award	
10-11 April	MCC Lands End Trial	H. L. Hadley	276	Premier Award	✿
29-30 May	MCC Edinburgh Trial	H. L. Hadley	206	Held Over	
17-18 July	MCC July Rally (Torquay)	P. H. J. Barugh	112	Silver	✿
7 November	MCC Sporting Trial (Buxton)	H. L. Hadley	113	Premier Award	
14 November	Bristol MC &LCC Fedden Trophy Trial	H. L. Hadley		Anthony Cup	
21 November	SUNBAC Shell/Vesey Cup	H. L. Hadley		Cup Winner, Team Prize	

1937

1-2 January	MCC Exeter Trial	H. L. Hadley	152	Premier Award	✿
27 February	SUNBAC Colmore Trophy	H. L. Hadley	24	First Class Award, Trial to Trial Trophy	✿
26-27 March	MCC Lands End Trial	H. L. Hadley	276	Retired	
24 April	SUNBAC Inter-Club Team Trial	H. L. Hadley			
1 May	MGCC Abingdon	H. L. Hadley	60		✿
14-15 May	MCC Edinburgh Trial	H. L. Hadley	204	Premier Award	✿
22 May	Bristol MC & LCC Whitchurch	H. L. Hadley	1	5th in Class	
16-17 July	MCC July Rally (Torquay)	H. L. Hadley	48	Premier Award	✿
30 October	Mid-Surrey AC Experts Trial	H. L. Hadley	31		✿
6 November	Sunbac Vesey Cup Trial	H. L. Hadley	26	Second Class Award	✿
13 November	Bristol MC & LCC Fedden Trophy Trial	H. L. Hadley		No Award	
20 November	Torbay & Totnes MC Riviera Trial	H. L. Hadley		Runner-up, Eric Perry Cup	
4 December	SUNBAC/NWLMC London to Gloucester	H. L. Hadley	76	Silver Medal, Second Class Award	✿

1938

7-8 January	MCC Exeter Trial	H. L. Hadley	213	Premier Award	✿
26 February	SUNBAC Colmore Trophy	W. S. Sewell	30	Third Class Award	
15-16 April	MCC Lands End Trial	H. L. Hadley	448	Non-starter	

COA 118

1937

19-20 June	Le Mans 24 Hour Race	C. L. Goodacre/C. D. Buckley	56	DNF	✿
24 July	Donington 12 Hour Sports Race	C. L. Goodacre/C. D. Buckley	2	3rd (11th)	✿

COA 119

1937

19-20 June	Le Mans 24 Hour Race	K. Petre/G. Mangan	55	DNF	✿
24 July	Donington 12 Hour Sports Race	K. Petre/P. Stevenson	3	5th (16th)	✿

1938

Date	Event	Driver	No.	Result	
31 July-5 Aug	Paris-Nice Rally	K. Petre/A. C. Itier	72	26th Winner of 750 class	⊛
11 September	IMRC Phoenix Park International GP	G. A. Mangan	42	Non Starter	
29 October	Mid-Surrey AC Experts Trial	H. L. Hadley	29		⊛
5 November	Sunbac Vesey Cup Trial	H. L. Hadley			
12 November	Bristol MC &LCC Roy Fedden Trophy	H. L. Hadley	3	Second Class Award	⊛
27 December	Ford Enthusiasts' Club Trial	H. L. Hadley		Winner, Supersports <1100cc	

1939

Date	Event	Driver	No.	Result	
11 February	NWLMC Coventry Cup Trial	H. L. Hadley	12	Runner-up, Whittingham Trophy, First Class Award	⊛
25 February	Colmore Trophy	H. L. Hadley	67	Second Class Award	⊛
26 February	Southsea President's Trophy	H. L. Hadley		1500 Cup, NWLMC Tankard	⊛
29 May	Plymouth Motor Club '200'	H. L. Hadley		Best Performance (Disqualified)	

1946

Date	Event	Driver	No.	Result	
9 March	SUNBAC Colmore Trophy	J. E. Wilson		No Award	⊛
	Scarborough 440	J. E. Wilson	51	Passenger Tommy Wise	⊛
	Yorkshire SCC Blackburn Trial	J. E. Wilson	32		⊛

1947

Date	Event	Driver	No.	Result	
Easter	Scottish SCC Highland 3 day Trial	J. E. Wilson		Team Award -Paige, Stevenson, Wilson	
May	Liverpool MC Jeans Gold Cup	J. E. Wilson		Third Class Award (<1500)	
	Yorkshire SCC Richmond Trial	J. E. Wilson			
	Bo'ness	J. E. Wilson			
	RAC Championship, Cheltenham	J. E. Wilson			

COA 121

1937

Date	Event	Driver	No.	Result	
19-20 June	Le Mans 24 Hour Race	C. J. P. Dodson/H. L. Hadley	57	DNF	⊛
24 July	Donington 12 Hour Sports Race	C. J. P. Dodson/H. L. Hadley	1	2nd (7th)	⊛
4 September	XI RAC International TT	C. J. P. Dodson	29	DNF	⊛
6 November	Sunbac Vesey Cup Trial	C. L. Goodacre		Premier Award	
13 November	Bristol MC & LCC Fedden Trophy Trial	C. L. Goodacre	48	First Class Award	⊛
20 November	Torbay & Totnes Riviera Trial	C. L. Goodcare			
4 December	SUNBAC/NWLMC London to Gloucester	C. L. Goodacre	75	Silver Medal, Second Class Award	⊛

1938

Date	Event	Driver	No.	Result	
7-8 January	MCC Exeter Trial	C. L. Goodacre	212	Premier Award	⊛
13 February	MGCC Ludlow Midland Centre Trial	W. H. Depper	20	Grasshopper Cup, First Class Award	⊛
26 February	SUNBAC Colmore Trophy	W. H. Depper	12	Third Class Award	⊛
15-16 April	MCC Lands End Trial	W. H. Depper	449	Premier Award	⊛
23 April	SUNBAC Inter-Club Team Trial	A. H. Langley		Winner	
14 May	MGCC Abingdon Trial	A. H. Langley	77	First Class Award	⊛
29 October	Mid-Surrey AC Experts Trial	A. H. Langley	11	Winner, Gliksten Trophy	⊛
5 November	SUNBAC Vesey Cup	A. H. Langley		Vesey Cup Winner	
12 November	Bristol MC & LCC Roy Fedden Trophty	A. H. Langley	20	Alexander Duckham Cup (4th)	⊛
3 December	SUNBAC/NWLMC London-Gloucester Trial	A. H. Langley			

1939

Date	Event	Driver	No.	Result	
12 February	MGCC Ludlow Midland Centre Trial	A. H. Langley		First Class Award	
25 February	Sunbac Colmore Trophy Trial	A. H. Langley		Third Class Award	
20 May	NWLMC Lawrence Cup Trial	W. H. Scriven	52		⊛

1949

Date	Event	Driver	No.	Result	
22 October	MCC Buxton Sporting Trial	R. Morley			

1950

Date	Event	Driver	No.	Result	
24 June	Chester MC Speed Trials, Queensbury	R. Morley			
10 July	Lancashire AC Morecambe Rally	R. Morley			
2 September	Lancashire AC Davis Trophy Trial	R. Morley	70		⊛
21 October	MCC Buxton Sporting Trial	R. Morley			

Photographs 1935 to 1939

Despite the poor quality of some of these images, collectively they provide a rare and invaluable record.

1935 MCC Lands End Trial 19-20th April

116. Orford getting away from the Barton Steep restart (AOV 343)
Light Car 26 April 1935

117. Richardson (AOX 4) on Darracott
Ian Moore Collection

1935 Le Mans 24 Hour Race 15-16th June

118. Goodacre (BOA 59) *Authors' Collection*

119. The Little 'uns in close company on the curve beyond the pits. The cars ahead of No. 56, the Misses Richmond and Simpson's MG Midget, are other Midgets and the "works" Austins.
Light Car 21 June 1935

120. 1934 AEK Speedy (CZ 6324) *Authors' Collection*

121. BOA 58 (No.60) *Ian Moore Collection*

1935 MCC July Rally (Torquay) 26-28th July

122. Milton (AOX 3) *Authors' Collection*

123. Richardson (AOX 4) *Authors' Collection*

124. Coachwork competition: AOV 343 (AOX 4 to its offside) *Ian Moore Collection*

125. Coachwork competition: AOX 4 in foreground, AOV 343 and AOX 3 far right of picture *Ian Moore Collection*

1935 MCC Members' Meeting, Brooklands 14th September 1935

126. AOX 4 (No. 47) *Ian Moore Collection*

127. AOX 4 (47) *Ian Moore Collection*

1935 MCC Exeter Trial 27-28th December

128. Goodacre (BOA 58) on Fingle Bridge *Austin Magazine February 1936*

1936 SUNBAC Colmore Trophy 22nd February

129. Orford (AOV 343) *Ferret Fotographics*

130. Richardson (AOX 4) *Ferret Fotographics*

131. Hadley (BOA 60) *Ian Moore Collection*

132. Hadley (BOA 60) towed to the start on Fish Hill *Autocar 28 February 1936*

133. Goodacre and Depper (BOA 59) *Ferret Fotographics*

134. Buckley's (BOA 58) first Grasshopper outing, ascending Kineton Hill *Austin Magazine April 1936*

1936 NWLMC Coventry Cup 14th March

135. Scriven (BOA 57) *Ferret Fotographics*

136. Scriven (BOA 57) *Authors' Collection*

137. Buckley (BOA 58) *Authors' Collection*

138. Goodacre (BOA 59) *Authors' Collection*

139. Hadley (BOA 60) tackling a rock-strewn climb, Cloutsham *Authors' Collection*

140. Hadley (BOA 60) *Ian Moore Collection*

1936 MCC Lands End Trial 10-11th April

141. Orford (AOV 343) makes light of the boulders on the new Bluehills *Light Car 17 April 1936*

142. Scriven (BOA 57) *Ferret Fotographics*

143. Hadley (BOA 60) *Authors' Collection*

144. Richardson (AOX 4) *Ferret Fotographics*

145. Buckley (BOA 58) *Ian Moore Collection*

146. Buckley (BOA 58) on Station Hill, Lynton *Austin Magazine May 1936*

147. Orford (AOV 343) *Ian Moore Collection*

148. Richardson (AOX 4) on Station Hill, Lynton *Ian Moore Collection*

149. Richardson (AOX 4) on Beggars Roost *Ian Moore Collection*

1936 MGCC Abingdon Trial 9th May

150. Orford (AOV 343) *Ferret Fotographics*

151. Buckley (BOA 58) *Ferret Fotographics*

152. Buckley driving BOA 58 *Authors' Collection*

1936 Lancashire A. C. Blackpool Rally 12-14th June

153. Buckley (BOA 58) and co-driver on the deserted Blackpool Front *Bacon*

154. Buckley (BOA 58) on the Sea front for the 'wiggle-woggle' special driving test *Austin Magazine August 1936*

1936 MCC July Rally (Torquay) 17-18th July

155. Buckley (BOA 58) slews sideways when pulling up in the braking area at the end of the second special test in Ilsham Road *Light Car 24 July 1936*

156. Orford (AOV 343) in the Acceleration Test *The Motor 21 July 1936*

157. P. H. J. Barugh (BOA 60) No. 112 *Ferret Fotographics*

1936 MCC Sporting Trial (Buxton) 7th November

158. Milton (AOX 3) *Ferret Fotographics*

159. Scriven (BOA 57) on Litton Slack *Authors' Collection*

160. Orford (AOV 343) on Jenkins Chapel *Ferret Fotographics*

1936 Bristol MC & LCC Fedden Trophy Trial 14th November

161. Scriven (BOA 57) at Hodgcombe Farm *Light Car 4 December 1936*

162. AOX 4 (No. 12) *Ian Moore Collection*

163. BOA 58 (10), BOA 57 (11) and AOX 4 (12) *Ian Moore Collection*

1936 SUNBAC Vesey Cup 21st November

164. Richardson (AOX 4) on Droppingwell *Light Car 27 November 1936*

1936 NWLMC/SUNBAC London – Gloucester 5th December

165. Buckley (BOA 58) *Austin Magazine January 1937*

166. Buckley (BOA 58) climbing Nailsworth Ladder *Light Car 11 December 1936*

1936 MCC Exeter Trial 1-2nd January 1937

167. Queuing at Fingle Bridge (BOA 59) *Light Car 8 January 1937*

168. Sewell (BOA 59) *Authors' Collection*

169. Scriven (BOA 57) *Michael J. Dorsett Collection*

170. Hadley (BOA 60) on Fingle Bridge Hill *Austin Magazine February 1937*

1937 SUNBAC Colmore Trophy Trial 27th February

171. Kineton Hill, Sewell (BOA 59) *Light Car 5 March 1937*

172. Buckley (BOA 58) Note the Le Mans style wings. This is the 1936 Gloucester picture, but the Austin Magazine has doctored the race number to '22' and assigned the photo to the 1937 Colmore! *Austin Magazine April 1937*

173. Buckley (BOA 58) on Juniper – note full wings! *Light Car 5 March 1937*

174. Orford and AOV 343 on Kineton Hill *Autocar 5 March 1937*

175. Scriven (BOA 57) *Ferret Fotographics*

176. Bill Sewell and Raleigh Appleby (BOA 59) *Harvey*

177. Hadley (BOA 60), Kineton *Roe*

1937 Lands End Trial 26-27th March

178. Richardson (AOX 4) *Ferret Fotographics*

179. Scriven (BOA 57) *Ian Moore Collection*

180. Buckley (BOA 58)
Ferret Fotographics

181. Buckley (BOA 58) on Beggar's
Roost *Light Car 2 April 1937*

182. Orford, Bluehills Mine (AOV 343)
Autocar 2 April 1937

183. Buckley (BOA 58) Darracott
Austin Magazine May 1937

184. Orford (AOV 343) Darracott
Austin Magazine May 1937

185. Scriven (BOA 57) Darracott
Austin Magazine May 1937

186. Orford (AOV 343) on
Bluehills *The Motor 30 March 1937*

187. 1937 Lands End Trial – W.J. Milton *Ferret Fotographics*

1937 SUNBAC Inter-Club Team Trial 24th April

188. Goodacre (BOA 59) on the right hand corner of Cowlow *Light Car 30 April 1937*

189. Depper (driving BOA 59) and Goodacre (passenger) *Authors' Collection*

1937 MGCC Abingdon Trial 1st May

190. Scriven (BOA 57) *Ferret Fotographics*

191. Buckley (BOA 58) *Ferret Fotographics*

192. Hadley (BOA 60) and Scriven (BOA 57) *Ferret Fotographics*

193. Hadley (BOA 60) *Ferret Fotographics*

194. Hadley (BOA 60) on Old Hollow *The Motor 4 May 1937*

195. Hadley on Tin Pan Alley after tipping BOA 60 into a ditch *Autocar 7 May 1937*

1937 MCC Edinburgh Trial 14-15th May

196. Milton (AOX 3) climbing Park Rash *The Motor 25 May 1937*

197. Scriven (BOA 57) on Park Rash *Authors' Collection*

198. Scriven with Charles Eaves (BOA 57) on Park Rash *Ferret Fotographics*

199. Buckley (BOA 58) makes easy work of Park Rash in Yorkshire *Authors' Collection*

200. Buckley (BOA 58) on Park Rash *Authors' Collection*

201. Hadley (BOA 60) climbing Park Rash *Ferret Fotographics*

1937 Lancashire AC Blackpool Rally 4-6th June

202. Buckley's BOA 58, and Scriven's BOA 57 in the foreground, parked on the promenade *Ferret Fotographics*

1937 Le Mans 24 Hour Race 19-20th June

203. Kay Petre (COA 119) posing at the start
Authors' Collection

204. Kay Petre in search of her starting position *www.imcdb*

205. Goodacre/Buckley '56' (COA 118) and Dodson/Hadley '57' (COA 121) *Authors' Collection*

206. Charles Dodson and Bert Hadley '57' and COA 121 in the pit *Canning-Brown*

207. COA 119 (No.55) *Ian Moore Collection*

208. Kay Petre (COA 119) *Authors' Collection*

209. COA 118 (No. 56) *Authors' Collection*

210. Hadley and Dodson (COA 121) *Authors' Collection*

1937 MCC July Rally (Torquay) 16-17th July

211. Orford (AOV 343) Braking Test
Authors' Collection

212. Orford (AOV 343) Garaging Test
Authors' Collection

213. Milton (AOX 3) *Authors' Collection*

214. Scriven (BOA 57) *Ian Moore Collection*

215. Buckley (BOA 58) *Ian Moore Collection*

216. Hadley (BOA 60) Stop & restart
Authors' Collection

217. Orford (AOV 343) *Authors' Collection*

218. Scriven(BOA 57) *Ian Moore Collection*

219. Buckley & wife (BOA 58) leading
Hadley and Simpson (BOA 60)
Ian Moore Collection

1937 Donington 12 Hours Sports Race 24ᵗʰ July

220. Dodson/Hadley (COA 121) *Authors' Collection*

221. Second massed Start (COA 118 & COA 119)
Light Car 30 July 1937

222. Petre/Stevenson (COA 119) slips behind a marshal *Authors' Collection*

223. Kay Petre/P. Stevenson *Ian Moore Collection*

1937 XI RAC International Tourist Trophy Donington 4ᵗʰ September

224. Dodson in action (COA 121)
Light Car 10 September 1937

225. Old Starkey to Melbourne hairpin (COA 121) *The Motor 14 September 1937*

226. Coppice Corner (COA 121)
The Motor 14 September 1937

Charles Martin on the Lagonda passes Dodson's Austin at Starkey's

227. Dodson is passed by a Lagonda at Starkey's
Speed Magazine October 1937

1937 Mid-Surrey Automobile Club Experts' Trial (Exmoor) 30th October

228. Buckley (BOA 58) and Langley (BOA 59) in background *Authors' Collection*

229. Langley (BOA 59) overlooked by a marshal *Authors' Collection*

230. Hadley (BOA 60) on Cloutsham Hill *Light Car 5 November 1937*

231. Hadley (BOA 60) *Authors' Collection*

232. Hadley (BOA 60) *Authors' Collection*

233. Hadley (BOA 60) skidding off Widlake's slippery rock on to the bank *Autocar 5 November 1937*

1937 SUNBAC Vesey Cup Trial 6th November

234. Hadley (BOA 60) at Cefn Splash *Light Car 12 November 1937*

235. Buckley (BOA 58) *Austin Magazine December 1937*

1937 Bristol MC & LCC Fedden Trophy Trial 13th November

236. Goodacre (COA 121) climbing Nailsworth Ladder *Speed Camera*

1937 NWLMC/SUNBAC London – Gloucester Trial 4th December

237. Scriven (BOA 57) after a gallant attempt at Breakheart
Light Car 10 December 1937

238. Scriven (BOA 57) waiting to be flagged off *Authors' Collection*

239. Buckley (BOA 58) *Authors' Collection*

240. Langley (BOA 59) *Authors' Collection*

241. Hadley (BOA 60) *Authors' Collection*

1937 MCC Exeter Trial 7-8th January 1938

242. Scriven (BOA 57) *Ferret Fotographics*

243. Buckley (BOA 58) on Fingle
Autocar 14 January 1938

244. Langley (BOA 59) *Ferret Fotographics*

245. Hadley (BOA 60) rounding the timed hairpin at the foot of Fingle Bridge
Austin Magazine February 1938

246. Goodacre (COA 121) also at the foot of Fingle Bridge
Light Car 14 January 1938

1938 MGCC Ludlow Midland Sporting Trial 13th February

247. Scriven (BOA 57) *Authors' Collection*

248. Scriven (BOA 57) on the Yeld
Ian Moore Collection

249. Buckley (BOA 58)*Ian Moore Collection*

250. Langley (BOA 59) on the Yeld *Light Car 18 February 1938*

251. Langley (BOA 59) tackling the Yeld *Wyatt*

252. Langley (BOA 59) *Authors' Collection*

253. Depper (COA 121) *Authors' Collection*

254. Depper (COA 121) *Authors' Collection*

1938 SUNBAC Colmore Trophy Trial 26th February

255. Scriven on Nailsworth Ladder (BOA 57)
Authors' Collection

256. Buckley (BOA 58) with either BOA 57 or BOA 60 in the background *Wyatt*

257. 1938 SUNBAC Colmore Trial - T.H. Cole *Ferret Fotographics*

258. Depper (COA 121) with lower door side-screens in place
Authors' Collection

259. Depper (COA 121) *Ferret Fotographics*

260. Richardson (AOX 4) on Nailsworth
Ladder *Ian Moore Collection*

261. Richardson (AOX 4) *Ian Moore Collection*

262. Richardson (AOX 4)
Ian Moore Collection

263. Depper (COA 121) resorts to the tow rope on Leckhampton
Autocar 4 March 1938

264. Depper (COA 121) Nailsworth
Authors' Collection

1938 MGCC S. W. Skurray's Scramble Trial 13th March

265. Buckley (BOA 58) acceleration and brake test
Motor Sport April 1938

1938 MCC Lands End Trial 15-16th April

266. T. H. Cole (AOV 343) *Ferret Fotographics*

267. Depper (COA 121) and Cole (AOV 343), New Mill Hill *Ferret Fotographics*

268. Buckley (BOA 58), Langley (BOA 59) and Scriven (BOA 57), New Mill Hill *Ferret Fotographics*

269. Scriven on Hustyn (BOA 57) *The Motor 22 April 1938*

270. Depper (COA 121) *Authors' Collection*

271. Depper (COA 121) *Ferret Fotographics*

272. Langley (BOA 59) New Mill Hill, near Boscastle
Austin Magazine June 1938

273. Richardson (AOX 4) New Mill Hill
Ian Moore Collection

1938 MGCC Abingdon Trial Challenge Trophy 14th May

274. Scriven (BOA 57)
Ferret Fotographics

275. Buckley (BOA 58)
Ferret Fotographics

276. Buckley (BOA 58) *Ian Moore Collection*

277. Langley (COA 121) on the aerodrome *Authors' Collection*

1938 Paris-Nice Rally, Automobile Club de Nice 31ˢᵗ July – 5ᵗʰ August

278. Mrs. Petre (Austin) and Yarburgh- Bateson (H.R.G.) on the ramp at Montlhéry *Motor Sport September 1938*

279. Kay Petre at la Turbie Hill Climb (COA119) *La Vie Automobile 10 September 1938*

280. COA 119 at the close of the Rally *La Vie Automobile 10 September 1938*

1938 Kirkcaldy & District MC 27ᵗʰ August

281. W. K. Stewart (AOX 4) making a determined attempt on Grassy Twist *Light Car 2 November 1938*

1938 Mid-Surrey Automobile Club Experts' Trial (Exmoor) 29ᵗʰ October

282. Starting Point, Dunster - BOA 57, COA 121, BOA 58 lined up ready for the start *Ferret Fotographics*

283. Market Place, Dunster –from another angle *Wheelspin website 'Allard' page*

284. Buckley (BOA 58) takes the first bend at Kersham *Light Car 4 November 1938*

134

285. Hadley in action with COA 119, Picked Stones Hill *Ferret Fotographics*

286. Hadley (COA 119) *Ferret Fotographics*

287. Hadley (COA 119) noses into the bank *Ferret Fotographics*

288. Langley (COA 121) mudhopping up Dytch Lane *Austin Magazine December 1938*

1938 Bristol MC & LCC Fedden Trophy Trial 12th November

289. Hadley (COA 119) Nailsworth Ladder *Ferret Fotographics*

290. Langley (COA 121) awaits the signal to go at the foot of Juniper *Light Car 18 November 1938*

1939 Lanarkshire MC & CC Half-Day Trial 4th February

291. Carlaw (BOA 59) on Southbrae *Light Car 10 February 1939*

1939 NWLMC Coventry Cup Trial 11th February

292. Hadley and Rose (COA 119) on Beechy Lees *Ferret Fotographics*

293. Hadley (COA 119) *Ferret Fotographics*

294. Hadley (COA 119) clears the summit *Ferret Fotographics*

295. Hadley (COA 119) *Ferret Fotographics*

1939 MGCC Midland Centre Ludlow Trial 12th February

296. Scriven (BOA 57) *Authors' Collection*

1939 SUNBAC Colmore Trophy Trial 25th February

297. Buckley (BOA 58) Lower Guiting
Autocar 3 March 1939

298. Observed Section: Buckley (BOA 58)
Authors' Collection

299. Observed Section: Hadley (COA 119)
Ferret Fotographics

300. Scriven (BOA 57) *Ferret Fotographics*

301. Scriven (BOA 57) *Ferret Fotographics*

302. Buckley (BOA 58) *Austin Magazine April 1939*

303. Buckley with Ron Norwood as passenger (BOA 58) *Authors' Collection*

1939 Southsea Club President's Trophy Trial 26th February

304. Hadley (COA 119) leaps into the air *Authors' Collection*

1939 Scottish Sporting Car Club Winter Half-Day Trial 4th March

305. B. L. Carlaw (BOA 59) on Carron Bridge *Light Car 10 March 1939*

1939 Edinburgh & District MC Trial 25th March

306. Valentine (AOV 343) negotiating the gulley at Princes Street *Light Car 31 March 1939*

1939 Highland Two-Day Trial 8-10th April

307. B. L. Carlaw (BOA 59) takes his Austin Grasshopper round the hairpin at Amulree *Light Car 14 April 1939*

1939 NWLMC Lawrence Cup Trial 20th May

308. Buckley (BOA 58)
Ferret Fotographics

309. Buckley (BOA 58) *Ferret Fotographics*

310. Scriven (COA 121) and Buckley (BOA 58)
Ian Moore Collection

311. Scriven (COA 121) – Red Road
Ferret Fotographics

312. Scriven (COA 121) *Ferret Fotographics*

1939 Caledonian MC Summer Trial 10th June

313. George Valentine (AOV 343) crossing Drumtain Ford
Authors' Collection

English Trial Photographs (To be identified)

314. Orford (AOV 343)
Ferret Fotographics

315. Buckley (BOA 58) No. 30: 1936 United Hospitals Trial, March 29th (curved badge bar, three badges – just as in April Lands End)? *Ferret Fotographics*

Scottish Trial Photographs (To be identified)

316. Valentine (AOV 343) and BOA 59 following
Authors' Collection

317. Valentine (AOV 343) and another Grasshopper below *Authors' Collection*

318. Carlaw (BOA 59) This picture, and the 3 below from the same trial *Authors' Collection*

319. Valentine (AOV 343) at the same point as the 2 accompanying pictures
Ferret Fotographics

320. Blyth (AOX 4) *Authors' Collection*

321. Carlaw (BOA 59) *Authors' Collection*

Additional Data

The two major shortcomings of the Grasshopper design when used off-road, were identified very early on; the first being a lack of low-down available power, overcome by fitting a supercharger; the second being poor ground clearance, solved through increasing the ride height by the use of military springs. These two changes offer a visual reference point to the evolution of the various cars. The first table shows the earliest available photograph of an individual car with military springs fitted.

Grasshopper Model	High chassis	Photo No.
AOV 343	15 April 1938 Lands End	266
AOX 3	13 February 1938 MGCC Ludlow Trial	19
AOX 4	26 February 1938 Colmore Trophy	260
BOA 57	4 December 1937 Gloucester Trial	238
BOA 58	4 December 1937 Gloucester Trial	239
BOA 59	4 December 1937 Gloucester Trial	240
BOA 60	4 December 1937 Gloucester Trial	241
COA 118	Remained on low chassis	
COA 119	11 February 1939 Coventry Cup	292
COA 121	6 November 1937 Vesey Cup	236

Drivers tended to personalise their Grasshopper in a variety of ways, noticeably through their choice of wings. At Brooklands or other track events, cars were either fitted with the short cycle-type wings, or ran without. Some drivers chose not to refit the heavier, flowing wings immediately afterwards. These latter wings offered more protection to the occupants when competing in reliability trials, so inevitably the trials and trials-adapted cars returned to this form, with the exception of **COA 121** with a unique arrangement all of its own. **COA 118** was never used in these events and is assumed to have retained its cycle-wings. **UI 3345** was fitted with 'trials' wings when sold by the Works. The change in style also provides a useful reference point when attempting to identify a specific event or period from surviving photographs.

AOV 343	AOX 3	AOX 4	BOA 57	BOA 58
Full Wings: From launch. **Cycle Wings:** Brooklands 25 Sept 1937 **Full Wings refitted:** Buxton 23 October 1937 onwards...	**Full Wings:** From launch	**Full Wings:** From launch. **Cycle Wings:** Brooklands 14 Sept 1935 Brooklands 26 Sept 1936 Fedden Trial 14 Nov 1936 Vesey Cup 21 Nov 1936 **Full Wings refitted:** Lands End 26 March 1937 onwards...	**Cycle Wings:** Le Mans 15-16 June 1935 **Full Wings:** Exeter 27 Dec 1935 onwards...	**Cycle Wings:** Le Mans 15-16 June 1935 **Full Wings:** Exeter 27 Dec 1935 **Cycle Wings:** Brooklands 26 Sept 1936 **Full Wings refitted:** Exeter 1-2 January 1937 onwards...
BOA 59	**BOA 60**	**COA 118**	**COA 119**	**COA 121**
Cycle Wings: Le Mans 15-16 June 1935 **Full rear, Cycle front:** Colmore 22 Feb 1936 **Full Wings:** Exeter 1-2 January 1937 **Cycle Wings:** Experts 30 October 1937 **Full Wings refitted:** Gloucester 4 Dec 1937 onwards...	**Full Wings:** From launch	**Cycle Wings:** Le Mans 19-20 June 1937 **Removed:** Donington 12 Hours Race 24 July 1937 **Cycle Wings refitted**	**Cycle Wings:** Le Mans 19-20 June 1937 **Removed:** Donington 12 Hours Race 24 July 1937 **Full Wings:** Paris-Nice 31 July-5 August 1938 onwards...	**Cycle Wings:** Le Mans 19-20 June 1937 **Removed:** Donington 12 Hours Race 24 July 1937 **Cycle Wings:** Donington ITT 4 Sept 1937 **Cycle-faired wings:** Vesey Cup 6 Nov 1937 onwards...

140

People and Cars

Appleby, Raleigh 'Ral', 'Rally', 'Rowley' *(1899-1980)*
Worked in the Competition Department - Mechanic and driver; co-driver to Bill Sewell, **BOA 59**.

Blyth, J. H. 'Jack'
Blyth was another Austin distributor, located in Dundee - Scottish Tartan Grasshoppers. Blyth purchased **AOX 4** from the works. He became a Lieutenant RN and was wounded in getting away from Dunkirk in June 1940.

Buckley, C. D. Charles 'Dennis'
Dennis was the son of Chris Buckley, the Austin Sales Manager. He became a Works Trials driver in 1936, previously competing with a 'white sports Austin' and was assigned **BOA 58**. Buckley competed very successfully in nearly all the Trials events up until 1939 and stayed with the same car. He was Charlie Goodacre's co-driver in the 1937 Le Mans, in **COA 118** and also competed in Brooklands events, speed trials and hill climbs, with the single seater racers.

Carlaw, B. L. 'Benby'
Scottish Tartan Grasshoppers; his family owned the Austin dealership in Glasgow; bought **BOA 59** from the works.

Clarkson, R. K. N. (Robert Kirkwood Nicol) 'Roy'
Owned **AOX 4** and used it in trials after the war. Clarkson competed in pre-war trials from 1935 with a Ford V8-LMB and fitted LMB independent front suspension to **AOX 4**. He was a dental surgeon in Yorkshire/Essex.

Cole, Thomas H.
Austin Trials Driver, 1937-38, **AOV 343/AOX 3**. T. H. Cole and Sons were a Birmingham Austin Dealership of Fordhouse Lane, Stirchley.

Depper, W. H. (William Henry) 'Bill' *(1893 - September 1973)*
Bill was an Austin apprentice and Works Driver (Trials), 1938, **COA 121**. He was the son of Alf Depper, the Experimental and Racing Department foreman, chief mechanic and Col. Arthur Waite's racing partner.

Dodson, Charles 'Charlie', 'Doddy' Joseph Pearson *(6 Dec 1901 – 26 Sept 1983)*

Son of a barrister from Didsbury, near Manchester, he was a successful motorcycle rider in 1925-1934 and Isle of Man T.T. winner in 1928 and 1929 (Sunbeam 500). In the 1930s he raced MG, Riley, Austin (Works driver) and Maserati. He won the Tourist Trophy in 1934 and 1936, first in a MG Magnette, then in a Riley, and won the 1938 British Empire Trophy with one of the Austin twin-cam racers. In the 1935 Le Mans he raced **BOA 58** and in the 1937 Le Mans he drove **COA 121** and again in the 1937 Donington 12 Hours. After WW2 in 1949 he raced a Jaguar sports car at Silverstone. Tragically, he died from injuries received after crashing a Sunbeam 90 TT bike at a Brands Hatch historic bike parade.

Driscoll, Leonard Patrick 'Pat' *(5 Dec 1900 – 8 June 1983)*

Born in Chiswick, Middlesex and died at Hayling Island, Hampshire. Sammy Davis overturned Leon Cushman's 4½ litre Invicta during the 1931 Easter Brooklands Mountain Race. Pat Driscoll, who was leading the race in a Lea Francis 'Hyper Sports', stopped to rescue Sammy, an act which was instrumental in bringing Pat into the Austin Team. Driscoll raced **BOA 57** in the 1935 Le Mans; he also raced the Works twin OHC single seaters in circuit and Speed Hill Climb events, until crashing at the Backwell Hill House Speed Hill Climb on 26th July 1936, thus ending his racing career with Austin.

Evans, Lloyd

An Austin dealer: Evans Motors Ltd, Priory Street, Carmarthen – He bought **COA 121** from the Works in 1940 at the same time as **COA 119** was sold. Ray Morley purchased it on 12 July 1949 for £310.

Goodacre, Charles Lindsay *(July 1909 -7 August 1989)*

Improver-mechanic in the racing shop, he shared digs with Freddie Henry at one time; Works Race Driver from 1930 to 1938: 1935 Le Mans, **BOA 59**; 1937 Le Mans and 1937 Donington 12 Hours Sports race in **COA 118**; (Trials) 1935 **BOA 58**, 1936-37 **BOA 59**, 1937-1938 **COA 121**; left Austin to join the Ethyl Export Company in February 1938 as a Consulting Engineer; Served as Engineer Officer in the RAF during the war.

Hadley, Herbert Lewis 'Bert' *(18 Apr 1910 - 31 Jul 1993)*

Born in Stirchley, Birmingham; Trained at the Austin Motor Company's Apprentice School; Seconded to the Racing and Experimental Department at Longbridge in 1930, first as a mechanic, then race-builder, test driver and finally as development engineer and leading driver. He was personally involved with all the competition cars, particularly with Murray Jamieson and the twin O.H.C. single-seaters. Bert claimed it was his idea to convert the failed Le Mans sports cars into what became the famous "Grasshopper" Trials Team. The PWA7C 'Grasshopper Challenge' series celebrates his success in this. He was seconded to the Ministry of Labour during the war, to co-ordinate the production facilities of Midlands engineering firms, towards the war effort. He remained with the ministry until his retirement. Hadley trialled **BOA 60** and **COA 119** and also raced **COA 121** in the 1937 Le Mans and Donington 12 Hour Sports Race. Bob Simpson was Hadley's passenger for many of the Trials, although he had various other passengers, including Amy Stallard (Rose), later to become his wife. He died in 1993 at Leamington Spa, Warwickshire.

Henry, Freddie *(1910-27 February 1997)*

Freddie, an ex-Austin Apprentice, started at Longbridge in 1926 and finished his apprenticeship in 1932 before being assigned to the personal staff of Col. Arthur Waite in the Works Competition Department as mechanic/driver; later co-driver to Wallis Milton, **AOX 3**. Vice-president of the Austin Ex-Apprentices Association, Past President of the Austin Seven Clubs' Association and member of 750 Motor Club. He died in Devizes Hospital.

Jamieson, Tom Murray *(27 September 1905 - 10 May 1938)*

At Brooklands, sometime in 1932, T. Murray Jamieson, of the Amherst-Villiers Organisation appeared with a white production 'Ulster' Seven, fitted with an Amherst-Villiers supercharger of his own design. The car was so much faster than the factory cars that Col. Waite bought it and Jamieson joined the racing shop at Longbridge, where he set to work designing a new side valve racer. He went on to develop the twin OHC racers and also the aluminium cylinder head and special camshaft used in the Grasshoppers. At the 1938 Easter Brooklands one of the Talbot racing team cars crashed into the crowded paddock; Murray Jamieson, who by now had left Austin to design the new E.R.A., was one of the casualties and died from his injuries three days later.

Rose-Itier, Anne Cécile *(1895-1990)*

Madame Itier co-drove **COA 119** with Kay Petre in the 1938 Paris-Nice Rally. Born in 1895 she was a leading woman driver in the 1930s in voiturette and GP races, particularly favouring Bugattis; she also competed in the 1935 and 1937 Le Mans races in a Fiat Balilla and an Adler; easily recognisable when driving as she sported pink overalls. She died on the Cote d'Azur in 1990.

Langley, Alfred Henry 'Alf' *(1897 – 1980)*

Trials Driver, **BOA 59**, **COA 121**. Langley was born in Kings Norton, Birmingham and died in Stourbridge. Before driving for Austin he drove for Singer and was part of the ill-fated Team competing in the 1935 Ards Circuit Tourist Trophy Race which saw the entire team crash in turn at the same corner.

Mangan, George 'Guy'

An Irish driver and co-driver to Kay Petre in her attempt at the 1937 Le Mans with **COA 119**. He was a salesman at Lincoln and Nolan, the Dublin Austin agents.

Milton, Wallis J. *(1890 – 12 August 1963)*

Born in the Bristol area and died in Romsey, Hants. Milton was an Invited driver, **AOX 3**; Herbert Austin's friend and a West End dental surgeon, Welbeck Street. He lived at 281 Burntwood Lane, London SW17 whilst practising. Milton raced Douglas motorcycles in earlier trials. Allegedly, Milton was the first person to trial an Austin Seven, in 1922.

Morley, Ray *(1906-2003)*

Ray was a successful trial driver of the '30s. He started competing with a 1927 AC Six and had many AC factory drives including the 1934 RAC Rally. In 1936 with an ex-works 16/80 he was most successful winning gold and silver awards on Exeter, Land's End and London-Exeter trials. Post war he swapped ACs for Grasshoppers, initially with **COA 121** with limited success, and from 1952 to 1957 in **BOA 59**, winning 3 silvers and 2 golds in the Lands End and Exeter Trials during that period.

Orford, J. G. 'Johnny' *(Born 1896)*

Works Driver, **AOV 343**.

Parish, C. (Cornelius) Donald *(1912 – 1972)*

Parish was a Hull garage owner and Austin Distributor who drove various Works cars from 1934, partnering Pat Driscoll in the 1935 Le Mans, driving **BOA 57.**

Petre, Kay - Kathleen Coad 'Kay' Petre, nee Kathleen Defries *(10 May 1903 - 10 Aug 1994)*

1937 Le Mans; Donington 12 hours; 1938 Paris-Nice Rally, **COA 119.** Born in Toronto, Canada; daughter to a barrister with clients in both England and South Africa. Her husband, solicitor Henry Aluysuis Petre, bought her a Wolseley Hornet in which she started racing. She also raced a Riley, Austins, Invicta, a Bugatti and the ex-Cobb 10.5 litre Delage. She became a good friend to Bernd Rosemeyer during his 1937 South Africa trip. Petre had a serious crash at the Brooklands Byfleet banking during practice for the 1937 BRDC 500 when her Austin was hit by the tail of Parnall's MG Magnette. She was taken to hospital with severe head injuries and even though she continued to rally and compete in Hill Climbs, she retired from circuit racing. Later she worked as a journalist and as a Consultant colour stylist for Austin. She died in Camden, London.

Richardson, R. J. 'Joe'

Invited driver (Trials), **AOX 4**, 1935 Le Mans co-driver, **BOA 58**. Family firm, Richardsons of Oldbury, were contractors to Austin Motor Co.

Scriven, W. H. 'Bill'

Ex-Austin apprentice; worked with Ral Appleby as race mechanic. Works retained Driver (Trials), **BOA 57**. Bought **COA 118** after he left Austin to use in short Speed Events – sold to George Symonds. Scriven fitted a Grasshopper engine and supercharger to his diminutive Ruby saloon for the May 1938 Scottish Rally!

144

Sewell, W. S. 'Bill' Capt.
Lord Austin's PA and Competitions Manager; competed in a number of 1937 Trials with **BOA 59**, but competed more often with the 10hp Sports, **AVP 505**, which also accompanied the 1937 Le Mans team to the race circuit.

Simpson, Bob
Bob was Hadley's regular passenger in trials events; mechanic in the Racing Department at Longbridge.

Stephenson, Percy
Co-Driver to Kay Petre, 1937 Donington 12 Hours, **COA 119** – Southport garagiste and sand racer, often with the 'Duck' single seat racing cars.

Symonds , George H.
Symonds bought **COA 118** from Bill Scriven. Experienced Trials driver; competed in numerous trials from 1926, initially with an Austin and later with a Triumph, Morris, MG and Singer.

Turner, Rodney F.
1935 Le Mans, **BOA 59,** co-driver to Charles Goodacre – He was a guest privateer, from Derby. A very successful campaigner of his red blown Ulster at Brooklands, Shelsley and Donington from 1931 to 1935 and shared a 'Duck' racer in the 1934 Brooklands 200 Mile Race.

Valentine, George
Scottish Tartan Grasshoppers; his family owned the Austin distributors for Perth and purchased **AOV 343** from the works.

Waite, Col. Arthur Cyril Roy "Skipper", MC. Ost J., DL., JP *(9 April 1894 – 25 January 1991)*
Waite was an Adelaide-born racing driver and became the son-in-law to Herbert Austin, marrying daughter Irene, whom he met in hospital after serving in Gallipoli. After World War I Captain Waite joined his father-in-law's firm, the Austin Motor Company; while in the employ of Austin, Waite was sent back to Australia, where in Melbourne, he established Austin Distributors. Prior to leaving for Australia he had established the firm's motor racing efforts, winning races himself at Brooklands and Monza. While in Australia he sent for his Austin 7 racing car in order to compete in the race that later became known as the 1928 Australian Grand Prix. A different car was sent however, but despite it being a relatively standard sports model it was a supercharged racing version of the Austin 7. Waite won the Grand Prix (held at Phillip Island). Later he was to become the Managing Director of Austin Export Corporation.

Wilson, John (Jack) E. 'Jock' *(14 March 1920 - 17 September 2006)*
Dunoon Austin agent; his mother bought **COA 119** from the works in 1940. He competed in many post-war trials. The car remains with the family in Argyll to this day.

Grasshopper Humour: The Grasshopper Story 1935-1940

"One of Our Grasshoppers is Missing!"

Reading List

Magazine Articles

<u>Autocar</u> 9th May 1941. *'Talking of Sports Cars - The Grasshopper Austin'* (AOX 4)
<u>Austin Seven Clubs Association Magazine</u>:
   1982A. *'A Brace of Grasshoppers'* Phil Baildon (Ray Morley).
   1992B. *'Le Mans 24 Hours'* Bert Hadley.
   1992C, 1992D. *'The Grasshoppers'* Bert Hadley.
   1994C. *'Grasshopper Notes'* Geoff Roe
   1995D. *'Grasshopper Reunion'* Peter Hornby (MG Cream Cracker reunion).
   2011D. *'Austin Sevens at Le Mans'* Bill Sheehan.
<u>The Automobile</u>:
   August 1995. *'MG Works cars reunion and Kimber Trial'*.
   January 2005. *'The Sporting Sevens'*.
<u>Light Car</u> February 1946. *'A Grasshopper Without a Hop'* (AOX 4).
<u>Motor Sport</u> January 1947. *'Entomological Dissection - The Grasshopper Austin Sevens'* H Biggs
<u>Vintage Austin Magazine</u> No.55, 2001/2. *'Grasshopper. An Australian Replica'* Graeme Steinfort.
<u>750 Bulletin</u>:
   April 1962. *'The Grasshopper Austin'* Maxwell Bennett (COA 118)
   May 1968. *'The Austin Seven Grasshopper'* Mike Eyre
   July 1995. *'Grasshopper Get-Together'* Peter Hornby (Cream Cracker Reunion)

Books and Publications

Bacon R. <u>The Golden Age of Motoring</u>. Promotional Reprint Company. (1995)
Boddy W. <u>The Austin Seven - Motor Sport Book</u>. Grenville Production Co. Ltd. (1972)
Canning-Brown B. <u>Austin Seven Competition History 1922-1939.</u> Quorum (2006)
Cowbourne D. <u>British Trial Drivers Their Cars and Awards 1929-1939.</u> *Smith Settle* (1998)
Eyre M. <u>Austin Seven Competition Cars 1922-1982.</u> 750 Motor Club (1982)
Garnier P. <u>The Motor Cycling Club.</u> David & Charles (1989)
Harrison R.C. <u>Austin Racing History.</u> Motor Racing Publications Ltd. (1949)
Harvey C. <u>Austin Seven.</u> Haynes (1985)
Henry F. <u>Austin From the Inside</u>. 750 Motor Club (1998)
May C.A.N. <u>Wheelspin - Competition Motoring from the Driver's Seat</u>. Foulis (1945)
May C.A.N. <u>More Wheelspin.</u> Foulis (1948)
Purves B. <u>The Austin Seven Source Book</u>. Haynes/Foulis (1989)
Roe G. <u>Bert Hadley - A Son of Birmingham.</u> Pre War Austin Seven Club (2013)
Sharrat B. <u>Men and Motors of The Austin.</u> Haynes (2005)
Thomas R.F. <u>M.G. Trials Cars</u>. Magna Press (1995)
Tompkins E.S. <u>Speed Camera - The Amateur Photography of Motor Racing.</u> Foulis (1946)
Wyatt R.J. <u>The Austin Seven - The Motor for the Million.</u> Macdonald (1968)
Wyatt R.J. <u>The Austin Seven - A Pictorial Tribute.</u> Motor Racing Publications Ltd. (1975)

Peter Hornby was born in Yorkshire at the end of the Second World War. Austin Seven memories from his formative years included trips to Scarborough in a 1937 Ruby (VN 7950) in the early fifties and a Pearl (AKW 924) fitted with a Nippy/65 engine and gearbox, used as family transport in the early sixties when his father was building a Rochdale Olympic. He acquired an Ulster in late teens, which was succeeded by a Grasshopper (UI 3345) in 1964. After a two year rebuild, the latter was used for a year at university in Edinburgh where the long 'high speed' trips to and from

Leeds took their toll, which included a broken front axle, before being retired for a short career of VSCC racing.

Following Edinburgh, in 1968 Peter joined the Army, spending the next 21 years in the Royal Engineers, racing an 'Ulsteroid' with the 750 Club and VSCC from 1980 to 1989. His career change from the Army to NHS management was 'interesting', and he finally retired in 2006.

He bought a second Grasshopper, BOA 59, in 1998, and this and his original car have been seen in MCC and other events over the last 15 years.

Michael Hanna was born in Yorkshire in the mid-fifties and worked in the service station of an American Air Force base, later managing a motorist discount store not so very far from Silverstone. He then trained and worked as an English teacher.

Basic mechanical skills were picked up fixing low-budget family runabouts, but only on retirement did a chore become a hobby with the purchase of a delightful Austin Seven Ruby.

An interest in Austin Sevens was first stirred as a small child on seeing family photographs of Grandfather Sam's chummy, EK 4969, and continued into his teens when playing around with an abandoned Ruby, BDG 248, left to rust in a field behind the local Hopcrofts Holt petrol station, Oxfordshire.

Although both Mick and wife, Anne-Marie, share a pleasure for the speedier world of motorcycling, the more sedate world of Austin Sevens has so far failed to impress her!